Current
Directions
in
ADULTHOOD
AND AGING

READINGS FROM THE
ASSOCIATION FOR
PSYCHOLOGICAL SCIENCE

Current
Directions
in
ADULTHOOD
AND AGING

EDITED BY

Susan T. Charles

University of California, Irvine

Boston • New York • San Francisco
Mexico City • Montreal • Toronto • London • Madrid • Munich • Paris
Hong Kong • Singapore • Tokyo • Cape Town • Sydney

Acquisitions Editor: Michelle Limoges
Series Editorial Assistant: Christina Manfroni
Marketing Manager: Kate Mitchell
Production Editor: Patty Bergin
Editorial Production Service: TexTech International
Composition Buyer: Linda Cox
Manufacturing Buyer: JoAnne Sweeney
Electronic Composition: TexTech International
Cover Administrator: Linda Knowles

For related titles and support materials, visit our online catalog at www.ablongman.com.

Between the time website information is gathered and then published, it is not unusual for some sites to have closed. Also, the transcription of URLs can result in typographical errors. The publisher would appreciate notification where these errors occur so that they may be corrected in subsequent editions.

Library of Congress Cataloging-in-Publication Data

Current directions in adulthood and aging / edited by Susan T. Charles.
    p. ; cm.—(Readings from the Association for Psychological Science)
"Reprinted as [they] originally appeared in Current directions in psychological science."
Includes bibliographical references.
ISBN-13: 978-0-205-59749-9
ISBN-10:   0-205-59749-1
1. Aging—Psychological aspects.   2. Brain—Aging.   3. Cognition—Age factors.
I. Charles, Susan T. (Susan Turk), 1969-   II. Association for Psychological
Science.   III. Current directions in psychological science.   IV. Series.
[DNLM: 1. Aging—psychology—Collected Works.   2. Adult.   3. Aged.
4. Aging—physiology—Collected Works.   5. Cognition—physiology—Collected
Works.   6. Cognition Disorders—Collected Works.   7. Dementia—Collected
Works. WT 145 C976t 2008]
BF724.55.A35C87   2008
155.67—dc22   2007051146

Printed in the United States of America

10 9 8 7 6 5 4 3 2 1   11 10 09 08

Contents

Introduction

When the science of psychology was in its infancy, the study of developmental processes already had a strong presence in the field. In the early 20th century, researchers were studying developmental stages of cognitive, psychological and social processes. Sigmund Freud stressed the importance of stages of development as his work paved the way for clinical psychology. Piaget turned his interests away from biology and to processes of cognitive development early in life, and Vygotsky was studying the importance of social and cultural context on cognitive processing throughout childhood. The study of adulthood and aging would begin in earnest only in the second half of this century. In 1945, the American Psychological Association decided to establish a new division focusing on adult development titled, "Maturity and Old Age." (Division 20 would later change its name to Adult Development and Aging in 1970). A year later, the first interdisciplinary journals on aging in the United States were published by the newly formed Gerontological Society of America. In 1961, the Gerontological Society of America devoted one of these journals only to research in the psychological sciences. In 1986, the American Psychological Association inaugurated their first journal devoted to adult development.

This compilation of *Current Directions* articles, focused exclusively on issues of adulthood, reflects the growing importance of studying adult development for gaining a comprehensive understanding of human behavior. Although these papers are divided into five sections, the reader will notice several common themes running through many of these readings. The first theme focuses on how cognitive processing changes throughout adulthood. The study of cognitive aging is important in its own right, but also when viewing changes in other psychological processes as well, such as emotional experiences and physical functioning. Another theme that pervades these articles is the importance of the environmental context when interpreting developmental findings. Research in adult development often relies on cross-sectional methodology (that is, when age differences are examined among a group, or cross-section, of people who vary in age). Interpreting cross-sectional findings necessarily involves teasing apart maturational effects from cohort effects. Cohort effects refer to the social and cultural mores and events that vary across groups of people born at different times in history. Adult developmental processes always occur in context, and researchers have grown sophisticated in their understanding of how these social contexts influence psychological processes. Additionally, researchers have illustrated how social attitudes of aging have resulted in the creation of different cultural contexts for people at different points along the life-span. Expectations of the self and others often change according to age. These 26 articles are designed to augment courses in life-span development that focus less on the first twenty years and more on the last eighty years of the human life span.

Section 1: Cognitive Aging

Since the time of the Greek philosophers, people have questioned how and why cognitive processes change across the adult life span. This section focuses on the nature of changes, potential reasons behind these changes, and possible activities that may influence cognitive declines in later life.

The first two articles provide an overview covering the how and why of cognitive aging. Timothy Salthouse, the author of the first article, "What and When of Cognitive Aging," received the Association for Psychological Science's William James Fellow Award for lifetime Achievement award for outstanding research contributions in 1998 and is recognized as one of the world's experts in cognitive development. He describes how aging is associated with general cognitive slowing that underlies multiple cognitive abilities. He discusses how these findings occur much earlier than most people may expect, beginning in the second decade of life. He also mentions possible reasons to explain why, given these decrements, older adults are still able to engage effectively in everyday activities of living.

The second article by Shu-Chen Li is titled, "Connecting the many levels and facets of cognitive aging." In this article, Li presents a compelling argument to explain the cognitive decline presented by Salthouse. She explains cognitive decline as the result of changes in catecholaminergic function, a perspective that departs from neuroanatomical explanations that had been the focus of early theories of cognitive decline. When describing these changes, she reviews findings from both animal and human studies to describe the role of neuronal noise in declines in cognitive processing.

The next three articles describe specific aspects of cognitive decline. In "False remembering in the aged," Larry Jacoby and Matthew Rhodes discuss declines in cognitive aging that place older adults at greater risk for false memories. They explain these age differences by the dual-process model of memory and present a series of findings to illustrate the mechanisms underlying age differences. They review studies where, under certain conditions, the memory of older adults can be improved, and in other situations younger adults make errors that mimic the effects of aging.

Deborah Burke and Meredith Shafto discuss how aging is related to specific linguistic errors in their article, "Aging and Language Production." They use a transmission deficit model that incorporates semantic, phonological and orthographic systems to describe why older adults have more tip-of-the-tongue experiences. The authors describe why these retrieval failures are more likely to occur for highly specific words as apposed to more general words, and why retrieval failures for younger adults look very different from the errors made by older adults.

The next article examines age differences in visual attention, outlining how the study of attention can illuminate age differences for other processes of cognition. David Madden outlines the importance of distinguishing between tasks requiring bottom-up versus top-down processing of visual information when summarizing age differences in his article, "Aging and visual attention". Although bottom-up processing shows reliable age-related changes, top-down processes remain relatively intact with age. He further provides a neurobiological explanation for this age-related pattern of similarities and age differences.

The final two articles of this section discuss the role of cognitive activity in late life, and how this activity may influence normal functioning as well as the probability of a dementia diagnosis. "Enhancing the cognitive vitality of older adults," authored by Arthur Kramer and Sherry Willis, discusses the effects of cognitive training among older adults to offset age-related declines. In this article, the authors provide an overview of age-related changes in cognition, and how experts engage in compensating strategies to mitigate their losses. Then, they review studies showing that older adults who underwent training sessions to learn cognitive strategies exhibited reductions in declines or even preserved performance on certain cognitive tasks.

In the last article in this section, Robert Wilson and David Bennett discuss the association between education level and the probability of an Alzheimer's diagnosis in their article "Cognitive activity and risk for Alzheimer's disease." They state the intriguing possibility that activities requiring greater cognitive demands may be protective against Alzheimer's disease. People with higher education levels generally engage in cognitively complex activities, and this engagement may explain their lower rates for this type of dementia.

What and When of Cognitive Aging

Timothy A. Salthouse[1]
University of Virginia

Abstract

Adult age differences have been documented on a wide variety of cognitive variables, but the reasons for these differences are still poorly understood. In this article, I describe several findings that will need to be incorporated into eventual explanations of the phenomenon of cognitive aging. Despite common assumptions to the contrary, age-related declines in measures of cognitive functioning (a) are relatively large, (b) begin in early adulthood, (c) are evident in several different types of cognitive abilities, and (d) are not always accompanied by increases in between-person variability.

Keywords

aging; cognition; reasoning; memory; speed

The phenomenon of cognitive aging has been noticed almost as long as the phenomenon of physical aging, but it is still not well understood. This is unfortunate because cognitive functioning can affect one's quality of life, and even the ability to live independently. Furthermore, cognitive functioning in early adulthood may be related to the development of pathologies such as Alzheimer's disease in later adulthood.

One way to conceptualize understanding is that it is equivalent to knowing answers to the questions of what, when, why, where, and how. In this article, I summarize some of the progress that has been achieved in describing the phenomenon of cognitive aging in terms of the questions of what and when. Although not much is yet known about why (what is ultimately responsible), where (in the nervous system), and how (via what mechanisms) age-related cognitive changes occur, a key assumption of my research is that answering these other questions will be easier as the characterization of what and when becomes more precise.

WHAT AND WHEN

It is often assumed that age-related effects on cognitive functioning are small, are limited to aspects of memory, begin relatively late in adulthood, and possibly affect only some people, so that any age-related declines are accompanied by increases in between-person variability. However, recent research in my laboratory and elsewhere suggests that these assumptions may all be incorrect. Evidence relevant to these issues can be illustrated with data aggregated across several recent studies in my laboratory (Salthouse, 2001a, 2001b; Salthouse, Atkinson, & Berish, 2003; Salthouse & Ferrer-Caja, 2003; Salthouse, Hambrick, & McGuthry, 1998; Salthouse et al., 2000). Participants in these studies were recruited through newspaper advertisements, appeals to community groups, and referrals from other participants. Nearly all of the participants reported themselves to be in good to excellent health, and they averaged approximately 16 years of education.

Four tests were common to most of these studies. A vocabulary test involved the examinee selecting the best synonyms of target words, in each case from a set of five alternatives. A speed test required the participant to classify pairs of line patterns as the same or different as rapidly as possible. Reasoning was assessed with the Raven's Progressive Matrices, in which each test item consists of a matrix of geometric patterns with one missing cell, and the task for the participant is to select the best completion of the missing cell from a set of alternatives. Finally, a memory test involved three auditory presentations of the same list of unrelated words, with the participant instructed to recall as many words as possible after each presentation. Data for the vocabulary, speed, and reasoning tests are based on 1,424 adults, and those for the memory test are based on 997 adults.

Because the raw scores for the four tests are in different units, all of the scores have been converted to z scores (by subtracting each score from the mean for that test and then dividing by the standard deviation) so that the age trends can be directly compared. The means for the z scores are plotted as a function of age in Figure 1. The bars above and below each point are standard errors, which represent the precision of the estimate (i.e., the smaller the bars, the more precise the estimate). Six important observations about the data in this figure can be noted.

First, scores on the vocabulary test were higher with increased age until about the mid-50s, after which they either remained stable or declined slightly. Findings such as these have been interpreted as indicating that knowledge accumulates with increased age, but compelling explanations for why this age function is curvilinear are not yet available (Salthouse, 2003).

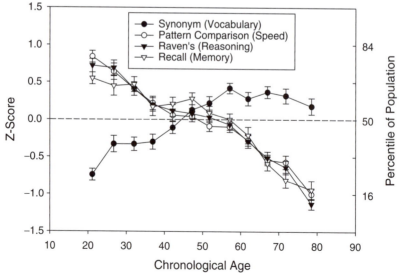

Fig. 1. Means (and standard errors) of performance in four cognitive tests as a function of age. Each data point is based on between 52 and 156 adults.

Second, similar negative age trends are evident in the measures of speed, reasoning, and memory. Although not represented in the figure, the correlations between age and these variables were also similar, as they were $-.47$, $-.48$, and $-.43$, respectively, for the speed, reasoning, and memory variables.

Third, the age-related effects on the speed, reasoning, and memory variables are fairly large. Not only are the age correlations for these variables greater than most correlations involving individual differences reported in the behavioral sciences, but the average performance for adults in their early 20s was near the 75th percentile in the population, whereas the average for adults in their early 70s was near the 20th percentile.

Fourth, the relations between age and the speed, reasoning, and memory variables are primarily linear. This observation is relevant to potential interpretations of the effects because the absence of obvious discontinuities in the functions suggests that transitions such as retirement, or menopause for women, are probably not responsible for much, if any, of the effects.

Fifth, the data in the figure indicate that age-related effects are clearly apparent before age 50. For some variables, there may be an acceleration of the influences at older ages, but age-related differences are evident in early adulthood for each variable.

And sixth, the age-related declines in these samples are not accompanied by increases in between-person variability. One way to express the relation between age and between-person variability is in terms of the correlation between age and the between-person standard deviation for the individuals in each 5-year age group. For the data in Figure 1, these correlations were $-.18$ for vocabulary, $-.80$ for speed, $-.74$ for reasoning, and $.13$ for memory. If anything, therefore, the trend in these data is for increased age to be associated with a smaller range of scores. Instead of a pattern of increased variability that might be attributable to some people maintaining high levels of performance and others experiencing large declines, the data show a nearly constant variability that is more consistent with a downward shift of the entire distribution of speed, reasoning, and memory scores with increased age.

Many of the patterns apparent in Figure 1 have been reported in a number of individual studies (see the earlier citations), and are also evident in data from nationally representative samples used to establish norms for standardized tests such as the third edition of the Wechsler Adult Intelligence Scale (Wechsler, 1997) and the Woodcock-Johnson III Tests of Cognitive Abilities (Woodcock, McGrew, & Mather, 2001). Results such as these suggest the following answers to the questions of the what and when of cognitive aging. With respect to what, many different types of cognitive variables are affected by increased age, and with respect to when, age-related differences appear to begin in early adulthood, probably in the 20s.

WHY ARE THE EFFECTS NOT MORE NOTICEABLE IN EVERYDAY LIFE?

The research I have summarized suggests that age-related cognitive declines are fairly broad, begin early in adulthood, and are cumulative across the life span.

A question frequently raised when findings such as these are mentioned is, why are there not greater negative consequences of the age-related cognitive declines? I suspect that there are at least four reasons.

First, cognitive ability is only one factor contributing to successful functioning in most activities. Other factors such as motivation, persistence, and various personality characteristics are also important, and they either may be unrelated to age or may follow different age trajectories than measures of cognitive functioning.

Second, very few situations require individuals to perform at their maximum levels because humans tend to modify their environments to reduce physical and cognitive demands. An analogy to physical ability and physical demands may be relevant here because there are well-documented age-related declines in strength, stamina, and speed, but these declines are seldom noticed in everyday life because of the relatively low physical requirements of most situations.

Third, many people may adapt to age-related changes by altering the nature and pattern of their activities. Examples of this type of adaptation are apparent in driving, because as they grow older, many adults make adjustments such as driving at different times and under different conditions, and possibly avoiding certain maneuvers, such as left turns. Accommodations such as these do not eliminate the declines, but they may serve to minimize their detrimental consequences.

And fourth, the greater experience and knowledge associated with increased age probably reduces the need for the type of novel problem solving that declines with age. Continuous age-related increases in knowledge may not be apparent in standardized tests because the tests are designed to be applicable to the general population, and much of the individual's knowledge may be increasingly idiosyncratic as he or she pursues progressively more specialized vocational and avocational interests. Nevertheless, very high levels of performance might be apparent among older adults, given the right combination of individuals and tasks. Research in my laboratory suggests, for example, that older adults demonstrate a high level of performance if they regularly work crossword puzzles and the task is solving crossword puzzles. In four recent studies, adults recruited because of their crossword-puzzle experience were asked to perform a number of activities, including spending 15 min attempting to solve a crossword puzzle taken from the *New York Times*. As can be seen in Figure 2, in general, the highest average level of crossword performance in every sample was achieved by adults in their 60s and 70s.

It could be argued that successful performance in solving crossword puzzles is primarily dependent on accumulated knowledge rather than on novel problem solving or abstract reasoning. This may be the case, but I suspect that the same is true in many real-world activities. That is, much of what we typically do may be more dependent on successful access and retrieval of what we already know than on our ability to solve novel problems or reason with unfamiliar material.

INVESTIGATING THE WHY, WHERE, AND HOW OF COGNITIVE AGING

Although the phenomenon of cognitive aging is fairly well documented in terms of the questions of what and when, there is much less consensus with respect to

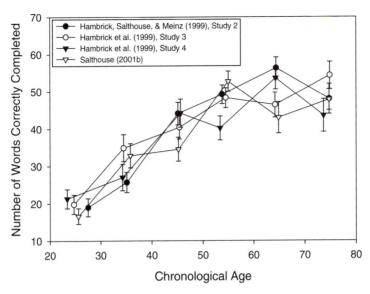

Fig. 2. Means (and standard errors) for the number of words in a *New York Times* cross-word puzzle correctly answered in 15 min as a function of age. Between 195 and 218 adults participated in each study. The crossword puzzles required either 76 or 78 words for their solutions.

the answers to, or even the best methods of investigating, the questions of why, where, and how. In fact, it can be argued that much of the current theoretical debate in the field of cognitive aging is not focused on distinguishing among alternative explanations, but rather is concerned with which approach is likely to be most productive in investigating causes of age-related differences in cognitive functioning. Several of the major issues can be described in terms of the following dichotomies, although it should be recognized that these are simplifications, and that this list is by no means exhaustive.

Micro Versus Macro

One theoretical issue is whether the primary focus should be on determining which specific aspects (e.g., theoretical processes or components) of cognition are most (or least) affected by aging, or whether several variables should be examined simultaneously to determine the extent to which the age-related effects on a particular variable are unique to that variable or are shared with other variables. Advocates of the former, micro, perspective point out that most cognitive tasks can be assumed to involve multiple processes, and thus an overall measure of performance in nearly any task is likely to represent an unknown mixture of theoretically distinct processes that may be difficult to interpret. Advocates of the latter, macro, perspective emphasize that a large number of cognitive variables have been found to be related to age, and that analyses have revealed that age-related influences on different types of cognitive variables are not statistically independent of one another. Researchers favoring the macro perspective have therefore argued that the age-related effects on particular cognitive tasks may be symptoms of a broader phenomenon, and consequently that it may not be very meaningful to attempt to provide a distinct explanation for the age differences in each variable.

Proximal Versus Distal

A second theoretical issue is whether researchers should concentrate on specifying characteristics (e.g., strategy, efficiency of specific hypothesized processes, adherence to particular sets of beliefs) associated with the performance differences of adults of different ages at the time of assessment (proximal factors), or whether researchers should try to identify factors occurring earlier in life that may have contributed to any differences observed at the current time (distal factors). The key question in this connection is whether it is more important to specify precisely how the performance of people of different ages differs at the current time or to investigate the role of earlier life experiences in producing those differences.

Moderation Versus Manipulation

A third issue relevant to the investigation of causes of cognitive aging arises from the fact that true experiments are not possible because the critical variable of age cannot be randomly assigned. Researchers differ in which of two approximations to true experiments they think will be most fruitful. On one side are those who say the focus should be on determining if particular characteristics (moderators) are associated with differences in the age-related trends on various cognitive variables. Their approach is to compare the age-related trends of preexisting groups (e.g., people sharing various lifestyle characteristics). On the other side are researchers who say that the most will be learned by attempting to alter people's current level of performance by some type of intervention. Using this approach, they hope to identify manipulations that influence the relation between age and level of performance.

Difference Versus Change

One of the perennial issues in developmental research is whether the results of cross-sectional comparisons can be considered informative about age-related changes, or whether all inferences about aging must be based on directly observed longitudinal changes. There is little dispute that people of different ages who are tested at the same point in time may also differ in other characteristics, and thus results of cross-sectional comparisons might not directly reflect effects of aging. There is also considerable agreement that there are several possible influences on longitudinal changes, including effects related to practice or learning from one occasion to the next and effects associated with changes in the society or culture in which the individual lives. However, there is much less consensus about the best method of distinguishing between "age" and "nonage" influences in each type of design. On the one hand, researchers favoring cross-sectional methods feel that it is plausible to assume that people who are of different ages and observed at the same point in time were similar in most important respects when they were at the same age, so that it is reasonable to make inferences about maturational changes on the basis of cross-sectional differences. On the other hand, researchers favoring longitudinal methods frequently assume that the maturational component of change can be distinguished from other components of change, such as practice effects and effects of sociocultural change, either because the latter are small relative to maturational effects or because they can be separated by statistical or other means.

It is probably healthy for a field to pursue different approaches to explanation when the level of understanding is relatively limited. However, it is probably also the case that progress toward answering the why, where, and how of cognitive aging will not be reached until there is some agreement among different theoretical perspectives on the best methods of addressing those questions.

CONCLUSION

To summarize, recent research in my laboratory and elsewhere has provided considerable information about the what and when of cognitive aging. We are also beginning to learn about the implications of this phenomenon for functioning outside of the research laboratory, but, perhaps because of different perspectives on the best methods of investigation, much less is currently known about the why, where, and how of this phenomenon.

Recommended Reading

Craik, F.I.M., & Salthouse, T.A. (2000). *Handbook of aging and cognition* (2nd ed.). Mahwah, NJ: Erlbaum.
Salthouse, T.A. (1991). *Theoretical perspectives in cognitive aging*. Mahwah, NJ: Erlbaum.

Acknowledgments—This research was supported by National Institute on Aging Grants AG06826 and AG19627 to the author.

Note

1. Address correspondence to Timothy A. Salthouse, Department of Psychology, P.O. Box 400400, University of Virginia, Charlottesville, VA 22904-4400; e-mail: salthouse@virginia.edu.

References

Hambrick, D.Z., Salthouse, T.A., & Meinz, E.J. (1999). Predictors of crossword puzzle proficiency and moderators of age-cognition relations. *Journal of Experimental Psychology: General, 128,* 131–164.
Salthouse, T.A. (2001a). Attempted decomposition of age-related influences on two tests of reasoning. *Psychology and Aging, 16,* 251–263.
Salthouse, T.A. (2001b). Structural models of the relations between age and measures of cognitive functioning. *Intelligence, 29,* 93–115.
Salthouse, T.A. (2003). Interrelations of aging, knowledge, and cognitive performance. In U. Staudinger & U. Lindenberger (Eds.), *Understanding human development: Lifespan psychology in exchange with other disciplines* (pp. 265–287). Berlin, Germany: Kluwer Academic.

Salthouse, T.A., Atkinson, T.M., & Berish, D.E. (2003). Executive functioning as a potential mediator of age-related cognitive decline in normal adults. *Journal of Experimental Psychology: General, 132,* 566–594.

Salthouse, T.A., & Ferrer-Caja, E. (2003). What needs to be explained to account for age-related effects on multiple cognitive variables? *Psychology and Aging, 18,* 91–110.

Salthouse, T.A., Hambrick, D.Z., & McGuthry, K.E. (1998). Shared age-related influences on cognitive and non-cognitive variables. *Psychology and Aging, 13,* 486–500.

Salthouse, T.A., Toth, J., Daniels, K., Parks, C., Pak, R., Wolbrette, M., & Hocking, K. (2000). Effects of aging on the efficiency of task switching in a variant of the Trail Making Test. *Neuropsychology, 14,* 102–111.

Wechsler, D. (1997). *Wechsler Adult Intelligence Scale–third edition.* San Antonio, TX: Psychological Corp.

Woodcock, R.W., McGrew, K.S., & Mather, N. (2001). *Woodcock-Johnson III Tests of Cognitive Abilities.* Itasca, IL: Riverside.

Critical Thinking Questions

1. At what point along the life-span does cognitive decline first appear, and for which cognitive processes?

2. If you were designing a test to minimize age differences, what type of questions would you include on this test? If you wanted to maximize age differences: what type of questions would best show age-related declines?

3. If age is associated with cognitive decline, what are several reasons why older adults are not performing noticeably worse in activities of everyday life?

This article has been reprinted as it originally appeared in *Current Directions in Psychological Science.* Citation information for this article as originally published appears above.

Connecting the Many Levels and Facets of Cognitive Aging

Shu-Chen Li[1]

Center for Lifespan Psychology, Max Planck Institute for Human Development, Berlin, Germany

Abstract

Basic cognitive mechanisms, such as the abilities to briefly maintain, focus, and process information, decline with age. Related fields of cognitive aging research have been advancing rapidly, but mostly independently, at the biological, information processing, and behavioral levels. To facilitate integration, this article reviews research on cognitive aging at the different levels, and describes a recent integrative theory postulating that aging-related deficiencies in neurotransmission cause increased noise in information processing and less distinctive cortical representation, which in turn lead to cognitive deficits. Aging-related attenuation of catecholaminergic modulation can be modeled by lowering a neural network parameter to reduce the signal-to-noise ratio of information processing. The performance of such models is consistent with benchmark phenomena observed in humans, ranging from age differences in learning rate, asymptotic performance, and interference susceptibility to intra- and interindividual variability and ability dedifferentiation. Although the details of the conjectured sequence of effects linking neuromodulation to cognitive aging deficits await further empirical validation, cross-level theorizing of the kind illustrated here could foster the coevolution of related fields through cross-level data synthesis and hypothesis testing.

Keywords

cognitive aging; catecholaminergic modulation; cortical representation; neural networks

Gradual declines in fundamental aspects of cognition pervade the aging process. Biologically, brain aging involves structural losses in neurons and the connections between them, along with deterioration in the neurochemical systems that support communication between neurons. Behaviorally, people's abilities to keep information in mind briefly (termed working memory), attend to relevant information, and process information promptly are compromised with age. Explanations for these cognitive aging deficits have been postulated at various levels. At the cognitive level, some researchers assume there is an aging-related reduction in processing resources, such as working memory, attention regulation, and processing speed. At the biological level, other researchers hypothesize there is an aging-related increase in neuronal noise (i.e., haphazard variations in neural information processing that reduce processing fidelity) or dysfunction of the prefrontal cortex, an area at the front of the cerebral cortex that is thought to be critical for working memory. Experimental designs used in neurobiological studies that involve animals are not always readily transferable to human cognitive studies, and vice versa. Therefore, until the recent advances with neuroimaging and related techniques that provide online measures of brain activity while people are performing cognitive tasks, data and theories of cognitive aging were mostly confined within their respective levels. The present article focuses on synthesizing what is known about cognitive aging in humans using a cross-level theory that postulates a sequence of events beginning at the mechanisms of neurotransmission and leading to the behavioral phenomena that have been documented.

AGING, CATECHOLAMINES, AND COGNITIVE PROCESSING RESOURCES

Although progressive neuroanatomical degeneration is characteristic of pathological aging such as Alzheimer's disease, there is now evidence suggesting that milder cognitive problems occurring during normal aging are mostly due to neurochemical shifts in still-intact neural circuitry (Morrison & Hof, 1997). In particular, the neurotransmitters referred to as catecholamines, including dopamine and norepinephrine, appear to play an important role in aging-related cognitive impairments.

There is consensus that catecholaminergic function in various regions of the brain, such as the prefrontal cortex and basal ganglia (a group of diverse structures, lying beneath the cortex, that regulate motor movements and category learning), declines with advancing age. Across the adult life span, in the various regions of frontal cortex and basal ganglia, the amount of dopamine and the number of protein molecules responding to the release of dopamine (i.e., dopamine receptors) decrease by 5 to 10% each decade (see Kaasinen et al., 2000, for review).

Research over the past two decades suggests that catecholamines modulate the prefrontal cortex's utilization of briefly activated cortical representations of external stimuli to circumvent constant reliance on environmental cues and to regulate attention to focus on relevant stimuli and appropriate responses (Arnsten, 1998). In addition, there are many findings indicating functional relationships between aging-related deficits in the dopaminergic system and reduced cognitive processing resources in terms of information processing speed and working memory. For instance, reduced density of dopamine receptors in old rats' basal ganglia decreases response speed and increases variability in reaction time (MacRae, Spirduso, & Wilcox, 1988). Drugs that facilitate dopaminergic modulation alleviate working memory deficits of aged monkeys who lose 50% of the dopamine in their pre-frontal cortex because of aging (Arnsten & Goldman-Rakic, 1985). In humans, aging-related attenuation of one category of dopamine receptors (i.e., the D2 receptors) is associated with declines in processing speed and word and face recognition (Bäckman et al., 2000).

MODELING AGING-RELATED DECLINE OF CATECHOLAMINERGIC MODULATION

Although there is growing evidence for the catecholamines' involvement in various aging-related cognitive impairments, the details of these functional relationships await further explication. Theoretical inquiries into general computational principles aimed at capturing how neuronal signals are processed and integrated might help unravel mechanisms underlying the associations between deficient catecholaminergic modulation of neurons' responsivity and cognitive aging deficits.

The specifics of catecholamines' roles in modulating neuronal responsivity notwithstanding, in general terms, catecholamines' effects can be conceptualized as altering the balance between the intensity of the to-be-processed neuronal signals and other random background neuronal activity in the brain (i.e., the signal-to-noise ratio), thus regulating the neurons' sensitivity to incoming signals. This effect can be modeled with artificial neural networks, computational models that consist of multiple interconnected layers of simple processing units whose responsivity can be regulated by a network parameter (Servan-Schreiber, Printz, & Cohen, 1990). Neural signal transmission in such systems is simulated by forwarding the effect of an external stimulus signal, represented by the activity profile across units at the input layer, to output units via the intermediate layer. The activity level (activation) of each of the intermediate and output units is usually defined by a mathematical equation describing the function relating input signals to output (the most commonly used equation is the S-shaped logistic function). The activation function transforms the input signal into patterns of activation at the subsequent layers. The thus-transformed activation profile across units at the intermediate layer constitutes the network's internal representation for a given external stimulus. The gain (G) parameter is a component of the activation function that determines its slope. Conceptually, the G parameter captures catecholaminergic modulation by altering the slope of the activation function, thus regulating a processing unit's sensitivity to input signals (Fig. 1a). The randomness inherent in mechanisms of neurotransmitter release can be implemented by randomly choosing the values for the G parameters of the network's processing units at each processing step. Reducing the mean of these values can then simulate aging-related decline in catecholaminergic function (Li, Lindenberger, & Frensch, 2000).

FROM DEFICIENT NEUROMODULATION TO NEURONAL NOISE AND REPRESENTATION DEDIFFERENTIATION

A classical hypothesis regarding cognitive aging is that it is due to an aging-related increase in neuronal noise; however, mechanisms leading to such an increase and its immediate consequences have not been unveiled thus far. Simulating aging-related decline of neuromodulation by attenuating the average of the G parameter hints at a possible chain of mechanisms that may be involved.

Reducing mean G reduces a unit's average responsivity to input signals (Fig. 1a). For instance, a given amount of difference between two inputs—say, an excitatory input (e.g., $+1$) and an inhibitory input (e.g., -1)—produces a much greater difference in activation when G equals 1.00 than when G equals 0.1. At the extreme case when G equals 0, the unit's response always remains at its baseline activation regardless of differences in inputs (see Fig. 1). Furthermore, when the values of a unit's G are randomly chosen from a set of values, the lower the average of that set, the more variable is the unit's response to a given external signal. An increase in the variability of activation within the network, in turn, decreases the fidelity with which signals are transmitted. Put differently, a given amount of random variation in G, simulating random fluctuations in release of neurotransmitters, generates more haphazard activation variability during signal processing if the average of the

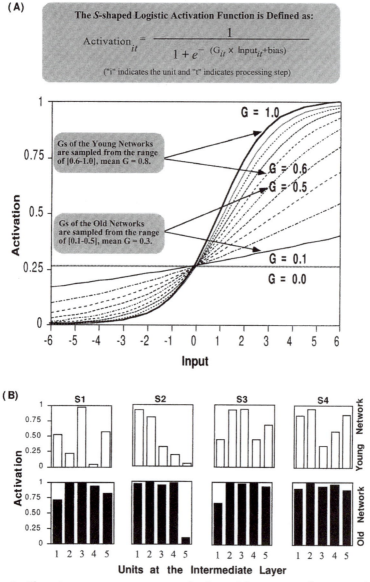

(A)

The *S*-shaped Logistic Activation Function is Defined as:

$$\text{Activation}_{it} = \frac{1}{1 + e^{-(G_{it} \times \text{Input}_{it} + \text{bias})}}$$

("i" indicates the unit and "t" indicates processing step)

Gs of the Young Networks are sampled from the range of [0.6-1.0], mean G = 0.8.

Gs of the Old Networks are sampled from the range of [0.1-0.5], mean G = 0.3.

G = 1.0
G = 0.6
G = 0.5
G = 0.1
G = 0.0

Activation

Input

(B)

Activation

S1 S2 S3 S4

Young Network

Old Network

Units at the Intermediate Layer

Fig. 1. The gain parameter: its impact on the slope of the activation function and the distinctiveness of activation patterns at the intermediate layer. The S-shaped logistic activation function is defined in (a), and graphed for different values of G. Values of G ranging from 0.6 to 1.0 were used in networks simulating young adults' performance, and values of G ranging from 0.1 to 0.5 were used in networks simulating older adults' performance. Internal activation patterns across five intermediate units of one "young" and one "old" network in response to four different stimuli (S1–S4) are shown in (b). From "Unifying Cognitive Aging: From Neuromodulation to Representation to Cognition," by S.-C. Li, U. Lindenberger, and P.A. Frensch, 2000, *Neurocomputing, 32–33*, p. 881. Copyright 2000 by Elsevier Science. Adapted with permission.

processing units' Gs is reduced. This sequence of effects computationally depicts a potential neurochemical mechanism for aging-related increase of neuronal noise: As aging attenuates neuromodulation, the impact of transmitter fluctuations on the overall level of neuronal noise is amplified in the aging brain.

Moreover, reduced responsivity and increased random variability in the activation within a network subsequently decrease the distinctiveness of the network's internal representations of external stimuli. Low representational distinctiveness means that the activation profiles for different external stimuli are less readily differentiable from each other at the network's intermediate layer. To illustrate, Figure 1b shows the activation levels across units at the intermediate layer of one "young" (higher average G) and one "old" (lower average G) network in response to four input signals. Clearly, the internal stimulus representations are much less distinctive in the old than in the young network. Thus, according to this simulation, as people age, at the cognitive level their mental representations of different events, such as various scenes viewed at an art exhibition, become less distinct, and therefore more confusable with each other.

A potential biological implication of this theoretical property is that as declining catecholaminergic modulation drives down cortical neurons' responsivity and increases neuronal noise in the aging brain, cortical representations (the presumed biological substrates of mental representations) elicited by different stimuli become less distinct (i.e., become dedifferentiated). Cognitive processing depends on the cortical representations created by perception and accessed by memory. Therefore, by causing less distinctive cortical representations of different events, deficient neuromodulation could have an influential impact on various aspects of cognitive functioning.

SIMULATIONS LINKING NEUROMODULATION WITH BEHAVIORAL DATA

The theoretical path from aging-related impairment of neuromodulation to increased neuronal noise in the aging brain to dedifferentiated cortical representation and on to cognitive aging deficits has been tested and supported by a series of neural network simulations.

Aging, Learning Rate, Asymptotic Performance, and Susceptibility to Interference

Behavioral memory research shows that as people get older, they take longer to learn paired associates (arbitrary word pairs, such as "computer-violin"). In agreement with these empirical findings, neural network simulations have shown that old networks also require more trials than young networks to learn paired associates (Fig. 2a). If old and young people differ only in how fast they can learn, one would expect that, given enough training, old people would eventually reach young people's performance level. Alas, ample data show that maximum (asymptotic) performance often exhibits an aging deficit as well. The lower asymptotic performance observed in people in their 60s and onward can also be accounted for by reducing average G, as old neural networks display poorer asymptotic performance than young neural networks (Fig. 2b).

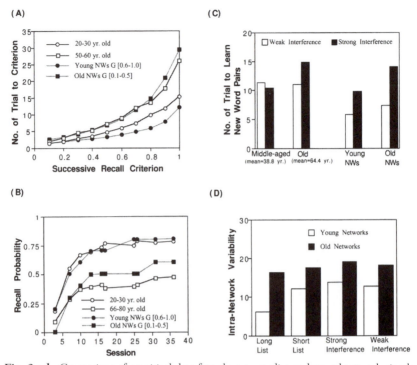

Fig. 2a-d. Comparison of empirical data from human studies and neural network simulations of aging-related cognitive deficits. The graph in (a) shows the number of trials needed to reach increasingly stringent criteria in paired associate learning, for young and older adults and for networks (NWs) with the G parameter set to high and low values (the empirical results can be found in Monge, 1971). Asymptotic performance of young and old adults and networks in paired associate learning is illustrated in (b), which shows the number of training sessions required to reach maximum-possible recall performance (the empirical results can be found in Baltes & Kliegl, 1992). Aging-related increase in susceptibility to interference during paired associate learning is illustrated in (c), which shows performance under conditions of weak and strong interference (the empirical results can be found in Lair, Moon, & Kausler, 1969). The effect of reduction in mean G on intranetwork performance variability across different study lists in four conditions is shown in (d). Intranetwork variability is reported in units of coefficient of variance (i.e., standard deviation divided by the mean). (Reviews of aging-related increase in intraindividual variability can be found in Li & Lindenberger, 1999.) Adapted from "Unifying Cognitive Aging: From Neuromodulation to Representation to Cognition," by S.-C. Li, U. Lindenberger, and P.A. Frensch, 2000, *Neurocomputing, 32–33*, pp. 884, 886. Copyright 2000 by Elsevier Science. Adapted with permission.

Another prominent cognitive aging deficit is older people's increasing susceptibility to distraction by irrelevant or no-longer-relevant information (i.e., increased susceptibility to interference). In the context of paired associate learning, 60-year-olds are more susceptible than 40-year-olds to interference of previously learned word pairs with subsequent learning of new pairs, and they need more trials to learn new word pairs if this interference is strong. In line with this empirical evidence, the simulations have shown that the degree of interference affects the rate at which new word pairs are learned more in old than in young networks (Fig. 2c).

Aging, Performance Variability, and Covariation

The behavioral data demonstrate not only decreases in performance levels, but also aging-related increases in performance variation within a person across time (or different tasks) and aging-related increases in differences between individuals. Furthermore, aging also seems to affect the relations between different cognitive abilities: Studies conducted since the 1920s have shown that as people age, performance levels on different tasks become more correlated with each other. These phenomena can also be accounted for by reduction in mean G, suggesting that aging-related increases in intraindividual performance variability, interindividual diversity, and ability dedifferentiation might in part be associated with declining neuromodulation (Li et al., 2000). For example, Figure 2d shows the results of a simulation in which intranetwork variability was tested. Performance variability across different study lists in four conditions of paired associate learning was larger in the old than in the young networks.

COEVOLVING FIELDS VIA CROSS-LEVEL DATA SYNTHESIS AND HYPOTHESIS GENERATION

Accumulating evidence indicates that catecholaminergic neuromodulation is an influential biological underpinning of many cognitive aging deficits. However, details of the effects causing this neurobiological-behavior link remain to be unraveled. Pieces of the puzzle are emerging from the various subfields, but the field as a whole needs overarching frameworks to integrate existing data and guide concerted research efforts. The cross-level computational theory described in this article is only an initial attempt to arrive at such integrative frameworks. Indeed, the theory's main tenet—that attenuated neuromodulation leads to increased neuronal noise and less distinctive cortical representations in the aging brain, and in turn to cognitive aging deficits—awaits more direct and vigorous empirical scrutiny in the future. However, the computational simulations conducted thus far integrate evidence of aging-related decline in catecholaminergic modulation with a broad range of cognitive aging effects that have been observed in humans—an integrative task that still cannot be easily implemented in animal neurobiological or human neuroimaging studies alone.

In addition to synthesizing data, the theory generates some cross-level hypotheses for future research. For instance, it suggests that neuromodulation might influence aging-related increases in intraindividual performance variability and interindividual diversity. Contrary to the traditional focus on average performance, this hypothesis motivates investigations of aging and intraindividual variability, an issue that is just now starting to be more broadly examined. Recent studies showed that intraindividual fluctuations in 60- to 80-year-olds' reaction times could be used to predict whether they had dementia (Hultsch, MacDonald, Hunter, Levy-Bencheton, & Strauss, 2000). In another study, fluctuations in 60- to 80-year-olds' gait and balance performance predicted verbal and spatial memory (Li, Aggen, Nesselroade, & Baltes, 2001). These results affirm that understanding aging-related performance variability and its sources may offer insight into aging-related changes in the brain-behavior link. At a different level, animal pharmacological studies could directly examine the effects of catecholamine agonists (drugs that facilitate the effects of catecholamines) on both intraindividual performance fluctuations and diversity of performance across individuals. Questions about how a drug affects performance levels and intraindividual fluctuations are commonly examined. However, issues relating to diversity across individuals are more rarely systematically addressed because individual differences traditionally play little role in animal research, despite the fact that such diversity is often observed in clinical settings.

Recent neuroimaging evidence suggests that many aspects of cortical information processing that involve either the left or the right hemisphere separately in young adults become less differentiated and involve activation of both hemispheres as people age. For instance, in several studies, people in their 60s and beyond showed activity in both brain hemispheres during memory retrieval and during both verbal and spatial working memory tasks. In young adults, verbal memory is processed primarily by the left hemisphere, and spatial memory is processed by the right hemisphere (see Cabeza, in press, for a comprehensive review). The fact that attenuating the average values of the G parameter causes less distinctive internal representations indicates that aging-related reduction in the extent to which the two hemispheres deal separately with different processes might, in part, be related to neurochemical changes in the aging brain. This suggests a new line of inquiry into how neuromodulation of the distinctiveness of cortical representations might affect the distribution of information processing across different neural circuitry, in addition to affecting working memory, attention regulation, and processing speed. Finally, given catecholamines' involvement in developmental attentional disorders (see Arnsten, 1998), investigations of whether normal cognitive development in children might be conceived as an increase in the efficacy of neuromodulation and cortical representations could aid the search for unifying accounts of cognitive development and aging.

Recommended Reading

Arnsten, A.F.T. (1993). Catecholamine mechanisms in age-related cognitive decline. *Neurobiology of Aging, 14*, 639–641.
Craik, F.I.M., & Salthouse, T.A. (Eds.). (2000). *The handbook of aging and cognition* (2nd ed.). Mahwah, NJ: Erlbaum.
Li, S.-C., Lindenberger, U., & Sikström, S. (2001). Aging cognition: From neuromodulation to representation. *Trends in Cognitive Sciences, 5*, 479–486.
Welford, A.T. (1981). Signal, noise, performance and age. *Human Factor, 23*, 97–109.
West, R.L. (1996). An application of prefrontal cortex function theory to cognitive aging. *Psychological Bulletin, 120*, 272–292.

Acknowledgments—With this review, I would like to commemorate Alan T. Welford (1914–1995), who more than four decades ago ventured to speculate about the neuronal-noise hypothesis. I thank the Max Planck Institute and Paul Baltes for sponsoring this research.

Note

1. Address correspondence to Shu-Chen Li, Max Planck Institute for Human Development, Lentzeallee 94, D-14195 Berlin, Germany; e-mail: shuchen@mpib-berlin.mpg.de.

References

Arnsten, A.F.T. (1998). Catecholamine modulation of prefrontal cortical cognitive function. *Trends in Cognitive Sciences, 2*, 436–447.

Arnsten, A.F.T., & Goldman-Rakic, P.S. (1985). Alpha 2-adrenergic mechanisms in prefrontal cortex associated with cognitive declines in aged non-human primates. *Science, 230*, 1273–1276.

Bäckman, L., Ginovart, N., Dixon, R., Wahlin, T., Wahlin, A., Halldin, C., & Farde, L. (2000). Age-related cognitive deficits mediated by changes in the striatal dopamine system. *American Journal of Psychiatry, 157*, 635–637.

Baltes, P.B., & Kliegl, R. (1992). Further testing the limits of cognitive plasticity: Negative age differences in a mnemonic skill are robust. *Developmental Psychology, 28*, 121–125.

Cabeza, R. (in press). Hemispheric asymmetry reduction in older adults: The HAROLD model. *Psychology and Aging*.

Hultsch, D.F., MacDonald, S.W.S., Hunter, M.A., Levy-Bencheton, J., & Strauss, E. (2000). Intraindividual variability in cognitive performance in older adults: Comparison of adults with mild dementia, adults with arthritis, and healthy adults. *Neuropsychology, 14*, 588–598.

Kaasinen, V., Vilkman, H., Hietala, J., Nagren, K., Helenius, H., Olsson, H., Farde, L., & Rinne, J.O. (2000). Age-related dopamine D2/D3 receptors loss in extrastriatal regions of the human brain. *Neurobiology of Aging, 21*, 683–688.

Lair, C.V., Moon, W.H., & Kausler, D.H. (1969). Associative interference in the paired-associative learning of middle-aged and old subjects. *Developmental Psychology, 5*, 548–552.

Li, S.-C., Aggen, S., Nesselroade, J.R., & Baltes, P.B. (2001). Short-term fluctuations in elderly people's sensorimotor functioning predict text and spatial memory performance. *Gerontology, 47*, 100–116.

Li, S.-C., & Lindenberger, U. (1999). Cross-level unification: A computational exploration of the link between deterioration of neurotransmitter systems and dedifferentiation of cognitive abilities in old age. In L.-G. Nilsson & M. Markowitsch (Eds.), *Cognitive neuroscience of memory* (pp. 104–146). Toronto, Ontario, Canada: Hogrefe & Huber.

Li, S.-C., Lindenberger, U., & Frensch, P.A. (2000). Unifying cognitive aging: From neuromodulation to representation to cognition. *Neurocomputing, 32–33*, 879–890.

MacRae, P.G., Spirduso, W.W., & Wilcox, R.E. (1988). Reaction time and nigrostriatal dopamine function: The effect of age and practice. *Brain Research, 451*, 139–146.

Monge, H.R. (1971). Studies of verbal learning from the college years through middle age. *Journal of Gerontology, 26*, 324–329.

Morrison, J.H., & Hof, P.R. (1997). Life and death of neurons in the aging brain. *Science, 278*, 412–429.

Servan-Schreiber, D., Printz, H., & Cohen, J.D. (1990). A network model of catecholamine effects: Gain, signal-to-noise ratio, and behavior. *Science, 249*, 892–895.

Critical Thinking Questions

1. What are catecholamines, and how are they related to cognitive functioning?

2. Define neuronal noise, and describe how this may explain age differences in cognitive processing.

3. You are working with two adults: one person performs in the average range on all tests, and the other person sometimes performs in the excellent range, but on other days performs at the below average level. Which person are you most worried about as far as his/her cognitive functioning, and why?

This article has been reprinted as it originally appeared in *Current Directions in Psychological Science*. Citation information for this article as originally published appears above.

False Remembering in the Aged

Larry L. Jacoby[1] and Matthew G. Rhodes
Washington University in St. Louis

Abstract

Researchers studying human memory have increasingly focused on memory accuracy in aging populations. In this article we briefly review the literature on memory accuracy in healthy older adults. The prevailing evidence indicates that, compared to younger adults, older adults exhibit both diminished memory accuracy and greater susceptibility to misinformation. In addition, older adults demonstrate high levels of confidence in their false memories. We suggest an explanatory framework for the high level of false memories observed in older adults, a framework based on the theory that consciously controlled uses of memory decline with age, making older adults more susceptible to false memories that rely on automatic processes. We also point to future research that may remedy such deficits in accuracy.

Keywords

memory; aging; memory accuracy

"As I told you, my mother is visiting this weekend and staying for two weeks. You agreed." Faced with an "I told you . . ." claim of this sort, one might wonder if one is being confronted with a false memory or, perhaps, a fraudulent attempt to create one. Are older adults more vulnerable to such mundane attempts to create false memories? As evidenced by warnings from the Federal Bureau of Investigation's Web site (Federal Bureau of Investigation, n.d.), there is a host of serious fraudulent schemes directed at older adults that rely on memory deficits that sometimes accompany old age. In this article, we describe results suggesting that older adults are more susceptible to such scams than are younger adults.

We begin by considering a common complaint about the memory performance of older adults: the repeated telling of stories. The greater tendency of older adults to unknowingly repeat stories can be understood in terms of a dual-process model of memory (Jacoby, 1999). According to such a model, repetition of a story has two effects, one of which is to "strengthen" or increase the familiarity of a story, making it more likely to be repeated. This automatic, habit-like influence of memory is opposed by "recollection," a more consciously controlled use of memory that allows unwanted repetition to be avoided by recollecting the specific prior telling of a story.

These two forms or uses of memory are illustrated by an experiment (Jacoby, 1999) whose results demonstrate that older adults are vulnerable to an ironic effect of repetition. In a first phase of that experiment, young adults and older adults (aged 65 and over) were presented with a list of words that they were instructed to read. Words in this list were presented one, two, or three times, with repetition intended to mimic the repeated telling of a story. Next, participants heard a list of words that they were told to remember for a subsequent memory test. For that test, participants were instructed to respond "yes" only if a word had been heard earlier and were correctly warned that the test would also include words that they had read earlier and should be rejected.

As Figure 1 shows, younger adults' false recognition of earlier-read items declined with increasing repetition. However, for older adults, the opposite pattern held, as repeated reading had the ironic effect of increasing the probability of falsely recognizing earlier-read items as having been heard. Thus, older adults were less able to counter an increase in the familiarity of a repeated item with a specific memory (recollection) of its prior occurrence, making them vulnerable to false memories. Younger adults forced to respond quickly also showed an ironic effect of repetition, exhibiting more false memories for repeated items. This elevation in false memories with repetition for younger adults, who presumably have intact recollection, suggests that recollection, in addition to being vulnerable to aging, may be slower than the more automatic processes that support familiarity.

False memories have also been studied using a paradigm initially reported by Deese (1959) and later revived by Roediger and McDermott (1995). In the Deese-Roediger-McDermott (DRM) paradigm, participants are first exposed to a list of semantically related words, such as *bed, rest, pillow*, etc. These words are all related to a central theme word (e.g., *sleep*), termed the critical lure, which is itself never presented. When later tested, however, participants often falsely recall or recognize the critical lure as an item that had been presented.

Several investigators have tested older adults in the DRM paradigm, with the evidence suggesting that in many cases older adults are more likely to report

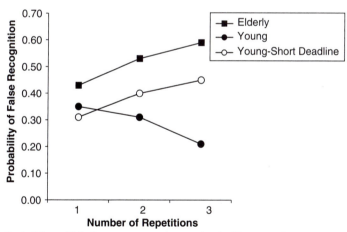

Fig. 1. Probability of falsely recognizing an item that had been read as one that had been heard. Participants read words one, two, or three times. They then heard a list of words and were given a recognition test with instructions to endorse only items that had been heard and to reject earlier-read words. Results showed that older adults' (filled squares) probability of false recognition of earlier-read words increased with repetition whereas younger adults' level of false recognition (filled circles) decreased with repetition. Younger adults made to respond quickly (unfilled circles) showed a pattern of data similar to that of older adults, being more likely to falsely endorse earlier-read items that had been repeated.

false memories for the critical lure than are younger adults (e.g., Norman & Schacter, 1997). Interestingly, manipulations that reduce false memories in younger adults are either partially or wholly ineffective for older adults. For example, McCabe and Smith (2002) demonstrated that warning younger adults about the nature of the DRM paradigm prior to study significantly reduced false recognition of the critical lure. Older adults exposed to the same manipulation exhibited approximately half the reduction in false memories evident for younger adults. In addition, when both groups were warned prior to a recognition test, only younger adults showed a substantial reduction in false memories.

Older adults' eyewitness memory may also be susceptible to striking inaccuracies. For example, Karpel, Hoyer, and Toglia (2001) had older and younger adults view a slide sequence depicting a theft and later administered a questionnaire about the theft. Several questions contained misleading information suggesting the presence of items that were never shown (e.g., "Did the thief pick up the glue . . . in front of the can of Coke?" when a can of Coke was never shown). When tested on their memory for the slide sequence, older adults were more likely to falsely recognize suggested items than were younger adults. They also showed higher levels of confidence for falsely remembered, suggested items and reported more vivid details for suggested items than younger adults did (see Kelley and Sahakyan, 2003, for a similar pattern of inaccuracy and overconfidence in older adults).

Taken together, these data suggest that older adults exhibit higher levels of false memories than younger adults do and that older adults' subjective experience of memory (in the form of confidence judgments) is less well attuned to their actual level of accuracy. In the next section, we discuss an explanatory framework for age-related differences in memory accuracy.

A DUAL-PROCESS MODEL OF MEMORY AGING

As noted previously, age-related differences in memory accuracy can be explained by a dual-process view of memory. This view suggests that older adults' greater susceptibility to false memories reflects a diminished ability to recollect specific events. A by-product of this reduced recollection is that easily accessible information may be mistakenly regarded as a memory (Jacoby, 1999). For example, Hay and Jacoby (1999) describe the case of an elderly math professor who, after attending a conference, was unable to locate his return airline ticket. He purchased another one and, arriving home, phoned his wife to pick him up at the airport. She responded that she would be unable to do so because he had driven their only car to the conference! The professor's action slip reflects a failure to recollect having driven to the conference along with a reliance on his usual habits that accompanied flying, such as calling his wife when he arrived at the airport.

Our contention is that the controlled processes necessary to support recollection and overcome habits change with age, rendering habits more influential and older adults more likely to exhibit false memories. We have used procedures to separately measure recollection and automatic influences of memory, such as habits; we illustrate these procedures by describing data reported by Hay and Jacoby (1999). The first phase of their experiment was meant to create habits of varying strength by exposing older and younger adults to pairs of associatively related words (e.g., *organ–music*). During that phase, cue words were paired with two different responses and the probability of pairings was varied. For example, the typical response word *music* appeared with the cue word *organ* on 75% of the trials, whereas, the atypical response *piano* appeared with *organ* on only 25% of the trials. In a second phase, participants studied short lists of word pairs. In some cases, the word pairs had been presented most frequently in the first phase. These *congruent items* can be contrasted with other studied pairs (e.g., *organ–piano*), termed *incongruent items*, that had been shown infrequently in the first phase. Following this study phase, participants were tested on their memory for words presented in the study phase, cued with the first word of the pair (e.g., *organ*_____). Younger and older adults were almost equally likely to report the correct response for congruent items. However, for incongruent items, older adults were more likely than younger adults to falsely recall the most typical response (e.g., *music*).

Results were analyzed with a dual-process model (Fig. 2). According to that model, correct recall of congruent items can result from recollection (R) or from reliance on habit (H) when recollection fails (1-R)—a situation expressed as the equation R + H(1-R). In contrast, for incongruent items, reliance on habit when recollection fails—expressed as H(1-R)—leads to false recall. These equations allow recollection to be estimated as the difference between correct recall on congruent items and false recall on incongruent items. Analyzing their data using these equations, Hay and Jacoby demonstrated that age differences in memory performance were fully accounted for by a difference in recollection (Fig. 3). Specifically, estimated habit did not differ for younger and older adults. Rather,

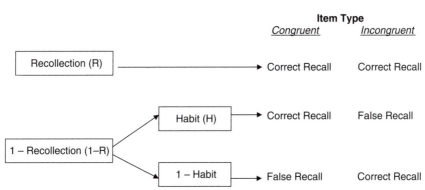

Fig. 2. Dual-process model of memory used by Hay and Jacoby (1999). In their experiments, participants first read pairs of words, some of which were presented more frequently (e.g., *organ–music*) than other pairs (e.g., *organ–piano*) to establish habits of varying strengths. For a second phase, participants studied short lists of word pairs and were tested on these pairs, cued with the first word of each pair (e.g., *organ–*_____). Two types of items are of interest. *Congruent items* were identical to the pairs presented most frequently and *incongruent items* were consistent with pairs presented less frequently. In this model, correct recall of congruent items occurs because of recollection or, failing that ("1–Recollection"), because of the habit established by presenting pairs frequently. False recall for an incongruent item occurs if one provides the response made most typical by habit and fails to recollect what was studied.

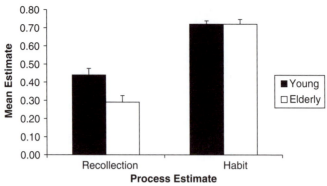

Fig. 3. Estimated recollection and habit for younger and older adults. Recollection was estimated by subtracting the probability of false recall for incongruent items from the probability of correct recall for congruent items. Habit can be estimated by dividing the probability of false recall on incongruent items by the estimated probability of a failure in recollection. Hay and Jacoby (1999) showed that younger and older adults did not differ on estimates of habit but did differ for recollection.

because estimated recollection was diminished in older adults, they relied on habit more often and produced more false memories.

MULTIPLE PROCESSES OF FALSE MEMORIES

More recent work has suggested that false memories can sometimes result because misleading information is so potent that older adults skip any further attempt to retrieve and mistakenly accept the misinformation as veridical. That is, older adults may be so "captured" by misleading information that they forgo engaging in recollection. Such deficits might make older adults more vulnerable to "I told you . . ." scams of the sort noted at the beginning of this article. For example, in one scam, a con man attempts to overcharge an older adult for a repair with the claim that "I told you that the repair cost X, and you agreed to pay." If the older adult is captured by this misinformation and falsely remembers specific details of the fraudulent oral contract, he or she will be victimized.

Jacoby, Bishara, Hessels, and Toth (2005) used an experimental procedure analogous to false "I told you . . ." claims to model the effects of misleading information on older adults. Their procedure was similar to that of Hay and Jacoby (1999), with the exception that, just prior to a test, a prime word was briefly presented that was either congruent or incongruent (misleading) with what had been studied. Results showed that presenting a misleading prime word disrupted memory accuracy, with older adults being much more likely than younger adults to mistakenly report the misleading prime as having been studied (i.e., a false memory). In addition, in one experiment, older adults were 10 times more likely to falsely "remember" details of the misleading prime than younger adults were. Using a variant of the model depicted in Figure 2, Jacoby et al. (2005) found that for older, but not younger, adults it was necessary to add a parameter (termed "capture") that indexed the probability that participants did not attempt recollection. That is, the misleading information was sometimes so powerful for older adults that they neglected any further attempt to remember what had been studied.

The notion of capture is consistent with other theories suggesting that older adults' memory deficits reflect a breakdown in processes important for ignoring irrelevant information (Hasher & Zacks, 1988). By this model, older adults are susceptible to misleading information because they are less efficient at suppressing such misinformation than younger adults are. Older adults' greater susceptibility to misinformation may also occur because they are less proficient at monitoring the source of misinformation (e.g., Henkel, Johnson, & De Leonardis, 1998). For example, older adults perform more poorly than younger adults do when asked to determine which of two sources (e.g., real vs. imagined events) a memory came from (Henkel et al., 1998).

IMPROVING MEMORY ACCURACY

For purposes of diagnosis and remediation, it is important to distinguish between different bases for cognitive control (Jacoby, Kelley & McElree, 1999). Cognitive control can be likened to quality control in manufacturing. For example, quality control can be achieved by using inspectors to monitor goods after they have been produced or by increasing the precision of production techniques to meet standards more reliably. Likewise, effective source monitoring could edit out false memories after they come to mind. Alternatively, as with improving production techniques, false memories could be avoided by elaborating on memory cues to constrain retrieval, such that what comes to mind is highly likely to be accurate— an *early-selection* means of cognitive control. We (Jacoby, Shimizu, Velanova, & Rhodes, 2005) have recently found that older adults are less likely to engage in early-selection processes that would help them avoid false memories. Such deficits may reflect deterioration in fronta-llobe functions thought to underlie cognitive control (e.g., Velanova et al., 2003). A goal for future research is to further delineate the precise neural mechanisms involved in controlled retrieval processes such as recollection and to understand how such mechanisms change with age.

Our present research is aimed at reducing older adults' vulnerability to false memories by training retrieval processes. In particular, we train older adults in situations that engender high levels of interference from misleading information and thus require a reliance on recollection to avoid misleading automatic influences of memory (see Jennings & Jacoby, 2003). As an example, we have examined the effects of training in a situation similar to that used by Hay and Jacoby (1999) to examine memory slips. Results have shown that providing feedback regarding the accuracy of responses reduced older adults' likelihood of producing confidently held false memories. We are continuing these initial efforts and are currently examining ways in which processes integral to early selection can benefit from remediation.

CONCLUSIONS

The data briefly reviewed here suggests that older adults (a) are more prone to reporting inaccurate memories; (b) may be more susceptible to misinformation;

and (c) may be largely unaware of this inaccuracy, as revealed by overconfidence. We do not suggest that these problems only afflict the memories of older adults, as college-aged younger adults exhibit similar patterns of data in some circumstances (e.g., when fast responding is required). Further, there exists great individual variability in older adults' likelihood of exhibiting false memories. However, the evidence does show a pervasive pattern of memory inaccuracy in older adults and sets an agenda for future research to enhance memory in the aged through training and to discover the neural substrates underlying the decline in accuracy. Our hope is that such training and research endeavors will not only help inoculate older adults against scams that prey on memory deficits but also contribute to our understanding of the changes in memory that accompany aging.

Recommended Reading

Balota, D.A., Dolan, P.O., & Duchek, J.M. (2000). Memory changes in healthy older adults. In E. Tulving & F.I.M. Craik (Eds.), *The Oxford Handbook of Memory* (pp. 395–409). Oxford, England: Oxford University Press.

Hoyer, W.J., & Verhaeghen, P. (2006). Memory aging. In J.E. Birren and K.W. Schaie (Eds.), *Handbook of the psychology of aging* (6th ed., pp. 209–232). San Diego, CA: Elsevier.

Rhodes, M.G., & Kelley, C.M. (2005). Executive processes, memory accuracy, and memory monitoring: An aging and individual difference analysis. *Journal of Memory and Language, 52,* 578–594.

Roediger, H.L. (1996). Memory illusions. *Journal of Memory and Language, 35,* 76–100.

Acknowledgments—Preparation of this article was supported by National Institute on Aging Grant AG13845.

Note

1. Address correspondence to Larry L. Jacoby, Department of Psychology, Washington University, Saint Louis, MO 63130; e-mail: lljacoby@artsci.wustl.edu.

References

Federal Bureau of Investigation. (n.d.). Fraud target: Senior citizens. Retrieved March 22, 2006, from http://www.fbi.gov/majcases/fraud/seniorsfam.htm

Deese, J. (1959). On the prediction of occurrence of particular verbal intrusions in immediate recall. *Journal of Experimental Psychology, 58,* 17–22.

Hasher, L., & Zacks, R.T. (1988). Working memory, comprehension, and aging: A review and a new view. In G.H. Bower (Ed.), *The psychology of learning and motivation* (pp. 193–225). San Diego, CA: Academic Press.

Hay, J.F., & Jacoby, L.L. (1999). Separating habit and recollection in young and older adults: Effects of elaborative processing and distinctiveness. *Psychology and Aging, 14,* 122–134.

Henkel, L.A., Johnson, M.K., & De Leonardis, D.M. (1998). Aging and source monitoring: Cognitive processes and neuropsychological correlates. *Journal of Experimental Psychology: General, 127,* 251–268.

Jacoby, L.L. (1999). Ironic effects of repetition: Measuring age-related differences in memory. *Journal of Experimental Psychology: Learning, Memory, and Cognition, 25,* 3–22.

Jacoby, L.L., Bishara, A.J., Hessels, S., & Toth, J.P. (2005). Aging, subjective experience, and cognitive control: Dramatic false remembering by older adults. *Journal of Experimental Psychology: General, 134*, 131–148.

Jacoby, L.L., Kelley, C.M., & McElree, B.D. (1999). The role of cognitive control: Early selection versus late correction. In S. Chaiken & Y. Trope (Eds.), *Dual-process theories in social psychology* (pp. 383–400). New York: Guilford Press.

Jacoby, L.L., Shimizu, Y., Velanova, K., & Rhodes, M.G. (2005). Age differences in depth of retrieval: Memory for foils. *Journal of Memory and Language, 52*, 493–504.

Jennings, J.M., & Jacoby, L.L. (2003). Improving memory in older adults: Training recollection. *Neuropsychological Rehabilitation, 13*, 417–440.

Karpel, M.E., Hoyer, W.J., & Toglia, M.P. (2001). Accuracy and qualities of real and suggested memories: Nonspecific age differences. *The Journals of Gerontology Series B: Psychological Sciences and Social Sciences, 56*, P103–P110.

Kelley, C.M., & Sahakyan, L. (2003). Memory, monitoring, and control in the attainment of memory accuracy. *Journal of Memory and Language, 48*, 704–721.

McCabe, D.P., & Smith, A.D. (2002). The effect of warnings on false memories in young and older adults. *Memory and Cognition, 30*, 1065–1077.

Norman, K.A., & Schacter, D.L. (1997). False recognition in younger and older adults: Exploring the characteristics of illusory memories. *Memorys Cognition, 25*, 838–848.

Roediger, H.L., & McDermott, K.B. (1995). Creating false memories: Remembering words not presented in lists. *Journal of Experimental Psychology: Learning, Memorys, Cognition, 21*, 803–814.

Velanova, K., Jacoby, L.L., Wheeler, M.E., McAvoy, M.P., Peterson, S.E., & Buckner, R.L. (2003). Functional-anatomic correlates of sustained and transient processing components engaged during controlled retrieval. *Journal of Neuroscience, 23*, 8460–8470.

Critical Thinking Questions

1. What is the dual-process model of memory, and how does this explain age differences in memory?

2. Under what conditions is the performance of younger adults most like the performance of older adults?

3. An attorney contacts you to ask you opinion about having an older adult provide an eye witness in court. What advice do you give her?

This article has been reprinted as it originally appeared in *Current Directions in Psychological Science*. Citation information for this article as originally published appears above.

Aging and Language Production

Deborah M. Burke[1]
Pomona College

Meredith A. Shafto
University of Oxford, Oxford, England

Abstract

Experimental research and older adults' reports of their own experience suggest that the ability to produce the spoken forms of familiar words declines with aging. Older adults experience more word-finding failures, such as tip-of-the-tongue states, than young adults do, and this and other speech production failures appear to stem from difficulties in retrieving the sounds of words. Recent evidence has identified a parallel age-related decline in retrieving the spelling of familiar words. Models of cognitive aging must explain why these aspects of language production decline with aging whereas semantic processes are well maintained. We describe a model wherein aging weakens connections among linguistic representations, thereby reducing the transmission of excitation from one representation to another. The structure of the representational systems for word phonology and orthography makes them vulnerable to transmission deficits, impairing retrieval.

Keywords

aging; word production; tip of the tongue; phonological retrieval; spelling

Older adults report that one of their most annoying cognitive problems is the inability to produce a well-known word. Although people of all ages suffer such word-finding failures, this type of error becomes more frequent with age, and older adults report that it is the cognitive problem most affected by aging. Understanding the nature and cause of word-finding failures is an important goal for aging research because these failures may diminish older adults' success in communicating, and weaken the evaluation of their language competence by themselves and others. Such negative self-appraisal promotes withdrawal from social interaction. Moreover, the age-related decline in word retrieval is theoretically significant because many language abilities are relatively well maintained in old age and models of aging must explain this pattern. For example, retrieval of the meaning of words and other semantic processes involved in understanding language show little change with aging. In this article, we focus on word production, that is, producing the sound or spelling for a word. (For age-related declines in other components of language production, see Kemper, Thompson, & Marquis, 2001.) We review evidence for the decline in word retrieval in old age and describe a cognitive aging model that explains why this language function declines.

MEASURING SPOKEN WORD PRODUCTION

One of the simplest methods for measuring the effect of aging on word retrieval is comparing young and older adults' ability to name pictures of objects. A number of studies have shown that older adults make more errors in naming pictures than young adults do (Feyereisen, 1997). During discourse, a more natural form of speech than picture naming, older adults produce more ambiguous references and more filled pauses (e.g., saying "um" or "er") and reformulate their words more than young adults do (Kemper, 1992; Schmitter-Edgecombe, Vesneski, & Jones, 2000). These dysfluencies suggest that older adults have difficulty retrieving the appropriate words when speaking.

Another type of dysfluency is a slip of the tongue in which the speaker produces one or more incorrect sounds in a word, for example, saying *coffee cot* when *coffee pot* was intended. Slips of the tongue have been an important source of data for developing models of speech production because they exhibit regular patterns that reveal production processes. Because slips of the tongue occur infrequently, techniques for inducing slips have been used to elevate their frequency in the laboratory. In a study by MacKay and James (in press), participants viewed written words containing either /p/ or /b/, and the task was to change the /p/ to /b/, or vice versa, and produce the reformulated word as quickly as possible. For example, the correct response for the stimulus "ribbed" was "ripped." An analysis of errors showed that older adults were more likely than young adults to omit sounds (e.g., saying "rip," given "ribbed"), whereas young adults were more likely than older adults to substitute a different sound (e.g., saying "tipped"). Older adults' omissions suggest they had difficulty retrieving the phonology (i.e., the sounds) of words; in contrast, young adults had multiple sounds available.

One of the most dramatic word production failures is the tip-of-the-tongue (TOT) experience—being unable to produce a word one is absolutely certain that one knows. Two studies investigating naturally occurring TOTs during everyday life demonstrated that older adults experience more TOTs than young adults (Burke, MacKay, Worthley, & Wade, 1991; Heine, Ober, & Shenaut, 1999). Participants kept diaries in which they recorded information about each TOT that they experienced during a 4-week interval. In both studies, the older participants reported more TOTs than young adults did. In one of the studies (Burke et al., in press), the majority of TOTs for both young and older participants involved proper nouns; the proper nouns for people were the names of people who had not been contacted recently. TOT words that were not proper nouns had a low frequency of occurrence in the language. Thus, although participants rated all TOT words as very familiar, they were words, including proper nouns, that were used neither frequently nor recently, making them vulnerable to retrieval failures.

W. James (1890) observed that a TOT produces a mental gap that "is intensely active," having the "wraith of the name" in it (p. 251). Indeed, people in the throes of a TOT recall bits of information about the form of the word they are trying to recall. They often report the first sound or number of syllables of the word, and this was true more often for young than older adults in the diary studies. Participants also reported that an alternate (but incorrect) word came to mind persistently, and this word tended to share its initial sound with the TOT word. For example, during a TOT for *eccentric*, the persistent alternate was *exotic*. As was the case for partial information, these alternate words were reported more often by young than by older adults.

Age differences in the TOT experience are supported by laboratory studies. In this research, TOTs are induced by asking participants questions that are correctly answered by single low-frequency words (e.g., "What word means to formally renounce a throne?"). Older adults experience more TOTs than young adults when answering such questions, although the age difference is reliable for proper nouns, but not always for other words. Further research is needed to clarify how age-related increases in TOTs vary for different types of words. Compared with young adults, older adults report less partial phonological information and fewer persistent alternates for lab-induced TOTs (e.g., Burke et al., 1991; Maylor, 1990). In the next section, we describe a model that accounts for these phenomena by postulating an age-related change in a fundamental word retrieval mechanism.

A MODEL OF AGING AND WORD RETRIEVAL FAILURES

Current models of language production postulate that verbal information is stored in a vast network of interconnected nodes organized into a *semantic system* representing word meanings and a *phonological* and *orthographic system* representing word sounds and spellings, as shown in Figure 1 (e.g., Dell, 1986; MacKay & Abrams, 1998). Word production starts with activation of semantic representations (propositional nodes) and transmission of excitation to lexical representations for words with these meanings. The lexical representation whose meaning corresponds most closely to the activated semantic information is then activated. Spoken production of this word requires activation of corresponding phonological representations.

TOTs occur when semantic and lexical representations corresponding to a word are activated, causing a strong feeling of knowing the word, but activation of phonological information about the word is incomplete. In the transmission-deficit model (Burke et al., 1991; MacKay & James, in press), activation of phonology fails because connections to phonological representations have become weak, reducing the transmission of excitation. For example, a TOT occurs for *pylon* (see Fig. 1) when weak connections transmit insufficient excitation to its phonological nodes. The model postulates three factors that weaken connections: aging of the speaker and lack of recent or frequent activation of representations. When a connection is sufficiently weak, it will transmit too little excitation to allow a representation to reach a threshold necessary for activation, resulting in production failure. This model explains why words that are produced infrequently are more likely than high-frequency words to be involved in TOTs. Moreover, age-related weakening of connections in older adults increases transmission deficits that cause both TOTs and omission errors in slips of the tongue.

Partial recall of the sounds of the target word during a TOT occurs when some but not all of the phonological nodes for producing that word are activated. Activated phonological nodes transmit excitation to other words that share these sounds, and if one of these words becomes activated, a persistent alternate will come to mind. For example, activation of the first syllable, /paɪ/, of *pylon* would send excitation to other lexical representations sharing this syllable, such as *pirate* and *pilot*, and one of these words may come to mind as a persistent alternate.

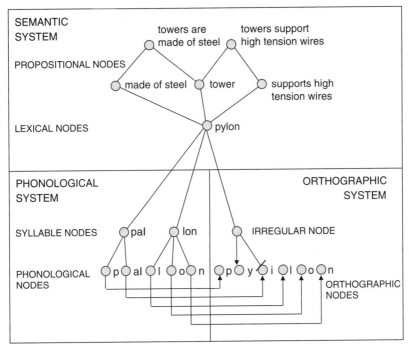

Fig. 1. Representation of semantic, phonological, and orthographic components of the word *pylon* (e.g., Burke, MacKay, Worthley, & Wade, 1991; MacKay & Abrams, 1998). Solid lines represent excitatory connections, and the broken line represents an inhibitory connection. All phonological nodes must be activated for spoken production of the word. Lateral connections between phonological and orthographic nodes produce correct spelling for regularly spelled words. However, because *pylon* is an irregularly spelled word, the lateral connections would lead to a misspelling; instead, the irregular node for *y*, connected to the lexical node, must be activated for the word to be spelled correctly. For the sake of simplicity, many nodes and connections have been omitted from this illustration.

Older adults report less partial phonological information and fewer persistent alternates than young adults because their weaker connections transmit less excitation to phonological nodes.

Why are age-related retrieval failures found for phonological but not semantic information? The architecture of the representational system renders the phonological system more vulnerable to transmission deficits than the semantic system because the functional effect of transmission deficits is more severe when one-to-one connections are involved than when connections are many to one. Because representations of semantic features of a word are highly interconnected (see Fig. 1), a transmission deficit in any one connection (e.g., *pylons are made of steel*) will be offset by other connections to the same feature (e.g., *towers are made of steel*). In retrieval of phonology, however, transmission of excitation diverges from lexical nodes along single connections to associated phonological nodes. A transmission deficit in a single connection will prevent retrieval of the phonology represented by that node.

TESTING THE ROLE OF PHONOLOGICAL RETRIEVAL IN TOTS

According to the transmission-deficit model, production of words sharing the sounds of a target word will reduce subsequent TOTs for the target word. This is because production of the phonologically related words strengthens weak phonological connections that cause TOTs. In one study (L.E. James & Burke, 2000), participants were asked a series of TOT-inducing questions, and whenever they responded "TOT" or "don't know," they were given 10 words to pronounce before the question was presented a second time. On some trials, half of these words shared some sounds with the answer to the question (e.g., "in*dig*ent" for the target "ab*dic*ate"). TOTs were more likely to be resolved following production of phonologically related rather than unrelated words. Further research has shown that production of the initial phonological component increases TOT resolution more than production of the middle or end sounds (White & Abrams, 2002).

If word retrieval deficits increase with aging because older adults have greater deficits in phonological retrieval, one would expect prior production of phonologically related words to have a greater beneficial effect for older than young adults. Under certain conditions, this age difference has been found. When participants attempted to name a picture of a famous person (e.g., Brad *Pitt*), prior production of the homophone for the surname (e.g., cherry *pit*) increased correct naming and reduced TOTs, but only for older, not young, adults (Burke, Locantore, Austin, & Chae, in press). Production of the homophone strengthened phonological connections that were especially weak in older adults, and this boosted their ability to produce a name corresponding to this phonology.

AGING AND ORTHOGRAPHIC RETRIEVAL

The transmission-deficit model predicts an age-related deficit in spelling that is parallel to the phonological deficit because retrieval of both orthography and phonology depends on single connections between nodes. A growing number of studies have demonstrated an age-related decline in the ability to spell words correctly. MacKay and Abrams (1998) used a dictation task to test the ability of young and older adults to spell words that had uncommon spellings for their speech sounds (e.g., *colonel*). Older adults made more errors than younger adults, and more errors were made for low- than high-frequency words. The age difference was larger for high- than low-frequency words, which was surprising because low-frequency words should be particularly vulnerable to retrieval failures in old age. The authors suggested that the young participants (undergraduates) may have been relatively unfamiliar with the low-frequency words, which would have led to high error rates. When familiarity was more controlled across participants by comparing the performance of 50- and 70-year-olds, the expected larger age difference for low- than high-frequency words was observed (Stuart-Hamilton & Rabbitt, 1997).

"Regular" words, such as *mint* or *worker*, are easy to spell because they follow the common spelling for their sounds; words with "irregular" segments, such as *yacht* or *beggar*, are difficult to spell because they follow uncommon spelling for their sounds. MacKay and Abrams (1998) found that most spelling errors involved irregularly spelled components of words, and the age decline in performance was greater for irregular than regular components. The misspellings of both young and older adults usually matched the correct pronunciation (e.g., *calender* instead of *calendar, spontanious* instead of *spontaneous*).

Models of aging and spelling ability must explain how aging differentially affects the spelling of irregular versus regular words. To account for the difficulty of irregular spelling, many models postulate two independent routes for retrieving orthography: an *indirect route* that uses sound-to-spelling correspondence rules and a *direct route* that connects lexical representations directly to the orthography. The indirect route can be used to spell regular words, whereas the direct route is critical for spelling irregular words. In Figure 1, the lateral connections between the phonological and orthographic units allow for regular sound-to-spelling mappings. When a word with an irregular spelling (e.g., "y" in *pylon*) is produced, an irregular node is activated and inhibits the regular spelling (e.g., "i"), while sending excitation to the irregular spelling, "y." The transmission-deficit model predicts greater age-linked deficits in retrieval of an irregular spelling because it depends on a one-to-one connection between nodes that are activated less frequently than the nodes for regular spelling (MacKay & Abrams, 1998).

CONCLUSIONS AND FUTURE DIRECTIONS

There is compelling evidence that normal aging selectively impairs certain language functions more than others: Although older adults maintain or improve their knowledge of words and word meanings, they suffer deficits in the ability to produce the spoken and written forms of words. The transmission-deficit model provides a framework for understanding this pattern of language change during adulthood, and points to important areas for future research. Inasmuch as these production deficits are caused by weak connections in the phonological and orthographic systems, recent and frequent word production should improve subsequent performance. Studies have supported this prediction. For example, prior production of the sounds of a target word facilitated its subsequent oral production and in some cases eliminated age differences in production. Further research is needed to identify the conditions of prior production that boost older adults' performance to the level of young adults'. Parallel effects need to be investigated for spelling: According to the transmission-deficit model, recent production of the orthography of irregularly spelled words should reduce age declines in spelling. This research will have important implications for models of language production, as well as for reducing decline in the everyday language production of older adults.

Recommended Reading

Brown, A.S. (1991). The tip of the tongue experience: A review and evaluation. *Psychological Bulletin, 10*, 204–223.
Burke, D.M., MacKay, D.G., & James, L.E. (2000). Theoretical approaches to language and aging. In T. Perfect & E. Maylor (Eds.), *Models of cognitive aging* (pp. 204–237). Oxford, England: Oxford University Press.
White, K.K., & Abrams, L. (2002). (See References)

Notes

1. Address correspondence to Deborah Burke, Psychology Department, 550 Harvard Ave., Pomona College, Claremont, CA 91711; e-mail: dburke@pomona.edu.

References

Burke, D.M., Locantore, J., Austin, A., & Chae, B. (in press). Cherry pit primes Brad Pitt: Homophone priming effects on young and older adults' production of proper names. *Psychological Science*.

Burke, D.M., MacKay, D.G., Worthley, J.S., & Wade, E. (1991). On the tip of the tongue: What causes word finding failures in young and older adults. *Journal of Memory and Language, 30,* 542–579.

Dell, G.S. (1986). A spreading-activation theory of retrieval in sentence production. *Psychological Review, 93,* 283–321.

Feyereisen, P. (1997). A meta-analytic procedure shows an age-related decline in picture naming: Comments on Goulet, Ska, and Kahn. *Journal of Speech and Hearing Research, 40,* 1328–1333.

Heine, M.K., Ober, B.A., & Shenaut, G.K. (1999). Naturally occurring and experimentally induced tip-of-the-tongue experiences in three adult age groups. *Psychology and Aging, 14,* 445–457.

James, L.E., & Burke, D.M. (2000). Phonological priming effects on word retrieval and tip-of-the-tongue experiences in young and older adults. *Journal of Experimental Psychology: Learning, Memory, and Cognition, 26,* 1378–1391.

James, W. (1890). *The principles of psychology* (Vol. 1). New York: Henry Holt & Co.

Kemper, S. (1992). Adults' sentence fragments: Who, what, when, where, and why. *Communication Research, 19,* 444–458.

Kemper, S., Thompson, M., & Marquis, J. (2001). Longitudinal change in language production: Effects of aging and dementia on grammatical complexity and propositional content. *Psychology and Aging, 16,* 600–614.

MacKay, D.G., & Abrams, L. (1998). Age-linked declines in retrieving orthographic knowledge: Empirical, practical, and theoretical implications. *Psychology and Aging, 13,* 647–662.

MacKay, D.G., & James, L.E. (in press). Sequencing, speech production, and selective effects of aging on phonological and morphological speech errors. *Psychology and Aging*.

Maylor, E.A. (1990). Age, blocking and the tip of the tongue state. *British Journal of Psychology, 81,* 123–134.

Schmitter-Edgecombe, M., Vesneski, M., & Jones, D. (2000). Aging and word finding: A comparison of discourse and nondiscourse tests. *Archives of Clinical Neuropsychology, 15,* 479–493.

Stuart-Hamilton, I., & Rabbitt, P. (1997). Age-related decline in spelling ability: A link with fluid intelligence? *Educational Gerontology, 23,* 437–441.

White, K.K., & Abrams, L. (2002). Does priming specific syllables during tip-of-the-tongue states facilitate word retrieval in older adults? *Psychology and Aging, 17,* 226–235.

Critical Thinking Questions

1. In your own words, define the tip of the tongue (TOT) phenomenon and provide an example of this effect. How does it vary for older and younger adults?

2. What type of information may help the performance of the older adults more than that of the younger adults?

3. Are age differences stronger for phonological or semantic systems? Why is one system more compromised by age than the other?

This article has been reprinted as it originally appeared in *Current Directions in Psychological Science*. Citation information for this article as originally published appears above.

Aging and Visual Attention

David J. Madden[1]
Duke University Medical Center

Abstract

Older adults are often slower and less accurate than are younger adults in performing visual-search tasks, suggesting an age-related decline in attentional functioning. Age-related decline in attention, however, is not entirely pervasive. Visual search that is based on the observer's expectations (i.e., top-down attention) is relatively preserved as a function of adult age. Neuroimaging research suggests that age-related decline occurs in the structure and function of brain regions mediating the visual sensory input, whereas activation of regions in the frontal and parietal lobes is often greater for older adults than for younger adults. This increased activation may represent an age-related increase in the role of top-down attention during visual tasks. To obtain a more complete account of age-related decline and preservation of visual attention, current research is beginning to explore the relation of neuroimaging measures of brain structure and function to behavioral measures of visual attention.

Keywords

visual perception; adult development; cognition; reaction time; neuroimaging

The frequently quoted observation by William James that "Every one knows what attention is" (James, 1890/1950, p. 403) is also applicable to the topic of visual attention, because "everyone knows" that there is age-related change in visual attention. Scientific research on attention over the past 100 years has continued to expand the definition of attention. Similarly, research on adult age-related differences, conducted over a more recent period, has provided additional insight into the changes in attention that occur during adulthood. The results of this research are important because they challenge the assumption that decline is the only form of age-related change. In addition, neuroimaging studies are providing a wealth of information regarding the brain mechanisms of attention. Thus, current accounts of age-related changes in attention reflect two influences: behavioral research focused on defining the role of attention in task performance and neuroimaging research directed towards identifying the relevant neural systems.

FEATURES OF ATTENTIONAL GUIDANCE

Continuum of Search Efficiency

In navigating the visual environment, people must attend to some objects and ignore others. Guiding attention to the relevant object is easy in some instances, as when noticing a red wine stain on a white carpet, but more difficult in others, as when attempting to identify objects in a blurry photograph. To quantify how attention is used in these perceptual tasks, behavioral research has relied extensively on analyses of *visual search*, in which observers attempt to find a predefined target item in a display of accompanying nontarget (distractor) items. The measure of interest is often the change in reaction time (RT) or accuracy for detecting the target, in relation to an increasing number of display items (display size). As illustrated in panel A of Figure 1, the search target (e.g., an upright T) may be a featural *singleton*, defined as an item that differs from all of the distractors in a particular feature (e.g., color, shape, or size). Detection of a singleton target is highly efficient, and RT is relatively unaffected by the number of distractor items. In contrast, when the target and distractors share features (Fig. 1, panel B), search is less efficient, and target detection requires additional time as display size increases.

Current theories of visual attention characterize the difference between panels A and B in Figure 1 in terms of a continuum of search efficiency, rather than as categorically different forms or stages of information processing (Wolfe & Horowitz, 2004). Search is highly efficient (as in panel A) when driven entirely in a *bottom-up* manner—that is, by salient differences among the features of the display items. In highly efficient search, the observer has the impression that the target pops out of the display, capturing attention automatically. Successful performance in more difficult search tasks (as in panel B) relies on *top-down* processing—that is, the observer's knowledge of the target and how it differs from

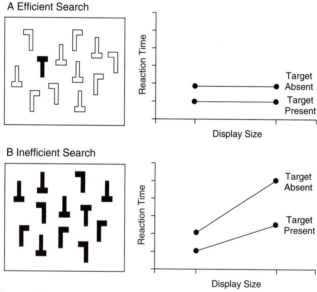

Fig. 1. Efficient (A) and inefficient (B) visual-search performance. In both cases, the target is an upright T. In the upper left panel, the target differs from the nontarget display items in a unique feature, color; as a result, target detection is highly efficient and reaction time is independent of the number of distractor items (display size; upper right). In this case, search is influenced primarily by the bottom-up process of feature salience. In the lower left panel, the nontarget features are similar to those of the target, leading to a less efficient, attention-demanding search process. The observer must search through the display items individually, leading to pronounced increase in reaction time as a function of display size (lower right). In this case, because the target cannot be distinguished from the nontarget items by local feature differences, performance is determined by the observer's top-down guidance of attention to the target.

the distractors. In this type of inefficient or difficult search, there is typically a direct increase in RT as a function of increasing display size, and thus the slope of the line of RT plotted against display size (or the RT × Display Size function) is useful as a metric of search efficiency.

Most instances of visual search, however, involve a combination of bottom-up and top-down effects. These effects do not occur in entirely separate processing stages but instead interact to determine performance. Top-down, knowledge-based processing can influence attentional guidance even when search is highly efficient (Wolfe, Butcher, Lee, & Hyle, 2003). Similarly, top-down knowledge of the relevant target feature can help observers to reduce or eliminate distraction from salient but irrelevant display items (Leber & Egeth, 2006).

Age-Related Changes in Attentional Guidance

In difficult search tasks such as those illustrated in panel B of Figure 1, the slope of the RT × Display Size function is typically higher for older adults than for younger adults, suggesting an age-related decline in the efficiency of search processes (Madden & Whiting, 2004). One goal of research on aging and attention is to clarify the relative contribution of the bottom-up and top-down components of age-related changes in visual attention. Older adults show declines in bottom-up visual processing at the sensory level, even when tested under best-corrected conditions (i.e., with glasses). When the visual target is a featural singleton, however, older adults typically exhibit the independence between RT and display size indicative of highly efficient search (Plude & Doussard-Roosevelt, 1989; Whiting, Madden, Pierce, & Allen, 2005). Thus, although age-related decline in bottom-up visual processing contributes to an overall slowing of perceptual processing speed for older adults, there is also some preservation of bottom-up attention, providing a basis for highly efficient search.

Cognitive-aging research has documented age-related decline in top-down attention, although researchers have expressed this conclusion in various ways. Several theories have been developed around the idea of age-related decline in executive processing, defined as processes involved in maintaining and updating information in working memory, in inhibiting irrelevant information, and in time sharing between tasks (Verhaeghen & Cerella, 2002). Older adults appear to be less successful than younger adults at using a top-down attentional set (i.e., maintaining mental preparation) for avoiding attentional capture by a salient but task-irrelevant display item (Colcombe et al., 2003). These findings suggest that older adults' decreased performance in visual-search tasks is not attributable entirely to bottom-up processing and includes some decline in top-down attentional control.

Other forms of top-down attention, however, do not completely conform to the predictions of executive-control theories, instead exhibiting a substantial degree of constancy as a function of adult age. In highly efficient search tasks, in which RT is independent of display size, advance knowledge of the target-defining feature leads to comparable levels of improvement in search performance for younger and older adults (Whiting et al., 2005).

Older adults are also successful in using some forms of top-down attention in more difficult search tasks. Madden, Whiting, Cabeza, and Huettel (2004) varied the probability that the target would be a color singleton (a red letter among gray letters). This was a difficult search task in which each display contained either four or six letters, and participants responded as to which one of two target letters (E and R) was present in the display. Across blocks of trials, participants performed two task conditions: "neutral," in which there was low probability (.17–.25) that the color singleton would be the E/R target, and "guided," in which there was higher probability (.75–.83) of singleton–target correspondence. Attending immediately to the singleton in the guided condition will thus facilitate identifying the target, and it will delay finding the target on those trials when it is not the singleton. The results indicated that the changes in search RT related to the target singleton were substantially greater in the guided condition than in the neutral condition, implying top-down attention to the target-relevant feature (color). The magnitude of this effect, in terms of the proportional change in RT, was comparable for the two age groups. Thus, although other forms of executive control exhibit age-related decline, older adults' top-down attention exhibits some degree of preservation.

The benefit in search performance associated with frequently occurring targets is due to two factors: the observer's conscious expectation that a particular feature or item will occur, and priming effects associated with repeating a particular feature across successive trials, independently of whether the observer is aware of that repetition. These two aspects of top-down attention are difficult to separate entirely. From the results of visual-search tasks that systematically varied the repetition priming of target and distractor features, it appears that both the repetition-priming and conscious-expectation aspects of top-down attention are preserved for older adults and that older adults place additional emphasis on the expectation of target-relevant features (Madden, Spaniol, Bucur, & Whiting, in press). This increased reliance on top-down attentional guidance may represent a compensatory response to age-related decline in bottom-up sensory processing.

COGNITIVE NEUROSCIENCE OF AGING AND ATTENTION

Brain Mechanisms of Attention

The age-related changes in visual attention discussed up to this point have been assessed in behavioral measures of visual search. How are the behavioral findings related to the brain mechanisms of attention? Neuroimaging studies of younger adults have led to some agreement on the broad outlines of these mechanisms (Kastner, 2004; Shulman et al., 2003). Much of this research has involved positron emission tomography (PET) and functional magnetic resonance imaging (fMRI), both of which measure the activation of cerebral gray matter, during the performance of cognitive tasks. A *frontoparietal network*, spanning the frontal and parietal lobes, on the lateral surface of the brain, appears to mediate performance in visual-search and detection tasks. Within this network, the dorsal regions (those on the upper surface) of the frontal and parietal lobes are particularly important for top-down attentional guidance during visual search. The network also contains a ventral component (on the lower surface of the frontal and parietal lobes), especially in the right hemisphere, mediating bottom-up attention. The ventral component acts as a "circuit breaker" that orients attention to unexpected or particularly relevant events.

Age-Related Changes in the Attentional Network

Neuroimaging studies of older adults have yielded evidence of age-related change within the dorsal component of the frontoparietal network. Activation of regions of the frontal lobe during cognitive tasks, for example, tends to increase as a function of adult age, which may reflect older adults' increased emphasis on the top-down attentional-control processes mediated by these regions (Cabeza, 2002; McIntosh et al., 1999). Less is known regarding age-related effects in the ventral component of the network. Activation of cortical regions mediating visual processing, situated in the occipital lobe (at the back of the brain), is often lower for older adults than it is for younger adults, which may reflect age-related decline in the quality of the bottom-up sensory input. Consistent with this type of decline, studies of nonhuman-primate brain anatomy have reported age-related degradation of white matter in the optic nerve, including both loss of axons (the extensions of nerve cells that conduct impulses to other nerve cells) and abnormalities of axons' myelin sheaths (the insulating coating that facilitates conduction). Neuro-imaging studies also suggest, however, that age-related decline in the volume of gray matter (nerve cells) is greater in the frontal lobe than it is in other brain regions. Thus, the relations between these structural and functional changes in the frontoparietal network, and their influence on attention, have not yet been completely defined.

In a recent fMRI study (Madden et al., 2007), my colleagues and I demonstrated that age-related changes in frontoparietal activation were associated specifically with top-down attentional guidance during visual search. In this experiment we used a letter-search task in which, as described previously, the probability that a color singleton would correspond to the search target was either high (guided condition) or low (neutral condition). One of the main findings, illustrated in Figure 2, was that activation in the frontal and parietal lobes was correlated with search performance for older adults, whereas activation in the occipital lobe was correlated with search performance for younger adults. Because this pattern held only in the guided condition (i.e., when the color singleton predicted target location) and not in the neutral condition, these data support the view that older adults' increased frontoparietal activation represents top-down attentional control.

In addition to measures of cortical activation from fMRI, we (Madden et al., 2007) also obtained measures of white-matter integrity from diffusion tensor imaging (DTI; a structural imaging measure that is sensitive to the rate and directionality of diffusion of water molecules in tissue). DTI provides a measure of the integrity of white-matter tracts, such as the degree to which axons are oriented in the same direction and possess intact myelin sheaths. We found that white-matter integrity was lower for older adults than for younger adults, particularly in prefrontal regions, although this effect was statistically independent of the age-related change in search performance. Further investigations of aging and DTI will be valuable, however, because age-related changes in white matter that lead to disconnections between components of the frontoparietal network

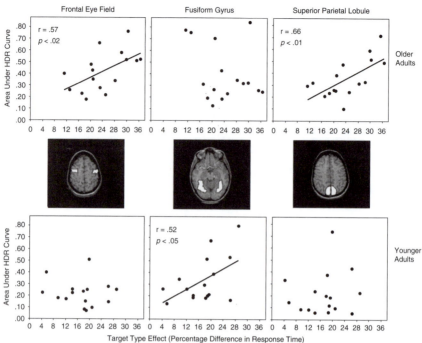

Fig. 2. Difference in the activation of three brain regions during top-down visual search for older (top) and younger (bottom) adults. Regions of interest included the frontal eye field (in the upper surface of the frontal lobe; left), the fusiform gyrus (in the lower surface of the occipital lobe; middle), and the superior parietal lobule (in the upper surface of the parietal lobe; right). Area under the HDR curve refers to the measure of activation during functional magnetic resonance imaging, defined by the area under the hemodynamic response (HDR) curve. The target-type effect refers to a behavioral measure of visual-search performance, the percentage change in reaction time for target-letter identification when the target is presented in a unique color (e.g., a red letter among gray letters), relative to when one of the nontarget items is presented in a unique color. The figure illustrates the finding that, when search involves top-down attention (i.e., the observer's expectation regarding the probability of the target's color), activation of the frontal and parietal regions (frontoparietal network) was correlated with search performance for older adults but not for younger adults. (Modified with permission from Madden et al., 2007.)

may be an important source of age differences in visual attention. The type of age-related increase in frontoparietal activation we reported (Madden et al., 2007), for example, may represent a compensatory response to decline in the bottom-up input from sensory pathways.

CONCLUSION AND FUTURE DIRECTIONS

Behavioral research on age-related change in visual attention suggests that decline occurs in bottom-up visual sensory processes and in some aspects of executive processing related to task control. Some forms of top-down attentional guidance, however, remain operative in older adulthood and may even play a larger role in the performance of older adults. Thus, one direction for future research is to determine the distinguishing features of top-down attention that separate it from executive processes exhibiting age-related decline. A related question is whether the age-related increase in top-down attention that has been observed in some visual-search tasks is a compensatory response to the decline in sensory processing. Neuroimaging findings lead to a compensatory interpretation, but additional evidence linking age-related increase in frontoparietal activation with higher levels of behavioral performance is needed. In addition, within the frontoparietal network, age-related changes are observed most frequently in the dorsal component mediating top-down attention. Little is known regarding age-related change in the ventral component mediating the detection of target-relevant features. Developing a more comprehensive account of aging and visual attention will involve integrating data from structural imaging (e.g., white-matter integrity), functional imaging, and cognitive performance.

Beyond these basic theoretical issues, researchers are also actively addressing the question of translation between laboratory and applied settings. In the case of visual attention, several studies have demonstrated correlations between laboratory measures of attention and automobile-driving performance (e.g., accident rates). Reports are also emerging to indicate that various forms of interventions designed to improve physical and cognitive vitality may lead to corresponding improvements in both the behavioral measures of attention and the brain structures related to them.

Recommended Reading

Kramer, A.F., & Madden, D.J. (in press). Attention. In F.I.M. Craik & T.A. Salthouse (Eds.), *The handbook of aging and cognition* (3rd ed.). Mahwah, NJ: Erlbaum.
Madden, D.J., Whiting, W.L., & Huettel, S.A. (2005). Age-related changes in neural activity during visual perception and attention. In R. Cabeza, L. Nyberg, & D. Park (Eds.), *Cognitive neuroscience of aging: Linking cognitive and cerebral aging* (pp. 157–185). New York: Oxford University Press.
Wolfe, J.M., & Horowitz, T.S. (2004). (See References)

Acknowledgments—Supported by Research Grants R37 AG02163 and R01 AG011622 from the National Institute on Aging. This article reports work conducted in collaboration with Scott Huettel, Roberto Cabeza, James Provenzale, Leonard White, Barbara Bucur, Julia Spaniol, and Wythe Whiting.

Note

1. Address correspondence to David J. Madden, Box 2980, Center for the Study of Aging and Human Development, and Department of Psychiatry and Behavioral Sciences, Duke University Medical Center, Durham, NC 27710; e-mail: djm@geri.duke.edu.

References

Cabeza, R. (2002). Hemispheric asymmetry reduction in older adults: The HAROLD model. *Psychology and Aging, 17*, 85–100.
Colcombe, A.M., Kramer, A.F., Irwin, D.E., Peterson, M.S., Colcombe, S., & Hahn, S. (2003). Age-related effects of attentional and oculomotor capture by onsets and color singletons as a function of experience. *Acta Psychologica, 113*, 205–225.
James, W. (1950). *The principles of psychology* (Vol. 1). New York: Dover. (Original work published 1890).

Kastner, S. (2004). Attentional response modulation in the human visual system. In M.I. Posner (Ed.), *Cognitive neuroscience of attention* (pp. 144–156). New York, NY: Guilford.

Leber, A.B., & Egeth, H.E. (2006). It's under control: Top-down search strategies can override attentional capture. *Psychonomic Bulletin & Review, 13,* 132–138.

Madden, D.J., Spaniol, J., Bucur, B., & Whiting, W.L. (in press). Age-related increase in top-down activation of visual features. *Quarterly Journal of Experimental Psychology*.

Madden, D.J., Spaniol, J., Whiting, W.L., Bucur, B., Provenzale, J.M., Cabeza, R., et al. (2007). Adult age differences in the functional neuroanatomy of visual attention: A combined fMRI and DTI study. *Neurobiology of Aging, 28,* 459–476.

Madden, D.J., & Whiting, W.L. (2004). Age-related changes in visual attention. In P.T. Costa & I.C. Siegler (Eds.), *Recent advances in psychology and aging* (pp. 41–88). Amsterdam: Elsevier.

Madden, D.J., Whiting, W.L., Cabeza, R., & Huettel, S.A. (2004). Age-related preservation of top-down attentional guidance during visual search. *Psychology and Aging, 19,* 304–309.

McIntosh, A.R., Sekuler, A.B., Penpeci, C., Rajah, M.N., Grady, C.L., Sekuler, R., & Bennett, P.J. (1999). Recruitment of unique neural systems to support visual memory in normal aging. *Current Biology, 9,* 1275–1278.

Plude, D.J., & Doussard-Roosevelt, J.A. (1989). Aging, selective attention, and feature integration. *Psychology and Aging, 4,* 98–105.

Shulman, G.L., McAvoy, M.P., Cowan, M.C., Astafiev, S.V., Tansy, A.P., d'Avossa, G., & Corbetta, M. (2003). Quantitative analysis of attention and detection signals during visual search. *Journal of Neurophysiology, 90,* 3384–3397.

Verhaeghen, P., & Cerella, J. (2002). Aging, executive control, and attention: A review of meta-analyses. *Neuroscience and Biobehav-ioral Reviews, 26,* 849–857.

Whiting, W.L., Madden, D.J., Pierce, T.W., & Allen, P.A. (2005). Searching from the top down: Ageing and attentional guidance during singleton detection. *Quarterly Journal of Experimental Psychology, 58A,* 72–97.

Wolfe, J.M., Butcher, S.J., Lee, C., & Hyle, M. (2003). Changing your mind: On the contributions of top-down and bottom-up guidance in visual search for feature singletons. *Journal of Experimental Psychology: Human Perception and Performance, 29,* 483–502.

Wolfe, J.M., & Horowitz, T.S. (2004). What attributes guide the deployment of visual attention and how do they do it? *Nature Reviews Neuroscience, 5,* 495–501.

Critical Thinking Questions

1. What are bottom-up versus top-down attentional strategies? Give some examples where each type of strategy is used.

2. Describe the areas where age-related declines and age-related preservation have been observed in tasks that have examined bottom-up and top-down processing in studies of visual attention.

3. What changes in the brain are believed to be responsible for the observed age differences in visual attention?

Enhancing the Cognitive Vitality of Older Adults

Arthur F. Kramer[1]
Beckman Institute, University of Illinois,
Urbana, Illinois (A.F.K.)

Sherry L. Willis
Department of Human Development
and Family Studies, Pennsylvania State University,
University Park, Pennsylvania (S.L.W.)

Abstract

Aging is associated with decline in a multitude of cognitive processes and brain functions. However, a growing body of literature suggests that age-related decline in cognition can sometimes be reduced through experience, cognitive training, and other interventions such as fitness training. Research on cognitive training and expertise has suggested that age-related cognitive sparing is often quite narrow, being observed only on tasks and skills similar to those on which individuals have been trained. Furthermore, training and expertise benefits are often realized only after extensive practice with specific training strategies. Like cognitive training, fitness training has narrow effects on cognitive processes, but in the case of fitness training, the most substantial effects are observed for executive-control processes.

Keywords

aging; plasticity; cognitive enhancement

One of the most ubiquitous findings in research on cognition and aging is that a wide variety of cognitive abilities show an increasing decline across the life span. Declines in cognitive function over the adult life span have been found in both cross-sectional and longitudinal studies for a variety of tasks, abilities, and processes. Cross-sectional studies, which compare the performance of one age group with that of another, have found linear decreases in a number of measures of cognition over the adult life span (Salthouse, 1996). Longitudinal studies, which range in length from a few years to more than 40 years, have found that the rate and onset of decline is variable, depending on the ability, and that accelerated decline occurs in the late 70s (Schaie, 2000). Although there are a number of factors that may be responsible for the different results obtained in the cross-sectional and longitudinal studies (e.g., differential attrition, non-age-related differences between age groups in cross-sectional studies, effects of practice, and study length in longitudinal studies), the important common observation is a reduction in cognitive efficiency with age.

Although age-related cognitive decline is quite broad, there are some notable exceptions. It has generally been observed that knowledge-based abilities (also called crystallized abilities) such as verbal knowledge and comprehension continue to be maintained or improve over the life span. In contrast, process-based abilities (also called fluid abilities) display age-related declines.

An important current issue concerns the source (or sources) of age-related declines in process-based abilities. A large number of mostly cross-sectional studies have found that age-related influences on different skills are highly related, prompting the suggestion that a common factor may be responsible for age-related declines (Salthouse, 1996). Many proposals concerning the source or mechanism responsible for this general decline have been advanced. For example, reduced processing speed, decreased attentional resources, sensory deficits, reduced working memory[2] capacity, impaired frontal lobe function, and impaired neurotransmitter function have all been cited as possible mechanisms of age-related cognitive decline.

Contrary to the general-decline proposals, a growing body of literature has pointed out a number of situations in which age-related differences remain after a general age-related factor has been statistically or methodologically controlled for (Verhaeghen, Kliegl, & Mayr, 1997). Such data suggest that a variety of different mechanisms may be responsible for age-related declines in information processing and that these mechanisms may be differentially sensitive to age.

DOES EXPERIENCE MODULATE AGE-RELATED COGNITIVE DECLINE?

Over the past several decades, researchers have examined whether previous experience in content areas (domains) such as driving, flying, and music serves to (a) reduce age-related decline in basic abilities, (b) aid in the development of domain-specific strategies that can compensate for the effects of aging on basic abilities, or (c) both reduce decline and help develop compensating strategies. In general, these studies have found that well-learned skills can be maintained at relatively high levels of proficiency, well into the 70s. However, these same studies have found that general perceptual, cognitive, and motor processes are not preserved in these highly skilled individuals. Thus, preservation of cognitive abilities for highly skilled individuals appears to be domain-specific and compensatory in nature. For example, Salthouse (1984) examined the performance of young and old adult typists and found a significant age-related decline in the performance of general psychomotor tasks, but no age-related deficit in measures of typing proficiency. Furthermore, the older typists were better able than the young typists to use preview of the text to decease their interkeystroke times, thereby enhancing their typing. Thus, the older typists were able to employ their accrued knowledge of the task domain to implement a strategy that compensated for declines in processing speed.

Krampe and Ericsson (1996) examined how amateur and expert pianists' expertise influenced their general processing speed, as well as performance on music-related tasks (i.e., single-hand and bimanual finger coordination). The general processing-speed measures showed an age-related decrement, regardless of the level of the individuals' music expertise. However, in the case of the music-related tasks, age-related effects were abolished for the expert pianists, although not for the amateur pianists. Furthermore, among the experts, high levels of deliberate practice over the past 10 years were found to be associated with decreases in age-related differences in music-related performance.

Despite the impressive cognitive sparing observed in the studies just discussed, as well as other studies, a variety of studies have failed to demonstrate an effect of expertise on age-related decline. The variability of the findings could be the result of several factors, including (a) the recency and amount of deliberate practice, (b) the degree to which the criterion tasks were specific to the domain of expertise, and (c) the age and health of the study participants.

In summary, the answer to the question of whether experience can reduce age-related cognitive decline is affirmative. However, this answer must be qualified. Sparing seems to be domain-specific, rather than general, and appears to depend on deliberate practice of the relevant skills and possibly also development of compensatory strategies.

CAN LABORATORY-BASED TRAINING REDUCE COGNITIVE DECLINE?

In this section, we discuss the results of laboratory-based practice and training studies on development and improvement of cognitive skills. We also address the specificity of these skills. We begin with a discussion of cross-sectional studies of the effects of training and conclude with an examination of longitudinal studies, in which specific individuals served as their own controls.

Cross-Sectional Training Studies

In general, old and young adults have been found to learn new tasks and skills at approximately the same rate and to show the same magnitude of benefit from training. Such data clearly suggest that older adults can learn new skills. However, given that older adults' baseline performance on most tasks is lower than that of younger adults, these data also suggest that age-related differences in level of performance will be maintained after training.

There have, however, been some interesting exceptions to these general observations. For example, Baron and Mattila (1989) examined the influence of training on the speed and accuracy with which young and older adults performed a memory search task; that is, the subjects memorized a set of items and then compared a newly presented item to the items in memory, to decide whether the new item was a member of the original memory set or not. Subjects were trained for 44 hr with a deadline procedure in which they were required to constantly increase the speed with which they performed the task. Prior to training, young and older adults performed the task with comparable accuracy, but the older adults were substantially slower. During training with the deadline procedure, both young and older adults performed more quickly, but with a substantially elevated error rate. Interestingly, when the deadline procedure was relaxed, the young and older adults performed with equivalent accuracies, and the speed differences between the groups were substantially reduced. Thus, these data suggest that the older adults improved their speed of responding more than the younger adults did.

A similar pattern of results was obtained in a study of training effects on dual-task performance (Kramer, Larish, Weber, & Bardell, 1999). Young and old adults were trained to concurrently perform two tasks, a pattern-learning task

47

and a tracking task (i.e., a task that involved using a joystick to control the position of an object so that it constantly matched the position of a computer-controlled object), with either of two training strategies. In the fixed-priority training condition, subjects were asked to treat the two tasks as equal in importance. In the variable-priority training condition, subjects were required to constantly vary their priorities between the two tasks. In both training conditions, subjects received continuing feedback on their performance.

Several interesting results were obtained. First, as in previous studies, young and old adults improved their dual-task performance at the same rate when using the fixed-priority training strategy. Second, variable-priority training led to faster learning of the tasks, a higher level of mastery, superior transfer of learning to new tasks, and better retention than did fixed-priority training. Finally, age-related differences in the efficiency of dual-task performance were substantially reduced for individuals trained in the variable-priority condition.

Although these studies and several others found that training decreased age-related performance differences, other studies have failed to demonstrate such training effects. What is the reason for these seemingly contradictory results? Although there is quite likely not a single answer to this question, one possibility centers on the nature of the training procedures. The training strategies in the two studies we just summarized explicitly focused on aspects of performance on which young and older adults showed large differences. For example, the deadline strategy employed by Baron and Mattila encourages individuals to emphasize speed rather than accuracy, something older adults are hesitant to do. Similarly, older adults have been observed to have difficulty in flexibly setting and modifying processing priorities among concurrently performed tasks. The variable-priority training strategy explicitly targets this skill. Thus, although additional research is clearly needed to further examine the situations in which the age gap in performance can be reduced, one potentially fruitful area of inquiry concerns targeting training strategies to specific difficulties encountered by older adults.

Longitudinal Studies of Practice and Training

A central focus of longitudinal studies has been to examine the extent to which training remediates or improves elders' performance on tasks for which there is long-term data. Given the wide individual differences in timing of age-related ability decline, two questions arise: First, is training effective in remediating decline for elders who have shown loss in a specific ability? Second, can training enhance the performance of elders showing no decline in a specific ability?

Data from the Seattle Longitudinal Study provide some initial answers to these questions. In this study, elders were classified as to whether they had shown reliable decline over a 14-year interval on two fluid abilities known to show early age-related decline—inductive reasoning and spatial orientation (Schaie & Willis, 1986). These individuals then received 5 hr of training on either inductive reasoning or spatial orientation. More than two thirds of elders who received training on each ability showed reliable improvement on that ability. Of those who had declined on the ability trained, 40% showed remediation, such that their performance was at or above their level of performance 14 years prior to the training. Elders who had not declined also showed reliable improvement. Moreover, the effects of training on inductive reasoning lasted up to 7 years after training (Saczynski & Willis, 2001).

Summary

Cross-sectional training research suggests that both young and old adults profit from training, but that strategies targeted at skills known to decline with age are particularly effective in training of elders. Longitudinal studies make it possible to identify abilities that have declined for a given individual and to assess whether the individual can benefit from training targeted at his or her specific deficits. Using the longitudinal approach, researchers can examine the range of plasticity (i.e., the extent to which an individual can benefit from training) over time within the same individual, rather than comparing the magnitude of training effects for different age groups. Both types of training research support the position that even individuals of advanced age have considerable plasticity in their cognitive functioning. The training findings also support the descriptive experiential studies of cognitive decline in showing that effects are specific to the particular domain that was practiced or trained.

FITNESS AND COGNITIVE SPARING?

The relationship between fitness and mental function has been a topic of interest to researchers for the past several decades. Their research has been predicated on the assumption that improvements in aerobic fitness translate into increased brain blood flow, which in turn supports more efficient brain function, particularly in older adults for whom such function is often compromised. Indeed, research with older nonhuman animals has found that aerobic fitness promotes beneficial changes in both the structure and the function of the brain (Churchill et al., in press).

However the results from human studies that have examined the influence of aerobic fitness training on cognition have been mixed. Some studies have demonstrated fitness-related improvements for older adults, but others have failed to show such improvements. Clearly, there are a number of potential theoretical and methodological reasons for this ambiguity. For example, studies have differed in the length and the nature of the fitness interventions, the health and age of the study populations, and the aspects of cognition that have been examined.

A recent analysis statistically combining the results of fitness intervention studies that have been conducted since the late 1960s (Colcombe & Kramer, in press) lends support to the idea that fitness training can improve cognitive functioning. Perhaps the most important finding obtained in this analysis was that the effects of fitness were selective rather than general. That is, aerobic fitness training had a substantially larger positive impact on performance of tasks with large executive-control components (i.e., tasks that required planning, scheduling, working memory, resistance to distraction, or multitask processing) than on performance of tasks without such components. Interestingly, substantial age-related deficits have been reported for executive-control tasks and the brain regions that support them. Thus, it appears that executive-control processes can benefit through either training or improved fitness. An important question for future research is whether such benefits are mediated by the same underlying mechanisms.

CONCLUSIONS AND FUTURE DIRECTIONS

The research we have reviewed clearly suggests that the cognitive vitality of older adults can be enhanced through cognitive training, in the form of domain-relevant expertise or laboratory training, and improved fitness. However, it is important to note that these benefits are often quite specific and have not been observed in all published studies (Salthouse, 1990). Therefore, one important goal for future research is to determine when these benefits are and are not produced. Clearly, there are some obvious candidate factors that should be examined in more detail. These include age, health conditions, medication use, gender, education, lifestyle choices, genetic profile, and family and social support.

The nature and length of training, whether cognitive or fitness training, bears further study. It is important to note that many of the previous studies of "training" have examined unsupervised practice rather than specific training procedures that might be well suited to the capabilities of older adults. The development of new methods, such as the testing-the-limits approach[3] (Kliegl, Smith, & Baltes, 1989), will clearly also be important in future studies of training and other interventions.

At present, psychologists have little understanding of the mechanisms that subserve age-related enhancements in cognitive efficiency. Possibilities include improvements in basic cognitive abilities, the development of compensatory strategies, and automatization of selective aspects of a skill or task (Baltes, Staudinger, & Lindenberger, 1999). Thus, the nature of cognitive and brain processes that support improvements in cognitive efficiency is an important topic for future research.

Finally, we would like to emphasize the importance of theory-guided research in the study of interventions targeted to enhancing the cognitive function of older adults. Theories of life-span change, such as the theory of selective optimization with compensation[4] (Baltes et al., 1999), offer great promise in this endeavor.

Recommended Reading

Charness, N. (1999). Can acquired knowledge compensate for age-related declines in cognitive efficiency? In S.H. Qualls & N. Ables (Eds.), *Psychology and the aging revolution: How we adapt to longer life* (pp. 99–117). Washington, DC: American Psychological Association.

Morrow, D.G., Menard, W.E., Stine-Morrow, E.A.L., Teller, T., & Bry-ant, D. (2001). The influence of expertise and task factors on age differences in pilot communication. *Psychology and Aging, 16,* 31–46.

Salthouse, T.A. (1990). (See References)

Notes

1. Address correspondence to Arthur Kramer, Beckman Institute, University of Illinois, Urbana, IL 61801; e-mail: akramer@s.psych.uiuc.edu.

2. Working memory refers to processes needed to both store and retrieve information over brief periods, as well as processes necessary to manipulate the stored

information (e.g., remembering a few weight measurements in pounds and converting them to kilograms).

3. Testing-the-limits examines the range and limits of cognitive reserve capacity as an approach to understanding age differences in cognitive processes.

4. This theory suggests that during aging, individuals maintain skill by focusing on selective aspects of broader skills, practicing these subskills often, and sometimes shifting strategies (e.g., shifting from speed to accuracy) to maintain performance.

References

Baltes, P.B., Staudinger, U.M., & Lindenberger, U. (1999). Lifespan psychology: Theory and application to intellectual functioning. *Annual Review of Psychology, 50*, 471–507.

Baron, A., & Mattila, W.R. (1989). Response slowing of older adults: Effects of time-contingencies on single and dual-task performances. *Psychology and Aging, 4*, 66–72.

Churchill, J.D., Galvez, R., Colcombe, S., Swain, R.A., Kramer, A.F., & Greenough, W.T. (in press). Exercise, experience and the aging brain. *Neurobiology of Aging*.

Colcombe, S., & Kramer, A.F. (in press). Fitness effects on the cognitive function of older adults: A meta-analytic study. *Psychological Science*.

Kliegl, R., Smith, J., & Baltes, P.B. (1989). Testing-the-limits and the study of adult age difference in cognitive plasticity of a mnemonic skill. *Developmental Psychology, 2*, 247–256.

Kramer, A.F., Larish, J., Weber, T., & Bardell, L. (1999). Training for executive control: Task coordination strategies and aging. In D. Gopher & A. Koriat (Eds.), *Attention and performance XVII* (pp. 617–652). Cambridge, MA: MIT Press.

Krampe, R.T., & Ericsson, K.A. (1996). Maintaining excellence: Deliberate practice and elite performance in young and older pianists. *Journal of Experimental Psychology: General, 125*, 331–359.

Saczynski, J., & Willis, S.L. (2001). *Cognitive training and maintenance of intervention effects in the elderly*. Manuscript submitted for publication.

Salthouse, T.A. (1984). Effects of age and skill in typing. *Journal of Experimental Psychology: General, 113*, 345–371.

Salthouse, T.A. (1990). Influence of experience on age difference in cognitive functioning. *Human Factors, 32*, 551–569.

Salthouse, T.A. (1996). Processing-speed theory of adult age differences in cognition. *Psychological Review, 103*, 403–428.

Schaie, K.W. (2000). The impact of longitudinal studies on understanding development from young adulthood to old age. *International Journal of Behavioral Development, 24*, 257–266.

Schaie, K.W., & Willis, S.L. (1986). Can decline in adult intellectual functioning be reversed? *Developmental Psychology, 22*, 223–232.

Verhaeghen, P., Kliegl, R., & Mayr, U. (1997). Sequential and coordinative complexity in time-accuracy functions for mental arithmetic. *Psychology and Aging, 12*, 555–564.

Critical Thinking Questions

1. Give some examples of how older adults may compensate for age-related declines in certain abilities.

2. What might explain the connection between cognitive abilities and physical activity?

3. If you were designing an intervention to decrease age differences in cognitive processes, what would you focus on that would best benefit older adults?

This article has been reprinted as it originally appeared in *Current Directions in Psychological Science*. Citation information for this article as originally published appears above.

Cognitive Activity and Risk of Alzheimer's Disease

Robert S. Wilson[1]

Rush Alzheimer's Disease Center (R.S.W., D.A.B.) and Departments of Neurological Sciences (R.S.W., D.A.B.) Chicago, Illinois

David A. Bennett

Psychology (R.S.W.), Rush-Presbyterian-St. Luke's Medical Center, Chicago, Illinois

Abstract

Recent research suggests that frequent participation in cognitively stimulating activities may reduce risk of Alzheimer's disease in old age. We review epidemiological evidence of such an association. We then consider whether cognitive activity can account for the association between higher educational and occupational attainment and reduced risk of Alzheimer's disease. Finally, we discuss the behavioral and neurobiological mechanisms that may underlie the association between cognitive activity and risk of Alzheimer's disease.

Keywords

Alzheimer's disease; cognitive activity; longitudinal studies

Recent scientific data suggest that people with higher educational and occupational attainment tend to have a lower risk of developing Alzheimer's disease than do people with lower educational and occupational attainment (Stern et al., 1994). The mechanism underlying this pattern is unknown. One hypothesis is that the effects of education and occupation are due to their association with frequency of participation in cognitively stimulating activities (Evans et al., 1997). Although the idea that frequent intellectual activity might help one's mental faculties in old age predates the Roman empire, it has only recently become the subject of rigorous scientific investigation.

COGNITIVE ACTIVITY AND ALZHEIMER'S DISEASE

The first problem encountered in this line of research is defining the construct of cognitive activity. Most human activities involve some degree of cognitive function, but it is uncertain how best to quantify that degree, particularly when comparing persons from diverse cultural and socioeconomic backgrounds. Nonetheless, researchers have developed a number of scales to measure frequency of cognitive activity. For these measures, respondents rate their current or past frequency of participation in activities judged to primarily involve seeking or processing information. These activities range from pursuits that most people would agree are cognitively stimulating (e.g., reading a book or playing a game like chess or checkers), to pursuits that seem less cognitively demanding (e.g., listening to the radio or watching television), but that also involve information processing that may be important, especially in old age, when physical infirmities and social isolation may limit access to certain kinds of activities. Various summary measures of frequency of participation in cognitively stimulating activities have been shown to be related to educational level and performance on cognitive tests, so they appear to have some validity (Wilson, Barnes, & Bennett, in press; Wilson et al., 1999, 2000).

Several prospective studies have examined the association between summary measures of participation in cognitively stimulating activities and risk of developing Alzheimer's disease. In one of these studies (Wilson, Mendes de Leon, et al., 2002), older[2] Catholic clergy members who did not have dementia rated how frequently they participated in several cognitively stimulating activities at the beginning of the study. During an average of about 5 years of follow-up, persons reporting frequent participation in cognitively stimulating activities had only half the risk of developing Alzheimer's disease compared with those reporting infrequent cognitive activity. This association between cognitive activity and incidence of Alzheimer's disease has been confirmed in several studies of older persons from geographically defined communities (Scarmeas, Levy, Tang, Manly, & Stern, 2001; Wang, Karp, Winblad, & Fratiglioni, 2002; Wilson, Bennett, et al., 2002).

Because Alzheimer's disease is the leading cause of dementia in older persons and few potentially modifiable risk factors have been identified, understanding the basis of the association between cognitive activity and disease incidence is a matter of substantial public-health significance. In the remainder of this article, we examine three issues bearing on this association. We first consider whether cognitive activity accounts for the association between educational and occupational attainment and risk of Alzheimer's disease. We then discuss what is known about the behavioral and neurobiological mechanisms underlying the association between cognitive activity and Alzheimer's disease.

COGNITIVE ACTIVITY AND EDUCATION

Because cognitive activity is related to both risk of Alzheimer's disease and education, in a recent study we examined whether cognitive activity could explain the association between educational attainment and disease risk (Wilson, Bennett, et al., 2002). In this 4-year longitudinal study of older residents of a biracial community, those who had completed more years of schooling had a reduced risk of developing Alzheimer's disease compared with those who had less educational attainment. The prestige of a resident's main occupation had a similar association with disease risk. When frequency of participation in cognitive activity was added to the analysis, however, the associations of educational and occupational attainment with disease risk were substantially reduced and no longer statistically significant. By contrast, the association between frequency of cognitive activity and disease risk was not substantially affected by adding educational level, occupational prestige, or both to the statistical model. These findings suggest that the association between educational attainment and risk of Alzheimer's disease may in large part be due to the fact that persons with more education tend to be more cognitively active than persons with less education.

53

BEHAVIORAL MECHANISMS UNDERLYING THE ASSOCIATION

What might account for the association between cognitive activity and risk of Alzheimer's disease? It seems likely that the positive correlation between cognitive activity and cognitive function is one contributing factor. On average, cognitively active persons are apt to begin old age at a higher level of cognitive function than their less cognitively active counterparts. As a result, a cognitively active person would need to experience more cognitive decline than a less active person before reaching a level of cognitive impairment commensurate with dementia.

A more fundamental way in which cognitive activity might affect risk of Alzheimer's disease is through an association with the primary manifestation of the disease, progressive cognitive decline. That is, not only might cognitively active people begin old age with better cognitive skills than less cognitively active people, but those skills may also be less subject to decline. Two studies have demonstrated such an effect (Hultsch, Hertzog, Small, & Dixon, 1999; Wilson, Mendes de Leon, et al., 2002). In each, frequent cognitive activity was associated with reduced cognitive decline in analyses that controlled for initial level of cognitive function. Thus, the higher level of cognitive function and reduced rate of cognitive decline that are associated with frequent cognitive activity probably both contribute to the association between frequent cognitive activity and reduced risk of Alzheimer's disease.

Cognitive training programs that provide strategic instruction and practice have been shown to have substantial and long-lasting beneficial effects on cognitive function in older persons (Ball et al., 2002), further supporting the idea that level of cognitive activity may be causally linked with risk of Alzheimer's disease. The benefits of cognitive training appear quite specific, with improved performance restricted to the skill that was trained.

Evidence of this specificity can also be discerned in observational studies. Thus, some studies have found that frequency of cognitive activity, but not of physical activity, is related to risk of Alzheimer's disease (Wilson, Bennett, et al., 2002; Wilson, Mendes de Leon, et al., 2002). In addition, cognitive activity appears to be primarily associated with reduced decline in processing skills like perceptual speed and working memory (Hultsch et al., 1999; Wilson, Mendes de Leon, et al., 2002). These skills are notable for being involved in nearly all kinds of intellectual activity, so it makes sense that they would benefit most from the frequency of such activity. Further, among people who already have Alzheimer's disease, level of reading activity prior to the onset of dementia is related to decline in verbal abilities but not nonverbal abilities (Wilson et al., 2000), providing further evidence that a particular cognitive activity benefits mainly the skills involved in that activity.

NEUROBIOLOGICAL MECHANISMS UNDERLYING THE ASSOCIATION

The neurobiological mechanisms through which cognitive activity reduces the risk of Alzheimer's disease are unclear. One possibility is that cognitive activity actually reduces the accumulation of pathology associated with cognitive impairment, such as neuritic plaques and neurofibrillary tangles,[3] which are forms of

Alzheimer's disease pathology, or cerebral infarction (i.e., stroke). Alternatively, cognitive activity may influence risk of Alzheimer's disease by affecting the development or maintenance of the interconnected neural systems that underlie different forms of cognitive processing.

Scientific interest has focused on the latter possibility for two main reasons. First, recent studies have found that the correlation of quantitative measures of Alzheimer's disease pathology with cognitive impairment or dementia are modest in size, which suggests that other neurobiological mechanisms are involved. Second, an extensive body of research has shown that environmental complexity is related to a variety of changes in the brains of adult animals, including formation of new neurons and connections between neurons, in brain regions that are critically involved in memory and thinking (Kempermann, Gast, & Gage, 2002; Shors et al., 2001). In humans, therefore, some researchers have hypothesized that cognitive activity contributes to structural and functional organization and reorganization that make selected neural systems more difficult to disrupt, so that more Alzheimer's disease pathology is needed to impair the skills mediated by those systems (Cummings, Vinters, Cole, & Khachaturian, 1998).

Support for this idea comes from a recent study (Bennett et al., in press) that examined the relation of education and a summary measure of Alzheimer's disease pathology to level of cognitive function near the time of death. Both years of education and amount of Alzheimer's disease pathology were related to level of cognitive function. Education was not related to measures of Alzheimer's disease pathology, but influenced the association between Alzheimer's disease pathology and cognitive function: A given amount of Alzheimer's disease pathology was associated with less cognitive impairment in a person with more education than in a person with less education. In other words, the deleterious impact of Alzheimer's disease pathology on cognitive function was reduced in persons with more education compared with those with less education. These data suggest that education—or variables related to education, such as cognitive activity— affects risk of cognitive impairment and dementia by somehow enhancing the brain's capacity to tolerate Alzheimer's disease pathology, rather than by altering the accumulation of the pathology itself.

Because Alzheimer's disease is thought to develop gradually over a period of years, another possibility is that a low level of cognitive activity is an early sign of the disease rather than an independent risk factor. The early-sign hypothesis is inconsistent with several observations, however. For example, excluding people with memory impairment, usually the first sign of Alzheimer's disease, or controlling for a well-established genetic risk factor for the disease (i.e., possession of an $\in 4$ allele from a gene on chromosome 19 that codes apolipoprotein E, a plasma protein involved in cholesterol transport), does not appear to substantially affect the association between cognitive activity and Alzheimer's disease. In addition, the specificity of the association between frequency of participation in cognitive activity and level of function in different domains of cognition is not easily reconciled with the early-sign hypothesis. Thus, although early Alzheimer's disease may contribute to reduced cognitive activity, such an effect does not appear to be sufficient to explain the association between cognitive activity and disease incidence.

CONCLUSIONS

Several large prospective studies have found an association between frequency of cognitive activity and subsequent risk of developing dementia or Alzheimer's disease. Evidence from observational studies and cognitive intervention research suggests that the association of cognitive activity with disease incidence may be causal. Because few potentially modifiable risk factors for Alzheimer's disease have been identified, this area of research has important public-health implications. Much remains to be learned, however.

A central question is whether the protective effect of cognitive activity depends on when it occurs during the life span. In particular, it is uncertain to what extent cognitive stimulation in late life, as opposed to early life or adulthood, is critical. Answers to this question are likely to require advances in how researchers assess cognitive activity and features of the environment that support it (Wilson et al., in press). Such research could help determine the feasibility of large-scale trials of cognitive intervention.

Another challenge is to elucidate the structural, biochemical, and molecular mechanisms that underlie individual differences in the ability to tolerate Alzheimer's disease pathology. These mechanisms may differ for cognitive activity during development compared with cognitive activity in adulthood and old age. For example, in experimental animal studies, environmental experiences during development appear to affect mainly the number of neurons that survive into adulthood, whereas experiences late in life may affect cognition more by maintaining neural connections than by changing their number. Understanding these mechanisms may make it possible to develop new preventive strategies aimed at augmenting the ability of the brain to withstand the deleterious effects of Alzheimer's disease pathology and possibly other neurodegenerative conditions as well. To that end, we have recently begun a large epidemiological study of older persons who have a wide range of educational and occupational backgrounds and have agreed to annual clinical evaluation and brain donation at death.

Finally, short-term clinical trials are needed to identify efficient and practical ways to train and strengthen cognitive skills. In addition, clinical trials of several years' duration are needed to determine whether cognitive training can reduce cognitive decline in old age.

Recommended Reading

Ball, K., Berch, D.B., Helmers, K.F., Jobe, J.B., Leveck, M.D., Marsiske, M., Morris, J.N., Rebok, G.W., Smith, D.M., Tennstedt, S.L., Unverzagt, F.W., & Willis, S.L. (2002). (See References)

Kempermann, G., Gast, D., & Gage, F.H. (2002). (See References)

Wilson, R.S., Bennett, D.A., Bienias, J.L., Aggarwal, N.T., Mendes de Leon, C.F., Morris, M.C., Schneider, J.A., & Evans, D.A. (2002). (See References)

Wilson, R.S., Mendes de Leon, C.F., Barnes, L.L., Schneider, J.A., Bienias, J.L., Evans, D.A., & Bennett, D.A . (2002). (See References)

Acknowledgments—This research was supported by National Institute on Aging Grants P30 AG10161, R01 AG15819, and R01 AG17917.

Notes

1. Address correspondence to Robert S. Wilson, Rush Alzheimer's Disease Center, 1645 West Jackson Blvd., Suite 675, Chicago, IL 60612; e-mail: rwilson@rush.edu.
2. We use "older" to refer to persons who are 65 years of age or older.
3. Neuritic plaques accumulate outside neurons and consist mainly of an abnormal protein called beta-amyloid. Neurofibrillary tangles are found inside neurons and are composed primarily of an abnormal protein called tau that appears like a tangled mass of filaments under a microscope. If sufficient numbers of plaques and tangles are present, a pathological diagnosis of Alzheimer's disease can be made.

References

Ball, K., Berch, D.B., Helmers, K.F., Jobe, J.B., Leveck, M.D., Marsiske, M., Morris, J.N., Rebok, G.W., Smith, D.M., Tennstedt, S.L., Unverzagt, F.W., & Willis, S.L. (2002). Effects of cognitive training interventions with older adults: A randomized controlled trial. *Journal of the American Medical Association, 288,* 2271–2281.

Bennett, D.A., Wilson, R.S., Schneider, J.A., Evans, D.A., Mendes de Leon, C.F., Arnold, S.E., Barnes, L.L., & Bienias, J.L. (in press). Education modifies the relation of AD pathology to level of cognitive function in older persons. *Neurology.*

Cummings, J., Vinters, H., Cole, G., & Khachaturian, Z. (1998). Alzheimer's disease: Etiologies, pathophysiology, cognitive reserve, and treatment opportunities. *Neurology, 51*(Suppl. 1), S2–S17.

Evans, D.A., Hebert, L.E., Beckett, L.A., Scherr, P.A., Albert, M.A., Chown, M.J., Pilgrim, D.M., & Taylor, J.O. (1997). Education and other measures of socioeconomic status and risk of incident Alzheimer's disease in a defined population of older persons. *Archives of Neurology, 54,* 1399–1405.

Hultsch, D., Hertzog, C., Small, B., & Dixon, R. (1999). Use it or lose it: Engaged lifestyle as a buffer of cognitive decline in aging? *Psychology and Aging, 14,* 245–263.

Kempermann, G., Gast, D., & Gage, F.H. (2002). Neuroplasticity in old age: Sustained fivefold induction of hippocampal neurogenesis by long-term environmental enrichment. *Annals of Neurology, 52,* 135–143.

Scarmeas, N., Levy, G., Tang, M.X., Manly, J., & Stern, Y. (2001). Influence of leisure activity on the incidence of Alzheimer's disease. *Neurology, 57,* 2236–2242.

Shors, T.J., Miesegaes, G., Beylin, A., Zhao, M., Rydel, T., & Gould, E. (2001). Neurogenesis in the adult is involved in the formation of trace memories. *Nature, 410,* 372–376.

Stern, Y., Gurland, B., Tatemichi, T.K., Tang, M.-X., Wilder, D., & Mayeux, R. (1994). Influence of education and occupation on the incidence of Alzheimer's disease. *Journal of the American Medical Association, 271,* 1004–1010.

Wang, H.-H., Karp, A., Winblad, B., & Fratiglioni, L. (2002). Late-life engagement in social and leisure activities is associated with a decreased risk of dementia: A longitudinal study from the Kungsholmen Project. *American Journal of Epidemiology, 155,* 1081–1087.

Wilson, R.S., Barnes, L.L., & Bennett, D.A. (in press). Assessment of lifetime participation in cognitively stimulating activities. *Journal of Clinical and Experimental Neuropsychology.*

Wilson, R.S., Bennett, D.A., Beckett, L.A., Morris, M.C., Gilley, D.W., Bienias, J.L., Scherr, P.A., & Evans, D.A. (1999). Cognitive activity in older persons from a geographically defined population. *Journal of Gerontology: Psychological Sciences, 54B,* P155–P160.

Wilson, R.S., Bennett, D.A., Bienias, J.L., Aggar-wal, N.T., Mendes de Leon, C.F., Morris, M.C., Schneider, J.A., & Evans, D.A. (2002). Cognitive activity and incident AD in a population-based sample of older persons. *Neurology, 59,* 1910–1915.

Wilson, R.S., Bennett, D.A., Gilley, D.W., Beckett, L.A., Barnes, L.L., & Evans, D.A. (2000). Premorbid reading activity and patterns of cognitive decline in Alzheimer's disease. *Archives of Neurology, 56,* 1718–1723.

Wilson, R.S., Mendes de Leon, C.F., Barnes, L.L., Schneider, J.A., Bienias, J.L., Evans, D.A., & Bennett, D.A. (2002). Participation in cognitively stimulating activities and risk of incident Alzheimer's disease. *Journal of the American Medical Association, 287,* 742–748.

Critical Thinking Questions

1. An older adult approaches you and states that he does not have to worry about Alzheimer's disease because he has an advanced degree, and education automatically confers a decreased risk for disease. What do you say in response?

2. If cognitive processing across multiple domains decline at a similar rate, then would an intervention focusing on reading and giving presentations help all aspects of cognition functioning? Why or why not?

3. How might the external environment play a role in cognitive functioning and cognitive abilities? Provide one example from this reading.

This article has been reprinted as it originally appeared in *Current Directions in Psychological Science*. Citation information for this article as originally published appears above.

Section 2: Cognition in Context

The previous section discussed general cognitive changes that occur with age, possible reasons behind these changes, and activities that may change the course of both normative cognitive decline and Alzheimer's disease. The current section places these age-related changes and age differences in cognition into the physical and social context of aging. The first two articles describe how age-related physical changes beyond those mentioned in the previous section influence cognitive processes. The first article titled, "Neurobiological consequences of long term estrogen therapy" by L.K. Marriott and Gary Wenk, discusses the importance of timing when discerning the role of estrogen and its relation to cognitive stability or cognitive decline. They review animal and human studies that discuss the short-term benefits of estrogen on cognition as well as the negative consequences that occur from the long-term use of this hormone among post-menopausal females. In the second article, Arthur Wingfield, Patricia Tun and Sandra McCoy discuss how hearing loss that commonly occurs in old age can compound age-related declines in memory and comprehension for aural information. Their article, titled "Hearing loss in older adulthood: What it is and how it interacts with cognitive performance" illustrates how cognition is related to physical indices not always considered when people are determining the effects of age. They discuss how hearing loss can exaggerate age-related declines in cognition, leaving people without the contextual cues often used to compensate for their declines.

The next two articles describe the importance of studying and understanding the environment for interpreting the effects of cognitive aging. The first article discusses cognitive challenges in everyday living and the need for psychologists to discover how older adults can best learn to use new technological advances to navigate their environment. Arthur Fiske and Wendy Rogers offer strategies for teaching people how to use technology to compensate for age-related losses in their article, "Psychology and Aging: Enhancing the lives of an aging population."

The focus around the environment takes a slightly different turn in the last article in this section. In "The Cognitive Neuroscience of Aging and Culture" Denise Park and Angela Gutchess describe the role that the cultural context can play when shaping the neurological substrates that underpin cognitive processing. In this article, the authors discuss the plasticity of the brain in response to environmental influences and the ramifications of living in different types of environments on age differences in cognitive processing. The authors disentangle the influences of both culture and age: for certain cognitive tasks, cultural differences play a stronger role than age. In other tasks, age-related processes override any differences observed across cultures.

Neurobiological Consequences of Long-Term Estrogen Therapy

L.K. Marriott and G.L. Wenk[1]

Division of Neural Systems, Memory & Aging, Arizona Research Laboratories, University of Arizona

Abstract

Postmenopausal women demonstrate an increased incidence of Alzheimer's disease (AD). Epidemiological evidence suggests that estrogen replacement therapy (ERT) may reduce the risk or delay the onset of AD, yet recent clinical trials found no cognitive benefits of ERT in women with mild to moderate AD. This review suggests that the timing of estrogen administration may explain these conflicting results. Chronic administration has neurobiological consequences that can affect neural and immune function, but a therapy designed to mimic the natural cycle of fluctuating hormones may more effectively slow the progression of AD in postmenopausal women.

Keywords

estrogen; Alzheimer's disease; luteinizing hormone (LH); immune; neuroprotection

Postmenopausal women demonstrate an increased incidence of Alzheimer's disease (AD), and many researchers have considered whether this heightened risk is linked to their low menopausal levels of the hormone estrogen. Indeed, epidemiological evidence suggests that postmenopausal estrogen replacement therapy (ERT) may reduce the risk and delay the onset of AD. Moreover, animal studies demonstrate that estrogen has beneficial effects on brain cell survival and cognition. Despite these positive indications, however, recent clinical trials found no benefits of ERT on cognitive function in women with mild to moderate AD (for a review, see Hogervorst, Williams, Budge, Riedel, & Jolles, 2000). In this review, we attempt to reconcile these conflicting findings, highlighting a potential misunderstanding of estrogen's action in the brain.

MENOPAUSE AND ERT

As women enter menopause, the amount of estrogen circulating in their blood declines, eventually reaching approximately 1% of the level found in younger women. This change results in numerous physiological consequences, including cognitive dysfunction, loss of attention, mood disorders, hot flushes, and increased risk of some diseases, including AD. ERTs were developed to compensate for diminished circulating hormones, thereby alleviating the undesirable symptoms associated with menopause. When epidemiological studies discovered that postmenopausal women taking estrogen had a reduced risk of developing AD, delayed onset of AD, and a milder progression of the disease, researchers undertook some initial studies to see whether women with AD might benefit from estrogen therapy. These early studies demonstrated improvements in attention, orientation, and mood (for a review, see Hogervorst et al., 2000), thereby instigating an extensive examination of estrogen outside its established role as a reproductive hormone. Animal studies supported the idea that short-term estrogen replacement might be beneficial by showing that cognition, neurotransmitter function, brain plasticity (the ability of brain cells to change), blood flow, and neuroprotection (the ability of nerve cells to survive a variety of toxic insults) were all enhanced by estrogen (for a review, see Norbury et al., 2003).

Three randomized, double-blind, placebo-controlled intervention studies in humans demonstrated less encouraging results regarding the effects of estrogen on the brain. In the largest of these studies, the effects of ERT were initially beneficial, much as in previous studies using smaller groups of patients and shorter treatment durations; however, over the longer term, performance on a scale measuring dementia declined significantly more among women receiving ERT than among those receiving a placebo (Mulnard et al., 2000). All three of these intervention studies concluded that ERT could not improve the cognitive abilities of women with mild to moderate AD (for a review, see Hogervorst et al., 2000). Thus, results of these clinical trials suggest that relatively short-term ERT has beneficial effects on cognitive function, but that these effects are attenuated, and possibly reversed, following much longer treatment regimens.

Investigators offered several hypotheses to reconcile the conflict in the findings of epidemiological, intervention, and animal studies. For example, intervention studies were criticized for their design and potential biases in subject selection. Researchers argued that women who typically take ERT are better educated, are healthier, and have a higher socioeconomic status than nonusers, and these factors have been associated with a reduced risk of AD. In contrast, the women enrolled in the ERT trials already had an ongoing disease process and may have been estrogen deprived for decades prior to receiving ERT, which may have altered the effectiveness of the therapy (for reviews, see Hogervorst et al., 2000, and Toran-Allerand, 2000).

CONSEQUENCES OF CHRONIC ESTROGEN

The positive and negative effects of estrogen appear to depend on the timing of estrogen exposure. Chronic administration of estrogen results in neurobiological consequences that can affect both neural and immune function. Premenopausal women experience cyclic fluctuations in estrogen levels that are not mimicked in postmenopausal women by the continuous replacement of estrogen through ERT.

Chronic Estrogen and Cognition

Animal experiments have shown that deficits in working memory (the temporary retention of information needed to solve a task) are not seen immediately following surgical removal of the ovaries (ovariectomy), which removes the major source of estrogen. Instead, working memory deficits develop after longer durations of estrogen withdrawal (for a review, see Markowska & Savonenko, 2002). Chronic administration of estrogen to ovariectomized animals does not improve their cognition if they already have detectable deficits when they begin the estrogen treatment (Markowska & Savonenko, 2002). These results parallel the absence of cognitive benefits associated with ERT in postmenopausal women who already have cognitive deficits resulting from AD. However, estrogen levels fluctuate when constant administration is combined with injections of estrogen, and this combined treatment dramatically improved working memory in previously impaired ovariectomized animals (Markowska & Savonenko, 2002). These findings are consistent with the hypothesis that compared with constant estrogen levels, fluctuating levels may more effectively enhance cognition in postmenopausal women (Marriott, Hauss-Wegrzyniak, Benton, Vraniak, & Wenk, 2002).

Effects on Estrogen Receptors

Estrogen receptors are specialized proteins that respond to estrogen by initiating a variety of cellular responses. A prolonged period of menopause followed by the typical regimen of estrogen replacement can produce constant estrogen levels that may lead to a decrease in estrogen receptors' number or function (downregulation), which in turn may underlie the limited effectiveness of chronic ERT (Toran-Allerand, 2000). Estrogen receptors are distributed throughout the brain and located on both brain cells (neurons and glia) and immune cells. Therefore, it is not surprising that the downregulation of these receptors can have wide-ranging and dramatic effects on many neural, endocrine, and immune processes.

Chronic Estrogen Induces Reproductive Aging

The endocrine system is tightly regulated and requires a series of precisely timed hormonal signals. These signals are typically initiated in the hypothalamus and pituitary of the brain. For example, the induction of ovulation in healthy young animals and humans begins when the hypothalamus releases bursts of luteinizing hormone-releasing hormone (LHRH). LHRH stimulates production and pulsatile release of luteinizing hormone (LH) and follicle-stimulating hormone (FSH) from the pituitary gland. In turn, LH and FSH stimulate the production of steroid hormones and ovulation from the ovaries. The steroid hormones produced by the ovaries, such as estrogen and progesterone, control the reproductive cycle by acting on the hypothalamus and pituitary (for a review, see Hung et al., 2003). Thus, hormonal signals normally function in a pulsatile and tightly regulated manner. With aging, however, there is a dysregulation in these hormonal signals. Aging rodents experience a delayed onset and attenuation of LH pulses, as well as a chronic elevation of circulating estrogen, ultimately ending hormonal cycling and signaling the reproductive aging of the animal (for a review, see Tsai & Legan, 2001).

Continuous, long-term administration of estrogen to young ovariectomized rats suppresses the LH pulses, mimicking changes seen with normal aging (Tsai & Legan, 2001). The suppression of the LH pulses also induces alterations in hypothalamic and pituitary function. It has been suggested that reproductive aging in the rat is influenced more by the timing and duration of estrogen exposure than by true chronological age (Hung et al., 2003). In summary, the cessation of reproductive function in animals depends on a critical pattern of chronic estrogen exposure (Desjardins, Beaudet, Meaney, & Brawer, 1995). In turn, reproductive aging can affect neural and immune function.

Irreversible Damage to the Hypothalamus

The hypothalamus is an important region for hormonal timing and control, and chronic estrogen can irreversibly damage it. For example, studies with rodents have shown that chronic estrogen can selectively destroy certain cells in the arcuate nucleus, a subregion of the hypothalamus. Specifically, more than 60% of β-endorphin neurons (brain cells that respond to β-endorphin, a type of opiate) are destroyed (for a review, see Desjardins et al., 1995). β-endorphin and other opiates are important chemicals in the brain because they directly affect reproductive function and ovulation by strongly inhibiting the pattern of LHRH release, and subsequently LH release as well. The degeneration of β-endorphin neurons might be expected to increase LH concentrations. In fact, however, the loss of these neurons leads to compensatory changes that make the hypothalamus supersensitive to residual β-endorphin and other naturally circulating opiates, thereby resulting in persistent inhibition of LH release and inducing reproductive aging of the animal.

The aging process shares many features with this hypothalamic pathology, including deficits in β-endorphin concentrations and β-endorphin cell loss (for a review, see Desjardins et al., 1995). Persistent suppression of LHRH and LH release, therefore, may underlie aspects of reproductive aging. The consequences of reproductive aging include alterations in endocrine and immune signals.

ENDOCRINE AND IMMUNE INTERACTIONS IN THE BRAIN

There is bidirectional communication between the endocrine and immune systems within the brain. Alterations in neuroendocrine signals can modulate immune function, just as alterations in immune function can have consequences for neuroendocrine function (Reichlin, 1998). Following hypothalamic damage induced by elevated estrogen levels, microglial cells (a type of immune cell in the brain) become activated (for a review, see Hung et al., 2003), releasing chemicals that can be either beneficial or destructive, depending on their timing and termination (Akiyama et al., 2000; Reichlin, 1998). For example, activated microglial cells release inflammatory cytokines, and chronic exposure to these chemicals can contribute to pathological conditions such as AD (Akiyama et al., 2000).

Interactions Affecting Neuroendocrine Function

LHRH and LH pulses are disrupted by activation of the body's inflammatory and stress pathways. Stimulation of inflammatory and stress pathways induces elevated levels of inflammatory cytokines, thereby suppressing LHRH and LH pulses and preventing ovulation (Karsch, Battaglia, Breen, Debus, & Harris, 2002). In addition, activation of the hypothalamic-pituitary-adrenal axis (the major stress pathway in the body, named for the structures it comprises) stimulates the adrenal gland to release stress hormones, including glucocorticoids, that can have consequences on other processes, such as cognition and aspects of immune function. These relationships illustrate the extensive communication between the immune and endocrine systems within the brain (for a review, see Reichlin, 1998).

Interactions Affecting Neuroinflammation

AD is characterized by a process of chronic neuroinflammation (for a review, see Akiyama et al., 2000), and one of the hallmarks of the neuroinflammatory response is an elevation in numbers of activated microglia. Because the brains of AD patients show evidence of inflammation and the incidence of AD is elevated in postmenopausal women, we recently examined how the interaction of chronic neuro-inflammation and either estrogen deprivation or chronic ERT affects cognitive function and the microglial response of rodents (Marriott et al., 2002).

Our results were similar to those of Markowska and Savonenko (2002), who showed that ovariectomy did not cause behavioral impairments unless deficits were already present, in that we found no cognitive impairment after ovariectomy. However, ovariectomized animals were impaired after they were administered either chronic estrogen or a treatment that caused chronic brain inflammation. Moreover, the cognitive deficit was exacerbated when chronic estrogen and inflammatory treatments were combined, a condition analogous to a postmenopausal woman with AD receiving ERT. Although a comparison between humans and rodents must be made with caution, it is interesting that continuous, long-term estrogen therapy immediately following ovariectomy in female rats led to an impairment that paralleled the cognitive deficit recently reported in postmenopausal women with AD who received continuous, long-term ERT initiated decades after the onset of menopause, after cognitive deficits were already present. However, we found no impairments in naturally cycling females receiving the same chronic inflammatory treatment that produced impairments in ovariectomized animals; these results are consistent with Markowska and Savonenko's finding that fluctuating estrogen improved working memory in previously impaired ovariectomized animals.

With regard to the microglial response, ovariectomized animals with chronic neuroinflammation showed a robust increase in activated microglia that was not affected by chronic administration of estrogen. The activated microglial cells were specifically localized to brain regions that regulate the autonomic nervous system, which modulates the internal state of the animal, including stress responses (e.g., the hypothalamic-pituitary-adrenal axis) and immune function. Interestingly, intact animals with neuroinflammation had approximately half the number of activated microglia, suggesting that fluctuating gonadal hormones can provide some protection from the consequences of chronic neuroinflammation.

Taken together, these results suggest that the consequences of chronic neuroinflammation, such as cognitive impairment and microglial response, depend on the internal state (including hormone status) of the animal. First, the data support other findings showing that fluctuating levels of gonadal hormones, such as estrogen, have a neuroprotective effect. Second, these results suggest that continuous, long-term ERT given to postmenopausal women with AD, or other diseases characterized by chronic neuroinflammation, may exacerbate existing cognitive impairments (Marriott et al., 2002).

TIMING IS EVERYTHING

Reproductive aging is a dysregulation of neuroendocrine signals that can affect neural and immune function. Continuous administration of hormones may mimic a component of this process by inducing inappropriate alterations in hypothalamic and pituitary function, such as suppression of pulsatile release of LHRH and LH. Bidirectional communication between the endocrine and immune systems may underlie aspects of the aging process, as dysfunctions in one system can have dramatic consequences in the other. These systems may work together to exacerbate dysfunctions associated with aging (for a review, see Straub, Miller, Scholmerich, & Zietz, 2000). Therefore, continuous, long-term administration of hormones, such as estrogen alone (Mulnard et al., 2000) or in combination with progestin (Shumaker et al., 2003), is likely to have negative consequences that may impair aspects of cognition and exacerbate existing diseases characterized by neuroinflammation, such as AD.

Epidemiological and intervention studies of chronic estrogen therapy have produced conflicting results. How can estrogen have deleterious effects when administered chronically to postmenopausal women yet seem to be beneficial in epidemiological studies using the same chronic ERT regimen? The answer may lie in a close examination of the timing of the initiation of estrogen therapy. Chronic estrogen cannot improve memory if cognitive deficits already exist (Markowska & Savonenko, 2002). It has been suggested that estrogen may decrease the risk of AD but may not alter the progression of AD if the disease process has already begun (Wise, Dubal, Wilson, Rau, & Liu, 2001). Thus, epidemiological studies may have included women who took ERT immediately following menopause, when cognitive deficits were not yet present and processes of chronic neuroinflammation stemming from the disease had not yet begun. ERT users tend to be better educated and healthier than women who do not take ERT, so epidemiological studies may skew their results by examining women who are taking ERT for noncognitive reasons (Hogervorst et al., 2000). Still, because chronic estrogen affects neural function negatively, through its effects on estrogen receptors, β-endorphin neurons, and LH pulses, the underlying explanations for the benefits seen in epidemiological studies remain unclear. The disparate results may be due to a modulatory interaction of gonadal hormones with neuroinflammation, which can regulate the output of the autonomic nervous system and the processes it controls, such as stress regulation and immune system function.

Estrogen has complex actions on the brain that may be beneficial or detrimental, depending on the timing of exposure. Current research suggests that continuous estrogen administration for long durations may have deleterious effects on endocrine and immune function, but that such effects may be mitigated by using a therapy designed to mimic the natural cycle of fluctuating hormones. Fluctuating administration of estrogen by itself, however, may be insufficient to protect against the consequences of neuroinflammation accompanying AD, as the physiology of young, intact animals is characterized by a more complex pattern of multiple fluctuating hormones. It may be necessary to mimic this physiology more closely in order to ameliorate the cognitive and neuroinflammatory components characteristic of AD.

Recommended Reading

Brinton, R.D. (2001). Cellular and molecular mechanisms of estrogen regulation of memory function and neuroprotection against Alzheimer's disease: Recent insights and remaining challenges. *Learning & Memory, 8,* 121–133.

Cholerton, B., Gleason, C.E., Baker, L.D., & Asthana, S. (2002). Estrogen and Alzheimer's disease: The story so far. *Drugs & Aging, 19,* 405–427.

Hung, A.J., Stanbury, M.G., Shanabrough, M., Horvath, T.L., Garcia-Segura, L.M., & Naftolin, F. (2003). (See References)

Acknowledgments—This work was supported by the U.S. Public Health Service (AG10546) and the Alzheimer's Association (IIRG-01-2654).

Note

1. Address correspondence to Gary L. Wenk, Neural Systems, Memory & Aging, 384 Life Sciences North, Tucson, AZ 85724-5115; e-mail: gary@nsma.arizona.edu.

References

Akiyama, H., Barger, S., Barnum, S., Bradt, B., Bauer, J., Cole, G.M., Cooper, N.R., Eikelenboom, P., Emmerling, M., Fiebich, B.L., Finch, C.E., Frautschy, S., Griffin, W.S., Hampel, H., Hull, M., Landreth, G., Lue, L., Mrak, R., Mackenzie, I.R., McGeer, P.L., O'Banion, M.K., Pachter, J., Pasinetti, G., Plata-Salaman, C., Rogers, J., Rydel, R., Shen, Y., Streit, W., Strohmeyer, R., Tooyoma, I., Van Muiswinkel, F.L., Veerhuis, R., Walker, D., Webster, S., Wegrzyniak, B., Wenk, G., & Wyss-Coray, T. (2000). Inflammation and Alzheimer's disease. *Neurobiology of Aging, 21,* 383–421.

Desjardins, G.C., Beaudet, A., Meaney, M.J., & Brawer, J.R. (1995). Estrogen-induced hypothalamic beta-endorphin neuron loss: A possible model of hypothalamic aging. *Experimental Gerontology, 30,* 253–267.

Hogervorst, E., Williams, J., Budge, M., Riedel, W., & Jolles, J. (2000). The nature of the effect of female gonadal hormone replacement therapy on cognitive function in post-menopausal women: A meta-analysis. *Neuroscience, 101,* 485–512.

Hung, A.J., Stanbury, M.G., Shanabrough, M., Horvath, T.L., Garcia-Segura, L.M., & Naftolin, F. (2003). Estrogen, synaptic plasticity and hypothalamic reproductive aging. *Experimental Gerontology, 38,* 53–59.

Karsch, F.J., Battaglia, D.F., Breen, K.M., Debus, N., & Harris, T.G. (2002). Mechanisms for ovarian cycle disruption by immune/inflammatory stress. *Stress, 5,* 101–112.

Markowska, A.L., & Savonenko, A.V. (2002). Effectiveness of estrogen replacement in restoration of cognitive function after long-term estrogen withdrawal in aging rats. *Journal of Neuroscience, 22,* 10985–10995.

Marriott, L.K., Hauss-Wegrzyniak, B., Benton, R.S., Vraniak, P., & Wenk, G.L. (2002). Long term estrogen therapy worsens the behavioral and neuro-pathological consequences of chronic brain inflammation. *Behavioral Neuroscience, 116,* 902–911.

Mulnard, R.A., Cotman, C.W., Kawas, C., van Dyck, C.H., Sano, M., Doody, R., Koss, E., Pfeiffer, E., Jin, S., Gamst, A., Grundman, M., Thomas, R., & Thal, L.J. (2000). Estrogen replacement therapy for treatment of mild to moderate Alzheimer disease: A randomized controlled trial. *Journal of the American Medical Association, 283,* 1007–1015.

Norbury, R., Cutter, W.J., Compton, J., Robertson, D.M., Craig, M., Whitehead, M., & Murphy, D.G. (2003). The neuroprotective effects of estrogen on the aging brain. *Experimental Gerontology, 38,* 109–117.

Reichlin, S. (1998). Neuroendocrinology. In J.D. Wilson, D.W. Foster, H.M. Kronenberg, & P.R. Larsen (Eds.), *Williams textbook of endocrinology* (9th ed., pp. 165–248). Philadelphia: W.B. Saunders.

Shumaker, S.A., Legault, C., Rapp, S.R., Thal, L.J., Wallace, R.B., Ockene, J.K., Hendrix, S.L., Jones, B.N., Assaf, A.R., Jackson, R.D., Kotchen, J.M., Wassertheil-Smoller, S., & Watctawski-Wende, J. (2003). Estrogen plus progestin and the incidence of dementia and mild cognitive impairment in postmenopausal women. *Journal of the American Medical Association, 289,* 2651–2661.

Straub, R.H., Miller, L.E., Scholmerich, J., & Zietz, B. (2000). Cytokines and hormones as possible links between endocrinosenescence and immuno-senescence. *Journal of Neuroimmunology, 109,* 10–15.

Toran-Allerand, C.D. (2000). Estrogen as a treatment for Alzheimer disease. *Journal of the American Medical Association, 284,* 307–308.

Tsai, H.W., & Legan, S.J. (2001). Chronic elevation of estradiol in young ovariectomized rats causes aging-like loss of steroid-induced luteinizing hormone surges. *Biology of Reproduction, 64,* 684–688.

Wise, P.M., Dubal, D.B., Wilson, M.E., Rau, S.W., & Liu, Y. (2001). Estrogens: Trophic and protective factors in the adult brain. *Frontiers in Neuro-endocrinology, 22,* 33–66.

Critical Thinking Questions

1. Describe the results of long-term and short-term use of estrogen replacement therapy (ERT) on cognitive processing.

2. Would you recommend estrogen replacement therapy for a woman with moderate cognitive impairment from Alzheimer's disease? Why or why not?

3. How does chronic exposure to estrogen affect the hypothalamus and both the immune and neuroendocrine systems?

This article has been reprinted as it originally appeared in *Current Directions in Psychological Science.* Citation information for this article as originally published appears above.

Hearing Loss in Older Adulthood[1]: What It Is and How It Interacts With Cognitive Performance

Arthur Wingfield, Patricia A. Tun, and Sandra L. McCoy

Department of Psychology and Volen National Center for Complex Systems, Brandeis University

Abstract

Adult aging is accompanied by declines in many areas of cognitive functioning, including reduced memory for new information. Potential sources of these declines are well established and include slowed processing, diminished working-memory capacity, and a reduced ability to inhibit interference. In addition, older adults often experience sensory decline, including decreased hearing acuity for high-frequency sounds and deficits in frequency and temporal resolution. These changes add to the challenge faced by older adults in comprehension and memory for everyday rapid speech. Use of contextual information and added perceptual and cognitive effort can partially offset the deleterious effects of these sensory declines. This may, however, come at a cost to resources that might otherwise be available for "downstream" operations such as encoding the speech content in memory. We argue that future research should focus not only on sensory and cognitive functioning as separate domains but also on the dynamics of their interaction.

Keywords

aging; verbal memory; hearing; speech perception; effort

It is a stark reality that the ability to remember new information and the cognitive resources necessary to support this ability often decline in older adulthood. These declines have been characterized by Salthouse (1991) in terms of the metaphors of time (a slowing of processing rates), space (reduced storage capacity in working memory), and energy (reductions in attentional capacity, whether conceptualized as limitations in the executive component of working memory or as a reduction in allocatable attentional resources). Working memory refers to the ability to temporarily hold and manipulate information in active use. The central executive component of working memory organizes and coordinates multiple mental operations to be performed. To this list of age-related slowing and reductions in the capacity of working memory and attention, one may add also a reduced ability to inhibit potential sources of interference both at the level of perception and in mental operations (Stoltzfus, Hasher, & Zacks, 1996). Beyond the recognition that age-related changes in auditory and visual acuity may affect an older adult's performance, less attention has been paid to how cognitive effort may ameliorate such effects, or the extent to which perceptual effort may drain processing resources and result in a negative effect on cognitive performance. We will argue that this latter effect may be a significant one.

Although the arguments we offer can be applied widely across many domains of cognitive aging, our focus here is on comprehension and memory for spoken language. Unlike reading, where one can control the rate of input with eye movements or reread sections of text, speech rate is controlled by the speaker and any processing not completed as the speech is occurring must be conducted on a fading trace in memory of what the listener has heard. The real-time nature of natural speech makes a significant demand on speed of processing and working memory, two domains in which aging takes a toll.

AGE AND HEARING LOSS

Although many adults retain good hearing well into old age, some degree of age-related hearing loss (presbycusis) is not uncommon among older adults. A general hearing loss can arise from less efficient transmission of sound through the eardrum and ossicles in the middle ear (conductive hearing loss), but of greatest concern in aging are changes in the cochlea in the inner ear; loss of hair cells in the high-frequency region of the basilar membrane causes a loss of acuity for high-frequency sounds (sensorineural hearing loss), which can be especially debilitating for speech perception.

These peripheral changes may be assessed behaviorally by audiometric measures such as pure-tone and speech reception thresholds (the lowest intensities at which tones of various frequencies or specially recorded words can be detected 50% of the time). In addition to these measures, loss of outer hair cells (structures in the cochlea that respond to sound) can be assessed by measuring distortion-product otoacoustic emissions (a byproduct of hair-cell movement); such emissions are absent or reduced in amplitude with hair-cell loss, which can compromise speech understanding. In spite of remarkable progress in hearing-aid technology, allowing selective amplification to match a user's audiometric profile and increasingly sophisticated signal processing, it has been estimated that 2 out of 3 older adults with hearing loss do not use hearing aids; nonuse is especially prevalent among people with mild hearing loss (National Academy on an Aging Society, 1999). In part, this may be due to a perceived social stigma associated with using hearing aids or delayed awareness of the hearing loss due to the gradualness of its onset. There are, however, additional factors that play a role.

In addition to the peripheral losses that hearing aids can help rectify, aging can also produce what we will refer to here as a deficit in central auditory processing: decreased efficiency of temporal resolution (the ability to detect and maintain the ordering of rapidly arriving sounds) and spectral resolution (isolation and discrimination of the frequency components of complex signals) as incoming sounds are processed. Although the loci of these deficits are a matter of interest in hearing science (Humes, Christopherson, & Cokely, 1992), there is no question that efficient spectral and temporal processing are critically important for speech perception.

Given that average speaking rates range from 140 to 180 words per minute in ordinary conversation, one can see how poor temporal resolution would have a negative impact on the recognition of speech and other complex signals. Difficulties with frequency discrimination may make it especially difficult to separate speech from background noise and the "babble" of other speakers (Gordon-Salant & Fitzgibbons, 1997; Schneider & Pichora-Fuller, 2000), a problem that adds to older adults' slowing in attention switching and declines in attentional focus at the cognitive level (Tun, O'Kane, & Wingfield, 2002). When these central auditory deficits are present, they cannot be ameliorated with simple sound amplification.

Adult Aging and the Sensory–Cognitive Processing Chain

Although in the simplest sense one might contrast between cognitive declines on the one hand, and hearing declines on the other, one should rather think in terms of three levels of information processing, each of which may show age-related decline: (a) peripheral hearing acuity, (b) central auditory processing, and (c) cognitive operations. There is considerable blurring at the boundaries and there are interactions among the different levels. For example, to comprehend spoken language, a listener needs to extract stable linguistic information from a constantly changing speech stream. This is referred to as normalizing the speech signal, to allow speech sounds to be recognized in spite of variability in pronunciation or accent from one speaker to another. In an elegant set of studies, Sommers (1996) has shown how such normalization may impose especially heavy processing demands on older adults' more limited resources. Normalization would clearly be affected by peripheral hearing loss at the high frequencies, by central auditory changes affecting temporal and frequency resolution, and, as Sommers has pointed out, by declines in cognitive resources.

We list these interacting operations and limitations schematically in Figure 1. The first operation depicted in Figure 1, labeled as perceptual operations, requires an adequate level of function in both peripheral and central auditory processing. The second two levels of information processing represented in the diagram are the cognitive operations of encoding in working memory and higher-level encoding. The diagram illustrates the principle of multiple processing operations drawing to varying degrees on a limited-capacity resource system that is generally presumed to decrease with age. Terms such as working memory capacity and processing resources coexist as characterizations of this resource-limited system; there is also a major question of whether there are process-specific resources that may not draw on general resource capacity.

Contextual Support Can Compensate for Sensory Loss

Although aging may be accompanied by performance declines at multiple levels, linguistic knowledge is well preserved into older adulthood. This knowledge can be effectively used by older adults in word recognition, whether the challenge comes from underarticulation of the speech signal, as is common in ordinary conversation (Wingfield, Alexander, & Cavigelli, 1994); from speech being masked by noise (Schneider & Pichora-Fuller, 2000); or from reduction of sensory richness due to presbycusis (Gordon-Salant & Fitzgibbons, 1997; Schneider & Pichora-Fuller, 2000). Older adults are also frequently adept at using linguistic knowledge to support recall by reconstructing missing elements to give coherence to what they have heard (Wingfield, Tun, & Rosen, 1995). That a weakened signal may be compensated for by context has been well documented in the literature. Only

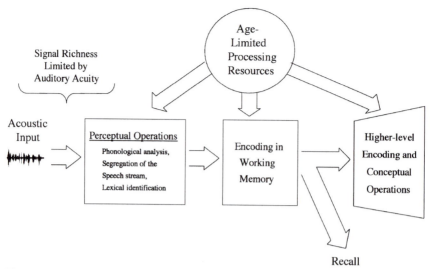

Fig. 1. Schematic diagram of the operations required for successful recognition of a speech message, beginning with the perceptual segregation of a continuous speech stream into its constituent words. The product of the perceptual analysis can be encoded in working memory for overt recall as well as serving as input to higher stages, such as understanding the input at the conceptual and discourse levels. Processing at each stage can be facilitated (or on occasion misled) by contextual support, such as the presence of a constraining linguistic context, when available. Age-related factors that may interfere with success include reduced signal richness consequent to peripheral hearing loss (such as a reduced ability to hear the high frequency sounds in speech) and central-auditory-processing deficits (such as reduced ability to discriminate the frequency components of complex auditory signals and to detect and maintain the ordering of rapid arriving sounds).

recently, however, has there been renewed attention to the possibility that this compensation may come at a cost.

A COST OF SUCCESSFUL PERCEPTION

When the older adult shows poorer recall for spoken stimuli, careful investigators typically take steps to insure that the stimuli (e.g., spoken word lists or sentences) can be correctly identified at the perceptual level. In addition to audiometric screening, having participants "shadow" speech (i.e., repeating each word as it is being heard) can help confirm this ability. Thus, if older adults can successfully shadow speech presented at the same intensity as the to-be-remembered stimuli, it might seem reasonable to exclude differences in hearing acuity as a contributing source of any age-related declines in recall that may be found.

We argue, however, that a consequence of even a mild peripheral or central auditory impairment in older adults may be the need to exert extra effort in order to achieve perceptual success. The concern here is that this more effortful processing in the initial stages of speech perception may come at the cost of processing resources that would otherwise be available for downstream operations, such as effective encoding of the material in memory for recall or performing higher-level comprehension operations. This "effortfulness" hypothesis was well-articulated over 30 years ago (Rabbitt, 1968). It has, however, only recently received renewed attention.

An Effortfulness Hypothesis

In a recall experiment, Rabbitt (1968, Experiment 2) gave young adults with normal hearing sets of spoken 8-digit lists, each list presented in two halves with a 2-second pause after the first 4 digits. He found that the first half of the list, even when presented clearly and without masking, was less well recalled when the second half of the list was heard in noise rather than in quiet. Rabbitt interpreted these findings as suggesting that the increased effort required to identify the noise-masked digits may have deprived the listeners of processing resources that might have been used to rehearse the previous digits for effective memory.

Rabbitt (1991) later reinforced this interpretation by showing better recall for older adults with good hearing than for those with a mild hearing loss, even when both groups could correctly repeat words heard at the same intensity levels as the to-be-remembered stimuli. Rabbitt argued that the older adults with a mild hearing loss had to allocate more processing resources to identify the spoken stimuli, thus reducing available resources that might otherwise have been deployed to support encoding of the materials in memory (Rabbitt, 1991; see also Dickinson & Rabbitt, 1991, for an analogous argument for degraded vision). Through the recent efforts of such investigators as Murphy, Craik, Li, & Schneider (2000), who studied memory performance with noise masking used to simulate a hearing loss in young and older adults, this effortfulness position has begun to receive considerable attention (Schneider & Pichora-Fuller, 2000; Tun et al., 2002).

How powerful is the effortfulness effect? To explore this question we compared word-list recall in older adults who had good hearing with that in older adults who had mild-to-moderate hearing loss. Participants heard 15-word lists that were stopped at random points, and all that was required of them was to recall just the last three words that they heard. As shown in Figure 2, we found that although both groups showed excellent recall for the final word of the three-word sets, recall of the two words that preceded it was poorer for the hearing-loss group than for the participants with better hearing, even though all three words were delivered at the same amplitude (volume). The data shown in Figure 2, which are taken from McCoy et al., 2005, are for sets of unrelated words unsupported by the constraints of context that are found in meaningful connected speech such as sentences or passages. In this same experiment we also showed that contextual constraints can significantly ameliorate this diminished recall among hearing-impaired participants (McCoy et al., 2005).

Because both of the groups could correctly report the final word of the three-word sets, we concluded that the reason for the hearing-loss group's failure to recall the previous two words was not that they had failed to correctly identify them. Consistent with Rabbitt's effortfulness hypothesis, we interpreted our results as showing that the extra effort the older adults with hearing loss had to expend to achieve their perceptual success came at the cost of processing resources that would otherwise have been available for encoding the words in

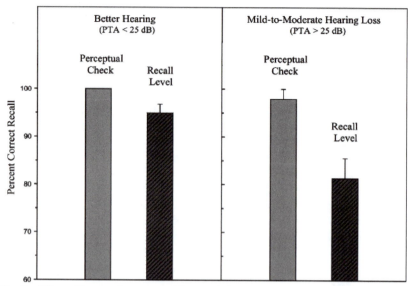

Fig. 2. Effect of hearing loss on word-list recall for two groups of older adults. Left panel shows percent correct recall for participants with better hearing, defined as a pure-tone average (PTA) of less than 25 dB (the ability to hear pure tones averaged across frequencies of 1000, 2000, and 4000 Hz for the better ear). The right panel shows corresponding data for age-matched participants with a mild-to-moderate hearing loss (PTA greater than 25dB). The left bar in each panel shows recall accuracy for the final word of the three-word recall sets as a perceptual check to insure that the stimulus words could be correctly identified at the intensities at which they were heard. The right bars in each panel show mean recall for the first two words of the three-word recall sets. To support the position that the greater number of errors in the poorer hearing group was due not to a failure of perceptual identification of the words but to a detrimental effect on memory encoding due to increased effort in processing the stimulus words, we show recall only for cases where the final words of the sets were recalled correctly (100% of the cases for the better hearing group; 97.0 % of the cases for the hearing loss group).

memory. It is especially noteworthy that this effect was so powerful as to influence memory performance for just a three-word memory set.

CAUTIONS, CONCLUSIONS, AND FUTURE DIRECTIONS

Results such as these suggest that the question of age differences in comprehension or memory for speech should not necessarily be framed simply in terms of whether poor performance on a test of memory or comprehension is due to poor hearing or to declines at the cognitive level. Certainly, sufficiently sensitive test procedures need to be developed to determine contributions at all three levels: peripheral, central, and cognitive. We have suggested, however, that these levels should not be seen as independent, but rather that the theoretical question that should engage researchers is one of how these levels interact. On the one hand, hearing scientists must determine the extent to which markers of central auditory decline such as declines in frequency or temporal resolution are independent of, or may be related to, peripheral hearing loss (e.g., Humes et al.,1992). On the other hand, we need also to pursue the apparent paradox implied by the effortfulness notion: that hearing loss can contribute to memory failure even when it can be demonstrated that all of the to-be-recalled stimuli could be correctly identified. In making this argument, we would not wish to imply that perceptual effortfulness is the only way in which poor hearing could affect recall of correctly identified spoken words. For example, poor hearing might strip the memory representation of extra-lexical features such as voice quality that might add distinctiveness to the memory trace.

As we caution against framing the sensory-cognitive interaction in either–or terms, we would also caution against rushing to conclude that sensory declines, whether visual or auditory, underlie all of the many cognitive, memory, and attentional declines that can accompany the aging process. That is, recognizing the importance of age-related sensory changes should not be seen as an argument against the existence of working-memory or other cognitive declines over and above these input limitations. Indeed, to the extent that older adults begin with more limited resources, the extra effort required at the sensory level could further add to the differential memory effects often seen in older adults' verbal recall.

In calling for a more comprehensive approach to broadening our understanding of sensory and cognitive declines in adult aging we would also encourage greater attention to individual-difference factors ordinarily associated with social and personality psychology, such as the potential effects of perceived self-efficacy on the degree of effort a person gives to a task. This broadening of the research scope could add further insight to the increasing evidence that cognitive performance may be reduced by perceptual effort even when, paradoxically, it can be shown that the to-be-remembered stimuli were correctly identified. These and related findings point to the need for awareness of the importance of sensory ability in studies of cognitive function in adult aging, as well as emphasizing the need for research that may better inform our understanding of the dynamics of sensory–cognitive interactions.

Recommended Reading

Rabbitt, P.M.A. (1968). (See references)
Schneider, B.A., & Pichora-Fuller, M.K. (2000). (See references)
Wingfield, A., & Stine-Morrow, E.A.L. (2000). Language and speech. In F.I.M. Craik & T.A. Salthouse (Eds.), *Handbook of aging and cognition* (2nd. ed., pp. 359–416). Mahwah, NJ: Erlbaum.

Acknowledgments—The authors' work is supported by National Institutes of Health Grants AG19714 and AG04517 from the National Institute on Aging.

Note

1. Address correspondence to Arthur Wingfield, Volen National Center for Complex Systems, MS 013, Brandeis University, Waltham, MA 02454-9110; e-mail: wingfield@brandeis.edu.

References

Dickinson, C.V.M., & Rabbitt, P.M.A. (1991). Simulated visual impairment: Effects on text comprehension and reading speed. *Clinical Vision Sciences, 6,* 301–308.

Gordon-Salant, S., & Fitzgibbons, P.J. (1997). Selected cognitive factors and speech recognition performance among young and elderly listeners. *Journal of Speech, Language, and Hearing Research, 40*, 423–431.

Humes, L., Christopherson, L., & Cokely, C. (1992). Central auditory processing disorders in the elderly: Fact or fiction? In J. Katz, N.A. Stecker, & D. Henderson (Eds.), *Central auditory processing: A transdisciplinary view* (pp. 141–150). St. Louis, MO: Mosby-Year Book, Inc.

McCoy, S.L., Tun, P.A., Cox, L.C., Colangelo, M., Stewart, R.A., & Wingfield, A. (2005). Hearing loss and perceptual effort: Downstream effects on older adults' memory for speech. *Quarterly Journal of Experimental Psychology, 58A*, 22–33.

Murphy, D.R., Craik, F.I.M., Li, K.Z.H., & Schneider, B.A. (2000). Comparing the effects of aging and background noise on short-term memory performance. *Psychology and Aging, 15*, 323–334.

National Academy on an Aging Society (1999, December). *Hearing loss: A growing problem that affects quality of life.* (Challenges for the 21st Century: Chronic and Disabling Conditions, No. 2). Washington, DC: Author.

Rabbitt, P.M.A. (1968). Channel capacity, intelligibility and immediate memory. *Quarterly Journal of Experimental Psychology, 20*, 241–248.

Rabbitt, P.M.A. (1991). Mild hearing loss can cause apparent memory failures which increase with age and reduce with IQ. *Acta Otolaryngologica, Supplementum, 476*, 167–176.

Salthouse, T.A. (1991). *Theoretical perspectives on cognitive aging.* Hillsdale, NJ: Erlbaum.

Schneider, B.A., & Pichora-Fuller, M.K. (2000). Implications of perceptual deterioration for cognitive aging research. In F.I.M. Craik, & T.A. Salthouse (Eds.), *Handbook of aging and cognition* (2nd ed., pp. 155–220). Mahwah, NJ: Erlbaum.

Sommers, M.S. (1996). The structural organization of the mental lexicon and its contribution to age-related declines in spoken-word recognition. *Psychology and Aging, 11*, 333–341.

Stoltzfus, E.R., Hasher, L., & Zacks, R.T. (1996). Working memory and aging: Current status of the inhibitory view. In J.R. Richardson (Ed.), *Working memory and cognition* (pp. 66–88). New York: Oxford University Press.

Tun, P.A., O'Kane, G., & Wingfield, A. (2002). Distraction by competing speech in younger and older listeners. *Psychology and Aging, 17*, 453–467.

Wingfield, A., Alexander, A.H., & Cavigelli, S. (1994). Does memory constrain utilization of top-down information in spoken word recognition? Evidence from normal aging. *Language and Speech, 37*, 221–235.

Wingfield, A., Tun, P.A., & Rosen, M.J. (1995). Age differences in veridical and reconstructive recall of syntactically and randomly segmented speech. *Journal of Gerontology: Psychological Sciences, 50B*, P257–P266.

Critical Thinking Questions

1. An older person with hearing loss has difficult understanding a speaker. The speaker talks louder so the older adult will understand her. After reading this article, you know this will not be very helpful. Why does talking louder not help the older adult, and what can the speaker do instead?

2. Why is listening to someone speak so much more difficult than reading?

3. Why would hearing difficulties affect cognitive functioning?

This article has been reprinted as it originally appeared in *Current Directions in Psychological Science*. Citation information for this article as originally published appears above.

Psychology and Aging: Enhancing the Lives of an Aging Population

Arthur D. Fisk[1] and Wendy A. Rogers
*School of Psychology, Georgia Institute of Technology,
Atlanta, Georgia*

Abstract

A pressing need for upcoming decades is ensuring that older adults, who constitute an increasing percentage of the population, are able to function independently and maintain an acceptable quality of life. One important concern is the usability of new technologies. Unfortunately, the science that could direct proper design and implementation of current and future technological advancement is underdeveloped and less mature than the engineering that supports technological advancement. We review data documenting age-related usability issues and how psychological science can remedy such problems. We also outline how training principles can be applied to older adults. We conclude that psychological science has much to contribute to the goal of enhancing the lives of older adults.

Keywords

cognitive aging; system design; training

From news reports or simple observation, it should be clear that within developed countries, the number of older adults is increasing faster than the number of their younger counterparts. Indeed, the life expectancy of the population in the United States and other countries is, collectively, increasing. Rowe and Kahn (1998) highlighted the dramatic nature of the increase in life expectancy when they estimated that of all humans who have ever lived to be 65 years or older, half of them are currently alive. This demographic shift brings with it certain challenges if society is to meet the needs of these older individuals. Psychological science is well positioned to help meet these challenges.

We use the term engineering psychology to refer to the applied science with the goal of understanding how humans sense, process, and act on information. Engineering psychology also applies that knowledge to the design of and training for new and existing technologies to make them safe, efficient, and easy to use. To accommodate older populations, it is necessary to understand age-related differences in sensing, processing, and acting on information. It is also necessary to apply that knowledge base to ensure that products and systems are safe, efficient, and easy to use by older adults.

Psychologists have conducted considerable research on the fundamentals of cognitive aging (see Craik & Salthouse, 2000, for specific reviews). These data serve as the starting point for designing products and systems that older adults can use.

ARE EXISTING SYSTEMS AND PRODUCTS EASY TO USE?

Are existing systems and products easy to use? In a word, no. They are not easy to use by individuals of any age, and usability problems may be exacerbated for older adults. In his book *The Psychology of Everyday Things*, Norman (1988) illustrated how many products and systems are difficult to use. The typical response of users who encounter a problem is to assume that they made a mistake and the problem lies with them. Not so—typically the problem lies with either the design of the system or the instructions provided for using it.

In a study examining usability problems with everyday products such as cleaners, toiletries, over-the-counter medications, and health care products (Hancock, Fisk, & Rogers, 2001), we found that 72% of the respondents reported experiencing some usability problems. Reported problems included difficulty understanding written materials (29% of respondents), trouble interpreting symbolic information (21%), perceptual problems such as inability to see print clearly (47%), memory problems such as forgetting actions to perform or procedures to follow (45%), and motor control and manipulation difficulties (84%). The survey respondents' age range was 18 to 91, but people of all ages reported similar types and frequencies of usability problems; the only exception was that people over age 65 reported more perceptual and motor problems than people under 35.

Many of the difficulties reported in this survey might be classified as "annoyance problems" (e.g., difficulty reading text or opening a bottle). However, many usability problems are not just annoyances but have the potential to be dangerous or even life threatening. Studies of home health care technologies illustrate this point.

Blood glucose meters are devices used to self-monitor glucose levels in the blood. Often these devices are advertised as simple to use: "It's as easy to use as 1, 2, 3. Just set up the meter, check the system, and test your blood." Yet these devices are not so easy to use. A detailed task analysis of one presumably easy system revealed more than 50 substeps for the performance of the three basic steps (Rogers, Mykityshyn, Campbell, & Fisk, 2001). Further, in an observational study of 90 users of blood glucose meters, 62% were found to make at least one clinically significant error (Colagiuri, Colagiuri, Jones, & Moses, 1990). Unfortunately, Colagiuri et al. engaged in the common practice of "blaming the user," as evidenced by their statement that "the most commonly encountered . . . errors resulted from a *general lack of care on the part of the patient* [italics added] in complying with the manufacturer's instructions" (p. 803). Such blame does not lead to understanding human error or minimizing future errors, and it ignores errors caused by system design or inappropriate instructional materials.

Design can induce errors, and design problems are often coupled with poorly written diagnostic aids. This point can be illustrated by an anecdote. A news crew was filming a story on our research concerning the usability of home medical devices. A reporter, skeptical of the usability issues we were reporting, attempted to set up a blood glucose meter, and it displayed the message "ERROR 2." To correct the problem, he went to the manual section labeled "What to do if errors" and found "ERROR 2—Device may not be working properly." After he admitted that there might be problems with the system design and the manual, we told him that he had the calibration strip in upside down. There were no markings on the strip to perceptually guide its insertion.

It is not only blood glucose meters that are difficult to use and to learn how to use. Home health care systems are often relatively complex, and existing instructions are not adequate (Gardner-Bonneau, 2001). Safe and effective uses of home health care technologies, especially those targeting older adult users, will require behavioral science–based design changes and development of adequate training materials.

CAN PSYCHOLOGICAL SCIENCE REMEDY THE USABILITY PROBLEMS?

In an effort to better understand how psychological science can improve the lives of older adults, we conducted a series of focus groups to document the usability problems older individuals encounter in their daily activities (Rogers, Meyer, Walker, & Fisk, 1998). Each reported problem was classified according to the activity the respondent was engaged in when he or she encountered the problem, the source of the problem (i.e., motor, visual, auditory, cognitive, external, or general health limitations), whether the problem was related to the inherent difficulty of the task or potential negative outcomes, and how the participant responded (e.g., stopped performing the task, compensated somehow).

Of the problems reported by the older adults in this study, 47% were due to financial limitations, health difficulties, or other general concerns not specific to the product's design. Each remaining problem was classified according to whether it could potentially be solved through redesign, training, or some combination of the two. Approximately 25% of the problems could potentially be remedied by improving the design of the systems involved to solve sensory or motor problems. For example, the possible remedies identified included lowering steps on buses, developing tools for grasping or scrubbing, improving chair design, and enlarging letter size on a label.

The remaining 28% of the reported problems had the potential to be solved through training, or through a combination of training and redesign. For example, an older person learning to drive for the first time would benefit from driver training tailored to his or her age-related needs. For other complex systems, such as personal computers or health care technologies, novices would need training; however, such systems clearly also have the potential for design changes that would improve their usability for users of all ages.

These data should not be interpreted as if the problems reported by older adults currently have solutions. Instead, the data imply that the potential exists to apply the science of psychology to enhance the lives of older adults. Design efforts must consider the capabilities and limitations of older adults, and the literature on cognitive aging provides a starting point for understanding more about this user population (e.g., Craik & Salthouse, 2000). In addition, the categories of usability problems we have reported in our studies (Hancock et al., 2001; Rogers et al., 1998) provide valuable information for design efforts. The application of task analysis and other tools used by engineering psychology to determine user requirements (see Salvendy, 1997, for a review of such tools) can be valuable for identifying both problems users have and how to minimize sources of design-induced errors (e.g., Rogers et al., 2001).

APPLICATION OF TRAINING PRINCIPLES

A goal of product design should be to minimize training requirements by designing systems that take into account the capabilities of users. However, even if products and systems are designed optimally, users often require training. Psychological science has much to contribute to efforts to optimize how younger and older adults are trained to use complex systems.

Training programs come in many forms and include materials ranging from written manuals to multimedia, experiential tutorials. What is the best way to develop such training programs? Theories of training abound in the research literature, but there has traditionally been a disconnect between developers of training theories and practitioners who could benefit most from the application of such theories (as discussed by Salas, Cannon-Bowers, & Blickensderfer, 1997). Applied psychology has the potential to serve as the bridge from the training principles in the literature to the development of training programs for practical applications. There must also be a link back to theory development to ensure that theories of training are refined on the basis of limitations that are discovered when the theories are applied to complex, real-world problems.

How, then, should trainers design programs for older adults to learn how to interact with technological systems? The background knowledge psychological science can bring to bear on such training is substantial. A review of the literature on skill acquisition and aging reveals basic principles: It is not the case that older adults cannot learn or that they always learn less or more slowly than younger adults; to understand age-related differences in learning, one must consider the task variables, the context, and the type and amount of training being provided (see Fisk & Rogers, 2000, for a review).

Older adults do exhibit declines in abilities important for learning and skill acquisition (Craik & Salthouse, 2000), such as working memory, perceptual speed, spatial ability, and fluid abilities in general (i.e., those abilities that are generally independent of processes that take advantage of the person's accumulated knowledge). Proper instructional design that capitalizes on intact abilities and compensates for declining abilities holds much promise for helping older adults obtain basic proficiency, as well as for improving their performance with additional training and helping them retain the levels of proficiency they achieve.

For example, we recently assessed the differential benefits of video-based versus user-manual-based training for younger and older adults learning to calibrate a blood glucose meter (Mykityshyn, Fisk, & Rogers, in press). The type of instruction was critical for determining older adults' performance. Older adults trained using the manual performed more poorly than all other groups. After only one calibration, older adults who received video training performed as accurately as the younger adults. Older adults' performance declined more than young adults' across a 2-week retention interval, but the benefit of the video training was maintained for the older adults. The video-based training provided environmental support for the learner by explicitly demonstrating the task sequence, and minimizing reliance on working memory (for visualizing) and reading comprehension (for drawing necessary inferences).

It is important to note that not just any video will result in superior performance. In one of our studies (Rogers et al., 2001), we demonstrated that the video provided by the manufacturer of a blood glucose meter was not sufficient for training users to operate the system. For a video to be effective, it must follow instructional principles.

Accurately assessing the expected benefits of a training approach is necessary for making informed selections among training options. Charness and Holley (2001) described one method for assessing the effectiveness of training using learning-curve data. A learning curve showing how many repetitions of an activity (i.e., trials) a particular group (e.g., older adults) needs to reach each of various levels of performance can provide the basis for making predictions. For example, by extrapolating from a learning curve, one can predict the number of trials that will be necessary to reach a higher level of performance than is shown in the curve itself. Rates of learning demonstrated after different kinds of training can be statistically compared to estimate their relative benefits. In addition, learning curves can be used to estimate how much training will be needed for a desired level of performance. Such predictions may be very useful in illustrating the effectiveness of training programs.

CONCLUSION

Through examples, we have highlighted opportunities for enhancing older adults' lives, particularly with respect to technology design and training. If research on training and system design is to be used to enhance performance of older adults, it can and should be driven by psychological theory. This view is shared by other scientists, as illustrated by a National Research Council (2000) report, *The Aging Mind*, which made recommendations for future cognitive research. One recommendation was to develop "knowledge needed to design effective technologies supporting adaptivity in older adults" (p. 35). The report also said that realizing such a goal "requires integrating behavioral science and engineering in a context of product design and development" (p. 36).

We agree and wish to extend this point. Certainly there still exists a gap between the knowledge base of the psychological scientist and the information needs of the nonscientist consumer of that knowledge. There is a crucial need for research programs aimed at clarifying how age-related changes in function affect older adults' ability to interact with technology successfully. To fulfill this need, researchers need to sample task environments, much as they sample participant populations (see Fisk & Kirlik, 1996, for examples). With such research, psychology will move toward fulfilling its promise of giving designers the science-based design principles they need for developing useful applications of current and future technologies.

Recommended Reading

Charness, N. (2001). Aging and communication: Human factors issues. In N. Charness, D.C. Park, & B.A. Sabel (Eds.), *Communication, technology, and aging: Opportunities and challenges for the future* (pp. 1–29). New York: Springer.

Czaja, S.J. (2001). Telecommunication technology as an aid to family caregivers. In W.A. Rogers & A.D. Fisk (Eds.), *Human factors interventions for the health care of older adults* (pp.165–170). Mahwah, NJ: Erlbaum.

Mead, S.E., Batsakes, P., Fisk, A.D., & Mykityshyn, A. (1999). Application of cognitive theory to training and design solutions for age-related computer use. *International Journal of Behavioral Development, 23,* 553–573.

Rogers, W.A., & Fisk, A.D. (2000). Human factors, applied cognition, and aging. In F.I.M. Craik & T.A. Salthouse (Eds.), *The handbook of aging and cognition* (2nd ed., pp. 559–591). Mahwah, NJ: Erlbaum.

Acknowledgments—Preparation of this manuscript was partially supported by Grants P01 AG17211, P50 AG11715, and R01 AG07654 from the National Institutes of Health (National Institute on Aging).

Note

1. Address correspondence to Arthur D. Fisk, School of Psychology, Georgia Institute of Technology, Atlanta, GA 30332-0170; e-mail: af7@ prism.gatech.edu.

References

Charness, N., & Holley, P. (2001). Computer interface issues for health self-care: Cognitive and perceptual constraints. In W.A. Rogers & A.D. Fisk (Eds.), *Human factors interventions for the health care of older adults* (pp.239–254). Mahwah, NJ: Erlbaum.

Colagiuri, R., Colagiuri, S., Jones, S., & Moses, R.G. (1990). The quality of self-monitoring of blood glucose. *Diabetic Medicine, 7,* 800–804.

Craik, F.I.M., & Salthouse, T.A. (Eds.). (2000). *The handbook of aging and cognition* (2nd ed.). Mahwah, NJ: Erlbaum.

Fisk, A.D., & Kirlik, A. (1996). Practical relevance and age-related research: Can theory advance without practice? In W.A. Rogers, A.D. Fisk, & N. Walker (Eds.), *Aging and skilled performance: Advances in theory and application* (pp. 1–15). Mahwah, NJ: Erlbaum.

Fisk, A.D., & Rogers, W.A. (2000). Influence of training and experience on skill acquisition and maintenance in older adults. *Journal of Aging and Physical Activity, 8,* 373–378.

Gardner-Bonneau, D. (2001). Designing medical devices for older adults. In W.A. Rogers & A.D. Fisk (Eds.), *Human factors interventions for the health care of older adults* (pp. 221–237). Mahwah, NJ: Erlbaum.

Hancock, H.E., Fisk, A.D., & Rogers, W.A. (2001). Everyday products: Easy to use . . . or not? *Ergonomics in Design, 9,* 12–18.

Mykityshyn, A.L., Fisk, A.D., & Rogers, W.A. (in press). Toward age-related training methodologies for sequence-based systems: An evaluation using a home medical device. *Human Factors.*

National Research Council. (2000). *The aging mind: Opportunities in cognitive research.* Washington, DC: National Academy Press.

Norman, D.A. (1988). *The psychology of everyday things.* New York: Harper Collins.

Rogers, W.A., Meyer, B., Walker, N., & Fisk, A.D. (1998). Functional limitations to daily living tasks in the aged: A focus group analysis. *Human Factors, 40,* 111–125.

Rogers, W.A., Mykityshyn, A.L., Campbell, R.H., & Fisk, A.D. (2001). Only 3 easy steps? User-centered analysis of a "simple" medical device. *Ergonomics in Design, 9,* 6–14.

Rowe, J.W., & Kahn, R.L. (1998). *Successful aging.* New York: Pantheon.

Salas, E., Cannon-Bowers, J., & Blickensderfer, E.L. (1997). Enhancing reciprocity between training theory and practice: Principles, guidelines, and specifications. In J.K. Ford, S.W.J. Kozlowski, K. Kraiger, E. Salas, & M.S. Teachout (Eds.), *Improving training effectiveness in work organizations* (pp. 291–322). Mahwah, NJ: Erlbaum.

Salvendy, G. (1997). *Handbook of human factors and ergonomics* (2nd ed.). New York: John Wiley and Sons.

Critical Thinking Questions

1. Are household products easy to use? What have studies shown about the ease of use for these products, and age differences in the reported difficulties?

2. Give one example of a type of training that is better than the usual manual-based technique for older adults

2b. The technique above reduces the demand placed on two cognitive processes that decline with age. What are these two cognitive processes, and how does this technique reduce the need to use such processes?

This article has been reprinted as it originally appeared in *Current Directions in Psychological Science*. Citation information for this article as originally published appears above.

The Cognitive Neuroscience of Aging and Culture

Denise Park[1]

University of Illinois at Urbana-Champaign

Angela Gutchess

Harvard University, and The Athinoula A. Martinos Center for Biomedical Imaging

Abstract

Research into the cognitive neuroscience of aging has revealed exciting and unexpected changes to the brain over the lifespan. However, studies have mostly been conducted on Western populations, raising doubts about the universality of age-related changes. Cross-cultural investigation of aging provides a window into the stability of changes with age due to neurobiology, as well as into the flexibility of aging due to life experiences that impact cognition. Behavioral findings suggest that different cultures process distinct aspects of information and employ diverse information-processing strategies. The study of aging allows us to identify those age-related neural changes that persist across cultures as well as the changes that are driven by culture-specific life experiences.

Keywords

cognition; aging; culture; cognitive neuroscience

There is compelling evidence for differences in cognitive function as a result of culture (Nisbett & Masuda, 2003). Behavioral evidence suggests that, because of cultural norms that focus on relationships and group function, East Asians develop a bias to monitor their environment more than Westerners do, resulting in greater attention to context (such as a picture's background) and more holistic encoding of stimuli. In contrast to East Asians, the individualistic society of Westerners produces a bias to attend more to focal objects and to engage in more analytic information processing (reviewed by Nisbett & Masuda, 2003).

In the present paper, we examine what is known and what can be learned about cognitive processes and human development from a joint exploration of culture and aging variables, and we show how neuroscience approaches to this issue can be particularly informative. The joint examination of cultural differences in a lifespan sample of adults permits an assessment of the interplay of experience (through culture) with neurobiology (through aging) in sculpting the neurocognitive system. Neuroimaging data indicate that the aging brain is different from the young adult brain, with the former continuously changing and adapting to its diminished efficiency (Reuter-Lorenz & Lustig, 2005). When aged brains show broad similarities across cultures in terms of neural recruitment patterns and structural integrity, we can be almost certain that these changes, relative to young brains, represent biological aging. If older adults, however, exhibit differences in neural circuitry and activation as a function of culture, this is likely because of experience and gives us a window into the plasticity of the aging neurocognitive system. Relatively little is known, behaviorally or neurally, about cultural differences in cognitive aging. The extant data involves contrasts between Western and East Asian cultures, and thus we limit our discussion to these cultures.

BEHAVIORAL EVIDENCE FOR DIFFERENCES IN COGNITIVE PROCESSES AS A FUNCTION OF AGE AND CULTURE

When one examines behavioral data on cognitive aging, the picture is one of decreased efficiency in basic cognitive processes such as speed, working memory, and long-term memory, although knowledge remains preserved or even grows (see Fig. 1). A framework for understanding the joint impact of culture and aging on cognition was proposed by Park, Nisbett, and Hedden (1999), taking into account these different cognitive domains. Park et al. (1999) propose that it is important to consider the distinction (discussed by Baltes, 1987) between basic cognitive hardware or *mechanics*—such as speed, working memory, and inhibition—and acquired knowledge (described as software or cognitive *pragmatics*) in understanding the impact of culture on cognitive aging. Park et al. (1999) suggest that when young adults evidence cultural differences in cognitive pragmatics, the differences will magnify with age, because they are based on acquired knowledge and older adults have more experience with the culture than younger adults do. Conversely, differences in basic processes (mechanics) that occur in young people will be minimized with age, as age-related decreases in capacity will operate to limit flexibility in mental operations, resulting in more similarity across cultures with age.

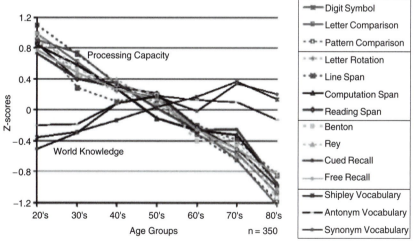

Fig. 1. The aging mind, showing regular decreases in various measures of processing capacity (including speed of processing, working memory, and long-term memory measures) but maintenance, or perhaps even augmentation, of knowledge of the world (as measured by vocabulary tests) over the lifespan. Adapted from "Models of visuospatial and verbal memory across the adult life span," by D.C. Park, G. Lautenschlager, T. Hedden, N.S. Davidson, A. Smith, and P.K. Smith, 2002, *Psychology & Aging, 17,* p. 305. Copyright 2002 by the American Psychological Association. Adapted with permission.

Research on old and young Chinese and Americans have provided some support for this model. For example, Hedden et al. (2002) studied backward digit span, which assesses participants' ability to manipulate a series of numbers in working memory and to repeat the numbers back in the reverse order in which they were originally presented. For this cognitive mechanic, the researchers found larger culture differences in young people than in old people. In contrast, Gutchess, Yoon, et al. (in press) examined the use of strategies for categorical clustering in a memory task (a strategy largely based on world knowledge) and found larger culture differences in old people than in young people.

Although cultural differences in cognition do exist, the behavioral evidence to date suggests that the impact of aging on cognitive mechanics is much greater than the impact of culture. Park et al. (1999) conducted a large study of young and old Chinese and Americans, and collected multiple measures of speed and working memory. They developed separate structural models for each of the four groups and found larger differences in the structural models due to age than due to culture. Similarly, in a study of source memory, in which subjects recalled the identity of speakers presenting facts in a video, no differences in source memory were observed as a function of culture, but large age differences were reported (Chua, Chen, & Park, in press). Likewise, elderly adults of both cultures recalled similar numbers of words in a free-recall task and recalled significantly fewer words than young people of both cultures did, even though

American elderly evidenced greater use of a categorical clustering strategy (Gutchess, Yoon et al., in press).

The relatively modest impact of culture and the strong effects of age on cognitive mechanics suggest that biological aging primarily drives age-related differences in resource-demanding, strategic functions. In contrast to these findings, the impact of culture, relative to age, on knowledge-based structures shows almost a complete reversal, with culture assuming a much larger role than age. In a recent study, Yoon et al. (2004) provided young and old Chinese and young and old Americans with the names of 105 categories. Subjects provided five exemplars for each category, providing a careful mapping of category structure as a function of age and culture. The results indicated that there were only 13 categories that were culturally equivalent across both age groups. Category exemplars were far more similar across age groups within a culture. Thus, in the development of knowledge structures, culture is much more important than age, suggesting that discriminating between types of cognitive processes is critical to understanding the impact of culture on cognitive aging. (Complete norms for categories, as well as for picture naming, which have been used in other studies, are available online at http:// agingmind.cns.uiuc.edu/ourresearch_cfdb.html.)

PATTERNS OF NEUROCOGNITIVE AGING

Neuroimaging techniques have added to our understanding of the aging mind. Consistent with behavioral data showing decreases in cognitive function (see Fig. 1), structural brain imaging reveals that the frontal cortex and, to a lesser extent, the medial temporal cortex exhibit significant loss of volume with age. In the face of declines in many cognitive systems, one might expect that neural activation would systematically decrease, paralleling the behavioral changes. Functional neuroimaging, however, has revealed that the aging brain is a dynamic system and that when young and old adults perform the same task, (a) neural activation is distributed across more brain sites and structures in old adults compared to young adults, (b) older adults frequently engage the same region in two hemispheres for tasks in which younger adults activate only one hemisphere, and (c) sometimes older adults show greater activation than young adults in the identical neural regions (Reuter-Lorenz & Lustig, 2005). Advances in neuroimaging have been largely responsible for views suggesting that the aging brain has residual plasticity, or cognitive reserve that can be utilized to reorganize neural circuitry to respond to the challenge of neurobiological aging.

Coincident with evidence that the brain responds to the challenge of neurobiological aging by reorganizing are neuro-imaging findings suggesting that neural structures may develop or change in response to sustained exposure to stimuli or repetitive events. For example, merely 3 months of juggling training increased grey matter, relative to the brains of nonjugglers (Draganski et al., 2004)—increases that were maintained 3 months later without additional juggling practice.

DEVELOPING A COGNITIVE NEUROSCIENCE OF CULTURE AND AGING

Evidence that experience affects neural functions and structures leads logically to the notion that differences in cultural values and customs could affect development of neural activation patterns, as well as create differences in the size of various neural structures (Park & Gutchess, 2002). In the first exploration of cultural differences in neural function, we hypothesized that East Asians and Westerners would differentially engage neural hardware in the ventral visual cortex that is specialized for processing different elements of a scene. Using functional magnetic resonance imaging (fMRI), we found that Americans showed more engagement of object-processing areas in the ventral visual cortex than did Chinese (Gutchess, Welsh, Boduroglu, & Park, in press). This pattern is consistent with behavioral evidence that Westerners show a bias to process object information whereas East Asians preferentially process background information (Nisbett & Masuda, 2003). In a later fMRI study, we presented young and old Singaporeans of Chinese descent with complex pictorial scenes and examined how specialized areas within the ventral visual cortex adapted to repetition of different elements of the scene. We found that the old Singaporean adults showed less activation than young adults did in object-processing areas (the lateral occipital complex), but old and young adults engaged background processing structures (the parahippocampus) equally (Chee et al., 2006). We then tested a matching group of young and old Americans to determine whether, as our cultural theories would predict, old Singaporeans showed less activation of object-processing structures than old Americans did. Preliminary results suggest that young Singaporeans and Americans showed relatively similar engagement of all of these specialized structures, but old Singaporeans showed a larger object-processing deficit than old Americans did, suggesting that cultural differences in neural response magnified over the lifespan. These data, combined with behavioral data revealing that East Asians show more eye fixations on backgrounds than on objects (Chua, Boland, & Nisbett, 2005), suggest that after a lifetime of culturally biased information processing the neural circuitry for looking at scenes may be sculpted in a culturally biased way.

We should note that cross-cultural neuroimaging research has many unique challenges. We are sensitive to the possibility that we could find cultural differences in neural activation due to data collection from different magnets (one in the United States and one in Singapore). To address this concern, we have conducted exhaustive studies of differences in signals between magnets by scanning the same individuals on the same task in both Singapore and the United States, and we have found compelling preliminary evidence for replicability across magnets. On a number of important dimensions, the difference in neural signal from an individual tested on identical model magnets at both sites is no greater than the difference in the signal from an individual tested twice using the same magnet. This finding provides clear evidence that we may appropriately attribute signal differences to actual differences in subjects tested rather than to hardware.

We also recognize that culture is more remote from the individual than most other variables psychologists study. This distal nature of culture, combined with possible genetic differences between samples, as well as differences in education, diet, and other variables, can make it difficult to definitively argue that differences observed in neural activation are due to cultural beliefs and practices. These problems can be minimized when cultural brain research is guided by specific behavioral hypotheses (e.g., that East Asians show less activation of object areas), so that the research is confirmatory rather than exploratory. We have also found that working in an area of the brain (the ventral visual cortex) in which highly specific functions have been isolated in young Western adults has enhanced the precision of cultural hypotheses and interpretation of findings. Cross-cultural research focused on activations in the frontal cortex will prove to be more challenging, as this is a highly flexible and strategic area of the brain, with more variability between subjects in activation patterns.

Despite these concerns, the cultural neuroscience of aging has great potential for separating the relative contributions of experience and biology to the process of aging. Cultural neuroscience work may hold the key to the "use it or lose it" hypothesis of cognitive aging—that is, that neurocognitive health is maintained by sustained intellectual engagement across the lifespan. If we can find some structures that are systematically engaged more by Asians compared to Westerners, we might expect that these structures will maintain volume and function across the lifespan better in the culture that uses them more. Similarly, if certain patterns of neural recruitment (such as bilateral engagement of the frontal cortex) are shown to be universal with age across cultures, we can be relatively certain that such recruitment patterns are a result of biological aging rather than experience.

SUMMARY

Through both behavioral and neuroimaging cross-cultural studies, we can learn much about the interplay between biology and environment as it affects cognitive aging. Our knowledge about cognitive aging (and even about cognition in general) is almost entirely limited to Western samples. At present, our research suggests that many cognitive processes decline similarly across cultures, revealing the universality of cognitive aging. At the same time, however, it appears that culture modulates neurocognitive aging, as demonstrated by the differences in activation of object-processing areas in old adults from Asian versus Western cultures. The study of culture, cognition, and aging can answer questions, not only about modifiability of neurocognitive processes across the lifespan but also about the nature of social-cognitive function in late adulthood. For example, representations of self differ across cultures (Markus & Kitayama, 1991), and fMRI allows us to examine the neural circuitry underlying such differences and how it evolves with age. Our understanding of stability and flexibility regarding self in late adulthood could also be greatly expanded by examining the neurocognitive processes that occur in old and young bicultural individuals when they switch from one cultural frame to another. Another critically important question is whether culturally determined neural differences observed in aging brains become hardwired (e.g., structural changes occur and circuitry is automatically engaged) or merely reflect neural circuitry associated with strategy differences that can readily be controlled by individuals with appropriate instructions. Most important, the emergence of a cultural psychology of aging will inform us about the plasticity of the neurocognitive system, as well as about biological imperatives associated with cognitive aging that are unchanged by any cultural context.

Recommended Reading

Li, S.-C. (2003). Biocultural orchestration of developmental plasticity across levels: The interplay of biology and culture in shaping the mind and behavior across the life span. *Psychological Bulletin, 129,* 171–194.

Nisbett, R.E. (2003). *The geography of thought: How Asians and Westerners think differently . . . and why.* New York: The Free Press.

Nisbett, R.E., Peng, K., Choi, I. & Norenzayan, A. (2001). Culture and systems of thought: Holistic versus analytic cognition. *Psychological Review, 108,* 291–310.

Park, D.C., Nisbett, R., & Hedden, T. (1999). (See References)

Acknowledgments—Funding from the National Institute on Aging (Grant R01 AG015047) supported preparation of this article.

Note

1. Address correspondence to Denise Park, 405 N. Mathews, The Beckman Institute, The University of Illinois at Urbana-Champaign, Urbana, IL 61801; e-mail: denisep@uiuc.edu.

References

Baltes, P.B. (1987). Theoretical propositions of life-span developmental psychology: On the dynamics between growth and decline. *Developmental Psychology, 23,* 611–626.

Chee, M.W.L., Goh, J.O.S., Venkatraman, V., Tan, J.C., Gutchess, A., Sutton, B., Hebrank, A., Leshikar, E., & Park, D. (2006). Agerelated changes in object processing and contextual binding revealed using fMR adaptation. *Journal of Cognitive Neuroscience, 18,* 495–507.

Chua, H.F., Boland, J.E., & Nisbett, R.E. (2005). Cultural variation in eye movements during scene perception. *Proceedings of the National Academy of Sciences, USA, 102,* 12629–12633.

Chua, H.F., Chen, W., & Park, D.C. (in press). Source memory, aging, and culture. *Gerontology.*

Draganski, B., Gaser, C., Busch, V., Schuierer, G., Bogdahn, U., & May, A. (2004). Changes in grey matter induced by training. *Nature, 427,* 311–312.

Gutchess, A.H., Welsh, R.C., Boduroglu, A., & Park, D.C. (in press). Cultural differences in neural function associated with object processing. *Cognitive, Affective, and Behavioral Neuroscience.*

Gutchess, A.H., Yoon, C., Luo, T., Feinberg, F., Hedden, T., Jing, Q., Nisbett, R.E., & Park, D.C. (in press). Categorical organization in free recall across culture and age. *Gerontology.*

Hedden, T., Park, D.C., Nisbett, R., Ji, L.-J., Jing, Q., & Jiao, S. (2002). Cultural variation in verbal versus spatial neuro-psychological function across the life span. *Neuropsychology, 16,* 65–73.

Markus, H.R., & Kitayama, S. (1991). Culture and the self: Implications for cognition, emotion, & motivation. *Psychological Review, 98,* 224–253.

Nisbett, R.E., & Masuda, T. (2003). Culture and point of view. *Proceedings of the National Academy of Sciences, USA, 100,* 11163–11170.

Park, D.C., & Gutchess, A.H. (2002). Aging, cognition, and culture: A neuroscientific perspective. *Neuroscience and Biobehavioral Reviews, 26,* 859–867.

Park, D.C., Lautenschlager, G., Hedden, T., Davidson, N.S., Smith, A.D., & Smith, P.K. (2002). Models of visuospatial and verbal memory across the adult life span. *Psychology & Aging, 17,* 299–320.

Park, D.C., Nisbett, R., & Hedden, T. (1999). Aging, culture, and cognition. *Journals of Gerontology Series B: Psychological Sciences and Social Sciences, 54,* P75–P84.

Reuter-Lorenz, P.A., & Lustig, C. (2005). Brain aging: Reorganizing discoveries about the aging mind. *Current Opinion in Neurobiology, 15,* 245–251.

Yoon, C., Feinberg, F., Hu, P., Gutchess, A.H., Hedden, T., Chen, H., Jing, Q., Cui, Y., & Park, D.C. (2004). Category norms as a function of culture and age: Comparisons of item responses to 105 categories by American and Chinese adults. *Psychology and Aging, 19,* 379–393.

Critical Thinking Questions

1. Discuss how pragmatics and mechanics change with age, and how these changes may influence cognitive functioning.

2. When comparing younger and older Chinese adults to younger and older American adults, what tasks show greater differences across culture than across age groups?

3. What does the area of cultural psychology and aging tell us regarding the role of environmental influences on neuroplasticity? Provide an example.

Section 3: Emotion and Cognition

The previous section discussed how physical and situational contexts shape cognitive processes. In the next series of articles, the topic turns to how changes in cognitive processing are related to changes in emotional experience and the processing of emotional information. In the first article, Fredda Blanchard-Fields discusses how age differences in problem solving vary according to the type of problem involved in her article, "Everyday problem solving and emotion." She reviews research showing that despite the reliable cognitive declines in aging, older adults are quite adept at solving problems of daily life, and particularly problems high in emotional salience. She illustrates situations where older adults are arguably more flexible in their decision-making than are younger adults. Next, Laura Carstensen and Joseph Mikels propose that older age is related to increases in emotional goals in their article, "At the intersection of cognition and emotion: The positivity effect." They use the theory of socioemotional selectivity to explain why emotions increase in importance with age, and they present a series of findings documenting a bias for older adults to remember more positive emotional information than negative emotional information compared to younger adults.

The next article offers a different theory to explain the interplay between cognitions and emotions. Gisela Labouvie-Vief presents her theory of dynamic integration in her work titled, "Dynamic integration: affect, cognition, and the self in adulthood." According to this theory, age-related changes fall under two processes: affect optimization and affect complexity. Optimization refers to maximizing the hedonic levels emotional experience, which is often captured by well-being measures. Affect complexity, which is characterized by complex representations of the environment, refers to how people process emotional information. Older age is related to greater affect optimization, but affect complexity exhibits a curvilinear pattern, highest in middle-age and lower earlier and later in life.

The last article in this section focus on attention and old age. The role of motivation in emotional processing is underscored in "Motivated gaze: The view from the gazer" by Derek Isaacowitz. He reviews research showing that people direct their attention towards information that is most relevant or important to them. Examining age differences in attention to emotional stimuli, then, provides insight into age differences in goals and desires. He further describes how the visual gaze of older adults reveals that they focus their attention on information that optimizes their well-being.

Everyday Problem Solving and Emotion: An Adult Developmental Perspective

Fredda Blanchard-Fields[1]

Georgia Institute of Technology

Abstract

Despite cognitive declines that occur with aging, older adults solve emotionally salient and interpersonal problems in more effective ways than young adults do. I review evidence suggesting that older adults (a) tailor their strategies to the contextual features of the problem and (b) effectively use a combination of instrumental and emotion-regulation strategies. I identify factors of problem-solving contexts that affect what types of problem-solving strategies will be effective. Finally, I discuss how this identification of factors affects what we know about developmental differences in everyday problem-solving competence.

Keywords

emotion regulation; everyday problem solving; emotions; life-span development; aging

Consider this example of an everyday problem situation. An older woman's daughter-in-law just gave birth to her fifth grandchild. However, the woman's daughter-in-law and son were quite insulting in instructing her on how to hold the baby. In order not to escalate the conflict, the older woman gently gave the baby back to the mother and left the hospital room to vent her emotions alone. She did not want to cause a fight with her family at such a vulnerable time. Regulating her emotional reaction to the situation made it easier for her to revisit the issue with her family later, undistracted by the emotional upheaval of the earlier moment. The older woman's primary use of emotion regulation was effective (and perhaps wise) given the context and her goal to avoid a fight. However, in another context, if this same older woman were administered a cognitive assessment battery, the extant cognitive aging research suggests that she would likely show cognitive decline on a number of tasks that assess working memory, attention, and executive abilities.

This contrast between loss in cognitive abilities in one context and gains in effective problem solving in another has become increasingly evident as more research on cognitive functioning in older adulthood is examined in a pragmatic and socioemotional context. For example, researchers find that, despite cognitive decline, emotional processing, social behavior, and emotion regulation remain intact and may even improve across adulthood (Blanchard-Fields, Jahnke, & Camp, 1995; Carstensen & Mikels, 2005). Furthermore, current neuropsychological models of aging show that cognitive decline in executive functioning is related to deterioration in specific brain regions such as the dorsolateral prefrontal area, whereas emotional processing and social behavior remain relatively intact and are related to the ventromedial prefrontal area (MacPherson, Phillips, & Della Sala, 2002).

These findings highlight the fundamental difference between age-related change in structures and mechanisms of cognition and the functional dynamics of everyday cognitive behavior. Functional dynamics include the skills and knowledge necessary to effectively adapt to the demands and opportunities presented in daily life. It is this latter approach that characterizes my current research on emotion and everyday problem solving from an adult developmental perspective. Two important questions follow from this approach. What are the skills, knowledge, and expertise that allow older adults to effectively solve everyday problems and regulate their emotions? What individual-difference factors are related to this form of everyday cognition?

ASSESSING EVERYDAY PROBLEM SOLVING

One approach to everyday problem solving is grounded in the psychometric intelligence tradition and focuses on well-structured problems with one single correct solution, such as calculating the correct medicine dosage or using tax forms correctly. This approach requires that older adults rely solely on basic cognitive abilities that decline with age in order to answer problems correctly. Older adults fare poorly on these tasks.

However, such an approach overlooks strategies used to solve ill-structured problem situations. My research takes a different approach that highlights the socioemotional nature of ill-structured problems, which are unpredictable and continually transforming. Such problems require individuals to appraise the causes and demands of the situation and to decide among many potentially effective solutions based on the particular trade-offs the person is willing to make. In such cases, older adults can draw on accumulated experience in socioemotional realms to solve problems effectively. In some situations, this may involve an immediate proactive plan of action, whereas in other situations it may involve first regaining emotional composure and then taking proactive action. Finally, effective problem solving needs to consider how the individual interprets the problem as reflected in an adaptive match between individual goals and strategy use. I shall now examine evidence for these forms of effective problem solving in older adulthood.

AGE DIFFERENCES AND EFFECTIVENESS IN EVERYDAY PROBLEM-SOLVING STRATEGIES

In a first set of studies, we presented hypothetical problem scenarios to participants ranging in age from 14 to 75 years. Some problems were emotionally laden or interpersonal (e.g., the decision to place your mother in a nursing home), whereas others were less emotionally charged and more instrumental (e.g., returning defective merchandise). One study asked participants how they would solve the problems (Blanchard-Fields et al., 1995). Other studies asked participants to rate the degree to which they would employ particular strategies (Blanchard-Fields, Chen, & Norris, 1997; Blanchard-Fields, Mienaltowski, & Baldi, in press). We examined two general categories of strategies: instrumental strategies (e.g., direct action taken to solve the problem) and passive emotion-regulation strategies (e.g., suppressing feelings, not trying to alter an uncontrollable situation).

In instrumental domains, most individuals across age groups tended to use action-oriented more than passive strategies. Furthermore, in some situations (e.g., consumer matters involving shopping strategies), older adults used more instrumental, less passive, and arguably more effective strategies than did young adults (Blanchard-Fields et al., 1997; in press). A different picture emerged when examining socioemotional problem situations. First, it is important to note that there were no age differences in the preference for direct action-oriented strategies. More importantly, older adults endorsed more passive emotion-regulation strategies than younger age groups in this domain did (see Fig. 1). However, it is not the case that older adults simply relied more on the regulation of their psychological state (e.g., withdrawal from an interpersonal conflict) in this context. They also engaged in a combined use of multiple strategies, including more action-oriented strategies (Watson & Blanchard-Fields, 1998). Thus, older adults' preference for more passive emotion-regulation strategies may not be a function of decline in adaptive functioning; instead it may be contingent on whether the emotional demands of the problem situation are high (i.e., tailoring strategies to the situation). Moreover, it is not the case that older adults do not have the energy to actively solve problems or that they are highly emotional. Instead, they may effectively recognize that not all problems can be fixed immediately or can be solved without considering the regulation of emotions.

To more directly examine the degree to which instrumental and passive emotion-regulation strategies are used adaptively, we assessed effectiveness of strategy choice. Effectiveness ratings for each strategy associated with each problem came from a panel of external judges (Cornelius & Caspi, 1987).[2] The match between judges' effectiveness ratings and participants' responses indicated that older adults were more effective than were young adults in their overall choice of strategies; and in particular, young adults were less effective than were older adults in their

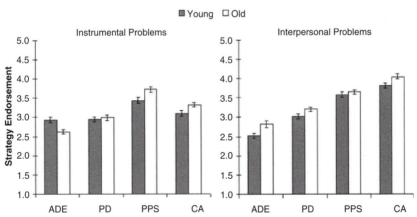

Fig. 1. Age-related differences in mean problem-solving-strategy endorsement for instrumental and interpersonal problems. The sample included young (n = 53; ages 18–27) and older adults (n = 53; ages 60–80). Passive strategies included avoidance-denial (ADE) and passive dependence (PD); instrumental strategies included planful problem solving (PPS) and cognitive analysis (CA).

strategy preferences for interpersonal problems (Blanchard-Fields et al., in press). Thus, we not only documented the degree to which older adults used more or less of a particular strategy that matched the problem context; we found that when they used strategies, they used them effectively (see Fig. 2).

However, external ratings by judges do not take into account how the individual interprets what is important about the problem context. Problems involve differential goals (e.g., to display one's competency vs. concern for others), which may guide selection of problem-solving strategies. In a recent study (Hoppmann, Heckman, & Blanchard-Fields, 2006) we examined effectiveness in terms of goal–strategy match. An effective strategy match for a generative goal (concern for the well-being of another) involves strategies directed toward the needs of the other person. Autonomy goals (concern for independence) should be linked to self-focused problem-solving strategies. Using an interview method, we asked 15- to 84-year-olds to generate a past problem and indicate how they solved the problem and to identify their goals associated with the problem. Age differences in goal–strategy match revealed that young adults exhibited more matches between autonomy goals and self-focused problem solving. Developmentally, autonomy goals fostering individuality and independent striving are more relevant in youth. Older adults showed a higher degree of goal–strategy match between generative goals and other-focused problem solving (e.g., strategies directed at maintaining relationships). Given that older adulthood is characterized by a greater concern for social connectedness and goals to achieve it, older adults appear to be employing effective strategies to achieve this goal. Young and older adults differentially approach problems because they focus on different goals related to their stage in life. Parenthetically, the goal–strategy match emphasized in older adulthood (involving social connectedness) suggests that older adults may be better at solving social problems.

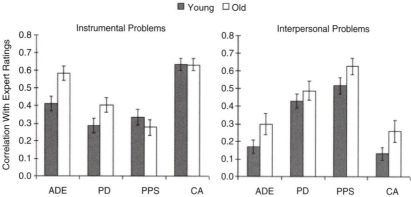

Fig. 2. Age-related differences in mean problem-solving effectiveness for instrumental and interpersonal problems. The sample included young ($n = 53$; ages 18–27) and older adults ($n = 53$; ages 60–80). Passive problem-solving strategies included avoidance-denial (ADE) and passive dependence (PD); instrumental strategies included planful problem solving (PPS) and cognitive analysis (CA).

Taken together, older adults' apparent use of a more diverse repertoire of problem-solving strategies and their effectiveness in using such strategies (effectiveness ratings and goal–strategy match) can lead to a more flexible application of problem-solving strategies to varying contexts. This is especially evident in their combined use of emotion-regulation strategies along with instrumental strategies in such contexts. In other words, older adults demonstrated an awareness of when to "do" (be instrumental), when to "let it be" (passively accept a situation), and when to use a combination of the two approaches. This supports past research indicating that older adults report that they are better at emotion regulation (Lawton, 2001); place more emphasis on emotional aspects of their environment (Carstensen & Mikels, 2005); and use more passive emotion-regulation coping when a stressful event is appraised as uncontrollable, in comparison with young adults (Blanchard-Fields & Irion, 1988). Our studies further suggest that this becomes evident in older adults' approach to socioemotional problem situations.

EMOTION REGULATION

Given the importance of emotions in older adults' lives, the next step was to focus more exclusively on the adaptive significance of older adults' ability to regulate emotions in a problem context. The focus of past research has been on passive emotion-regulation strategies. Interestingly, the stress-and-coping literature views passive emotion regulation as less effective than more instrumental or proactive strategies, suggesting that older adults may rely to a greater extent on less-adaptive strategies. However, the use of passive emotion-regulation strategies needs to be placed in a life-span developmental context. Passive emotion-regulation strategies may play a beneficial role for adaptive functioning, particularly in older adulthood. For example, passive strategies such as suppressing or avoiding negative emotions may help maintain tolerable levels of arousal given increased vulnerability and reduced energy reserves in older adulthood (Consedine, Magai, & Bonanno, 2002; Leventhal, Patrick-Miller, Leventhal, & Burns, 1998).

This becomes even more evident when specific emotions are considered. In a recent set of studies, we examined age differences in how individuals regulate emotions in problem situations. Using an interview procedure, participants ranging in age from 14 to 84 years generated interpersonal problems they had experienced in the previous year and described how they had handled specific emotions they had experienced throughout the problem situations. We expanded our previous coding scheme to include both passive (e.g., denial, withdrawal, suppression) and proactive (e.g., seeking out emotional support, directly confronting emotions) emotion-regulation strategies. We were now able to determine the degree to which older adults used both passive and proactive emotion-regulation strategies.

As expected from previous work, older adults tended to use more passive emotion-regulation strategies in comparison to younger age groups when handling emotions evoked from interpersonal problems (Blanchard-Fields, Stein, & Watson, 2004). Even more interesting, this age difference was qualified when we examined the regulation of anger and sadness separately (Blanchard-Fields & Heckman, 2006). Anger and sadness pose different regulatory challenges. Sadness may be more tolerable, requiring less allocation of resources to proactively regulate it (Consedine et al., 2002). Anger is higher in intensity and requires greater allocation of resources toward proactive strategies to reduce arousal.

Accordingly, we found that older adults were less likely to report feeling angry than were young adults, and this statistically accounted for the age differences in the use of proactive strategy use (i.e., older adults reported less proactive strategy use than young age groups did). Thus, a viable possibility why older adults use fewer proactive emotion-regulation strategies could be their decreased experience of anger. Problems reported by older adults in past research were most likely disproportionately low in evoking anger. Given that anger poses more of a physical challenge to older adults, it may be optimal for such individuals to allocate more effort to preventing the experience of that emotion (e.g., withdrawing from the situation to prevent its escalation). Thus, in reporting emotions experienced in problem situations, older adults report other, less-taxing emotions such as sadness.

However, we found that when older adults did feel angry they used proactive strategies. In contrast, when experiencing sadness they primarily used passive emotion-regulation strategies. When discrete emotions are taken into consideration, older adults appear to be differentiated in their use of emotion-regulation strategies and do not exclusively rely on passive strategies (i.e., using proactive strategies to handle anger). Therefore, it appears that with the development of emotion-regulation skills, older adults may consider a broader range of strategies. Emotion researchers such as Klaus Scherer (1986) have put forth the idea that differential emotional experience results from individuals continually performing evaluation checks on the environment using functionally defined criteria. Lawton (2001) extends this idea into a developmental context by observing that "Emotion may act as an intrusive element in social decisions among developmentally immature people, but as a source of differentiation among social situations for mature people" (p. 122).

Thus, in answer to the first question posed, the skills and knowledge older adults possess that allow them to effectively solve everyday problems appear to be related to their dynamic use of strategies that correspond to the nature of the problem situation encountered (e.g., interpersonal/emotionally charged vs. instrumental) and the specific discrete emotions they are managing in these situations.

PREDICTORS OF EMOTION-REGULATION STRATEGIES

With respect to the second question, cognitive abilities were not related to strategy use in socio-emotional problem solving. The question remains, what factors predict emotion-regulation strategy use? We are beginning to address this issue. Our research suggests that affect complexity and emotional expressivity may be promising candidates. Affectively complex individuals are those who are able to integrate emotional and cognitive aspects of themselves and their environment (Labouvie-Vief, 1998). At high levels of affect complexity, emotion is seen as jointly reflecting internal states and external contexts. We were interested in individual differences within older adults in their use of passive emotion-regulation strategies as indexed by affect complexity and emotional expressiveness. In a recent study we presented adults ranging in age from 18 to 80 years with hypothetical problem situations that evoked either anger or sadness (Heckman & Blanchard-Fields, 2006). Participants were then presented with a list of passive and proactive emotion-regulation strategies as well as instrumental problem-solving strategies and were asked which strategies they would use to manage anger and sadness. We also administered assessments of affect complexity and emotion expressivity.

We found that there were individual differences in older adults' use of passive strategies. Those older adults who were lower in affect complexity (i.e., who were less able to think in complex ways about the role emotions play in the context of everyday situations) were the ones who were more likely to use passive emotion-regulation strategies. Again, taking into consideration this finding and those reviewed above, it is not simply that older adults uniformly prefer passive strategies. Instead this preference is multiply determined by level of affect complexity and context–strategy match, among other variables. Future research needs to determine the extent to which these and other factors interact and contribute to the use of passive strategies. For example, it may be that older adults with lower levels of affect complexity prefer passive strategies across situations, whereas older adults with high levels of affect complexity prefer passive strategies only when the context demands it. Finally, we found that individuals who were more expressive when experiencing sadness were also more likely to rely on direct, action-related strategies than were individuals who were less expressive.

CONCLUSIONS AND FUTURE DIRECTIONS

In conclusion, the above research suggests that older adults effectively solve everyday problems because of their ability to balance emotion regulation with proactive instrumental strategies. Due to an accumulation of experience, older adults are more likely than young people to deal with the hassles of life with a wider array of problem-solving techniques and, even more importantly, to use these strategies more effectively. Furthermore, older adults are more likely than young adults to combine (a) actions directly targeted to the source of their problems with (b) emotion-regulation strategies that buffer psychological stress. This suggests that when solving everyday problems older adults display more complex, flexible, and emotionally mature functioning than otherwise expected. These findings stand in stark contrast to stereotypes of "rigidity" in older adulthood, as well as to traditional evidence of declines in reasoning that are often associated with advancing age. Of course this applies to normal-functioning older adults and not to individuals with creeping dementia, who do seem to become more rigid and less adaptive with increasing age. In other words, although normal advancing age may be associated with cognitive decline, such declines do not readily translate into impaired everyday problem-solving effectiveness. Furthermore, we have a better understanding of when it is advantageous for older adults to regulate their emotions as well as balance emotional and instrumental aspects of the problem situation. This could guide researchers in developing intervention programs that take into consideration the role emotion plays in effective strategy use—for example, when elderly people need to make important medical and health decisions.

These conclusions raise some interesting questions for future research. Of particular importance to our understanding of health and quality-of-life issues in the elderly is that the criteria for effective everyday problem solving needs to be extended to both psychological and bodily well-being. Most studies on emotion regulation are based on self-report data and not on observed performance. Thus, there is a clear need for well-controlled studies of emotion regulation examining naturally occurring emotional and physiological states that occur in association with on-line problem solving and emotion-regulation strategy use. In this way we can observe problem solving as it occurs over time. For example, anticipating heightened emotions before they arise could promote subsequent effective problem solving as time progresses. In this case, it may be quite effective to recognize the limitations of immediate proactive action and manage strong emotional reactions before acting. This approach could build on our finding that older adults use multiple strategies by examining the sequential ordering of strategy use.

Another important question involves the costs and benefits of older adults' emphasis on emotion regulation when handling everyday problems. What are the costs for older adults who selectively allocate resources toward regulating emotions and consequently reduce cognitive resources available to process other information? What are the other benefits of strategies used to regulate on-line emotional experiences, above and beyond improved emotion-regulation outcomes (e.g., an increase in positive feelings)? Finally, future research needs to substantiate our findings in an experimental context. For example, one could manipulate problem problem-solving goals under controlled laboratory conditions. This would reveal if participants adjust their strategies in accordance with their goals. Furthermore, investigating problems in people's ongoing daily life would help determine whether those whose problem-solving strategies match their goals are more effective in down-regulating negative affect and increasing their well-being.

Recommended Reading

Blanchard-Fields, F. (1998). The role of emotion in social cognition across the adult life span. In K.W. Schaie & M.P. Lawton (Eds.), *Annual review of gerontology and geriatrics* (Vol. 17, pp. 206–237). New York: Springer.
Blanchard-Fields, F., Stein, R., & Watson, T. (2004). (See References)
Watson, T.L., & Blanchard-Fields, F. (1998). (See References)

Acknowledgments—The preparation of this review was supported by National Institute on Aging research grant AG-11715 to Fredda Blanchard-Fields. I would like to thank Cynthia Adams, Randy Engle, Abby Heckman, Christiane Hoppmann, Michelle Horhota, Andrew Mienaltowski, and Antje Stange for their invaluable comments on this manuscript.

Notes

1. Address correspondence to Fredda Blanchard-Fields, School of Psychology, Georgia Institute of Technology, 654 Cherry St., Atlanta, GA 30332-0170; e-mail: fb12@prism.gatech.edu.

2. Cornelius and Caspi (1987) recruited 23 judges to determine which of four strategies could be used to effectively solve a series of everyday problems. Of these 23 people, 18 were "laypersons without formal training in psychology," and five were "graduate students majoring in developmental psychology" (p. 146). Overall, the panel consisted of young ($n = 9$, ages 24–40, $M = 28.4$), middle-aged ($n = 8$, ages 44–54, $M = 50.3$), and older adults ($n = 6$, ages 62–72, $M = 67.3$). Ten members of the panel were men and 13

were women. Participants' responses were correlated with the judges' ratings to determine degree of effectiveness.

References

Blanchard-Fields, F., Chen, Y., & Norris, L. (1997). Everyday problem solving across the adult life span: Influence of domain specificity and cognitive appraisal. *Psychology and Aging, 12*, 684–693.

Blanchard-Fields, F., & Heckman, A. (2006). *Emotions in everyday problems: Age differences in elicitation and regulation.* Manuscript submitted for publication.

Blanchard–Fields, F., & Irion, J. (1988). The relation between locus of control and coping in two contexts: Age as a moderator variable. *Psychology and Aging, 3*, 197–203.

Blanchard-Fields, F., Jahnke, H.C., & Camp, C. (1995). Age differences in problem solving style: The role of emotional salience. *Psychology and Aging, 10*, 173–180.

Blanchard-Fields, F., Mienaltowski, A., & Baldi, R. (in press). Problem solving effectiveness in older adulthood. *Journals of Gerontology, Series B: Psychological Sciences.*

Blanchard-Fields, F., Stein, R., & Watson, T.L. (2004). Age differences in emotion-regulation strategies in handling everyday problems. *Journals of Gerontology, Series B: Psychological Sciences, 59B*, P261–P269.

Carstensen, L.L., & Mikels, J.A. (2005). At the intersection of emotion and cognition: Aging and the positivity effect. *Current Directions in Psychological Science, 14*, 117–121.

Consedine, N., Magai, C., & Bonanno, G. (2002). Moderators of the emotion inhibition-health relationship: A review and research agenda. *Review of General Psychology, 2*, 204–228.

Cornelius, S., & Caspi, A. (1987). Everyday problem solving in adulthood and old age. *Psychology and Aging, 2*, 144–153.

Heckman, A., & Blanchard-Fields, F. (2006). *Emotion regulation in interpersonal problem situations: The role of affect complexity and expressivity.* Manuscript submitted for publication.

Hoppmann, C., Heckman, A., & Blanchard-Fields, F. (2006). *The role of personal goals on age differences in problem solving effectiveness.* Manuscript submitted for publication.

Labouvie-Vief, G. (1998). Cognitive-emotional integration in adulthood. In K.W. Schaie & M.P. Lawton (Eds.), *Annual review of gerontology and geriatrics* (Vol. 17, pp. 206–237). New York: Springer.

Lawton, M.P. (2001). Emotion in later life. *Current Directions in Psychological Science, 10*, 120–123.

Leventhal, H., Patrick-Miller, L., Leventhal, E.A., & Burns, E.A. (1998). Does stress-emotion cause illness in elderly people? *Annual Review of Gerontology and Geriatrics, 17*, 138–184.

MacPherson, S.E., Phillips, L.H., & Della Sala, S. (2002). Age, executive function, and social decision making: A dorsolateral prefrontal theory of cognitive aging. *Psychology and Aging, 17*, 598–609.

Scherer, K.R. (1986). Vocal affect expression: A review and a model for future research. *Psychological Bulletin, 99*, 145–165.

Watson, T.L., & Blanchard-Fields, F. (1998). Thinking with your head and your heart: Age differences in everyday problem-solving strategy preferences. *Aging, Neuropsychology, and Cognition, 5*, 225–240.

Critical Thinking Questions

1. How does the pattern of age differences vary for the type of everyday problems assessed?

2. Under what conditions might passive problem-solving strategies be useful?

3. How do goals determine the type of problem-solving strategy used? How do goals vary between older and younger adults?

This article has been reprinted as it originally appeared in *Current Directions in Psychological Science*. Citation information for this article as originally published appears above.

At the Intersection of Emotion and Cognition: Aging and the Positivity Effect

Laura L. Carstensen[1] and Joseph A. Mikels
Stanford University

Abstract

Divergent trajectories characterize the aging mind: Processing capacity declines, while judgment, knowledge, and emotion regulation are relatively spared. We maintain that these different developmental trajectories have implications for emotion–cognition interactions. Following an overview of our theoretical position, we review empirical studies indicating that (a) older adults evidence superior cognitive performance for emotional relative to non-emotional information, (b) age differences are most evident when the emotional content is positively as opposed to negatively valenced, and (c) differences can be accounted for by changes in motivation posited in socioemotional selectivity theory.

Keywords

aging; emotion; cognition; memory; attention

One of the most interesting discoveries in basic social science in recent years is that human aging, long thought to be characterized by intractable and steady decline, is a more complex and more malleable process than was initially presumed. Arguably even more interesting than the weaknesses are the relative strengths that older people display, making clear the potential resource that the growing older population offers. Findings provide remarkably convergent evidence that self-regulation, especially of emotional functioning, is spared from age-related decline, if not enhanced with age (Charles & Carstensen, 2004).

This pattern stands in contrast to the one characterizing many aspects of cognitive aging. A substantial body of literature documents age-related declines in abilities and processes that are effortful, deliberative, and resource-intensive. Processing speed declines with age, as do working memory (the short-term maintenance and manipulation of information), free and cued recall from long-term memory, source memory (memory for the source or context of information rather than the information itself), selective attention, effortful divided attention, mental imagery, as well as reasoning and problem solving. The fact that gains in emotional functioning occur against a backdrop of well-documented declines in effortful cognitive processing raises intriguing questions about potential developmental changes in domains that draw heavily on both emotional and cognitive processes. In fact, these opposing trajectories map perfectly onto the two core sets of strategies centrally involved in decision and judgment: intuition, which involves relatively fast automatic processing that often draws on emotion; and deliberative reasoning, which is relatively slow, controlled, and effortful (Kahneman, 2003). Given the critical role that these strategies play in daily life, age-related changes in basic cognitive and emotional functions may have important consequences in the lives of older adults. Yet, with few exceptions, researchers of aging have studied either emotional or cognitive processing and not both. To the extent that functioning is maintained in one domain and degraded in another, abilities preserved in one area could be recruited to bolster other, weakened areas. Thus, although emotion–cognition interaction issues are important for all of psychology, they are especially important for the study of aging.

The work we describe below is grounded in socioemotional selectivity theory, a life-span theory of how time horizons shape human motivation (Carstensen, Isaacowitz, & Charles, 1999). We first describe the theory and then return to issues concerning the intersection of emotion and cognition.

SOCIOEMOTIONAL SELECTIVITY THEORY

According to socioemotional selectivity theory, goals are always set in temporal contexts. When people perceive time as expansive, as they typically do in youth, they tend to focus on preparing for the future. They value novelty and invest time and energy in acquiring information and expanding their horizons. In contrast, when people perceive boundaries on their time they direct attention to emotionally meaningful aspects of life, such as the desire to lead a meaningful life, to have emotionally intimate social relationships, and to feel socially interconnected.

Because old age heralds a natural ending, socioemotional selectivity theory predicts age-related changes in motivation. Importantly, however, the theory does not hold age itself as causal; similar changes in motivation are observed in younger people suffering from life-threatening illnesses (e.g., Carstensen & Fredrickson, 1998). However, because of the strong association of advanced age and mortality, age differences in motivation emerge.

Socioemotional selectivity theory posits that people place increasing value on emotionally meaningful goals as they get older, and invest more cognitive and social resources in obtaining them. This shift in motivation toward emotional goals promotes emotion regulation (control over the emotions that an individual experiences and expresses). To the extent that people are motivated to prioritize goal-relevant information, attention to and memory for emotional information is expected to vary by age.

MOTIVATION, EMOTION, AND COGNITION

Plasticity in cognitive performance has been well documented. Until recently, however, the degree to which motivation systematically influences cognitive performance in the elderly was not fully appreciated. Recent findings—from a number of research laboratories—demand qualifications about the degree and the specificity of age-related memory decline. Hasher and her colleagues, for example, found that memory performance in older and younger adults was equivalent when testing instructions stressed "learning" instead of "memory," suggesting that the former instruction motivated older adults whereas the latter did not (Rahhal, Hasher, & Colcombe, 2001); and despite considerable evidence for age-related deficits in source memory, older people performed significantly better when questions about the source of the information to be remembered concerned emotionally significant characteristics of people than when questions concerned the gender of the person

(Rahhal, May, & Hasher, 2002). Although alternative explanations for this difference remain—for example, there may be differential atrophy in neural substrates involved in emotional and non-emotional processing—experimental findings suggest that motivation is an important factor.

We postulated that if people increasingly prioritize emotion regulation as they get older, their cognitive processing of emotional material may remain relatively intact compared to their processing of other types of material. There was some indication in the literature that this was so. In studies of memory for real and imagined events, for example, Johnson and colleagues had reported that older people recalled relatively more information about their own thoughts and feelings than about perceptual and contextual details (Hashtroudi, Johnson, & Chrosniak, 1990).

Our research team began to systematically test hypotheses about age differences in memory for and attention to emotional material. Our initial studies drew on the memory and persuasion literatures, which show clearly that people are more likely to remember and be persuaded by messages that are relevant to their goals. Given evidence that goals increasingly favor emotionally relevant matters with age, we reasoned that advertisements promising emotionally meaningful rewards would be more effective with older people than those that promise to increase knowledge or expand horizons (Fung & Carstensen, 2003). Relative to younger people, older people remembered emotional slogans—and the products they touted—better than other types of slogans. For example, in a camera ad, the slogan used to invoke emotionally meaningful goals read, "Capture those special moments"; the version used to invoke information-seeking goals read, "Capture the unexplored world." We also showed participants both the emotion-slanted and information acquisition-slanted versions of the same advertisement and asked them to indicate their preferred version. Some were simply asked to indicate the one they liked best. Others were presented with the following instruction and then asked to indicate their preference: "Imagine that you just got a call from your physician who told you about a new medical advance that virtually insures you will live about 20 years longer than you expected in relatively good health. Please look at these ads and tell us which one you prefer." In the time-expanded condition, age differences were eliminated.

THE POSITIVITY EFFECT

We had predicted that memory for emotional information would be better than memory for non-emotional information in older people. However, socioemotional selectivity theory was equivocal on the question of whether it would make a difference if emotional information were positive or negative. Studies have found that younger adults have a tendency to process negative information more thoroughly than positive information and to weigh negative information more heavily in impression formation, memory, and decision making (Baumeister, Bratslavsky, Finkenauer, & Vohs, 2001). Reasoning from socioemotional selectivity theory, there are two ways (at least) that emotional goals might influence older adults' attention and memory. The first possibility is that all information relevant to their emotional goals is made more salient. This "emotionally relevant" focus would bias attention and memory in favor of both positive and negative information.

The second possibility is that information that furthers emotional satisfaction is favored exclusively. This "emotionally gratifying" focus would bias attention and memory in favor of material that optimizes emotion regulation (i.e., positive material) even if there are costs to focusing only on such material.

We conducted two studies in which younger (ages 18–29), middle-aged (ages 41–53), and older adults (ages 65–85) viewed positive, negative, and neutral images on a computer screen and were subsequently tested for recognition and recall memory (Charles, Mather, & Carstensen, 2003).[2] In the first study, the ratio of positive to negative material accurately recalled by participants increased with age, despite an overall deficit in performance with age (see Fig. 1). A second study was conducted using essentially the same images and procedures but in which event-related functional magnetic resonance imaging was used to examine activation in the amygdala (a brain area integrally involved in the processing of emotion) while participants viewed the images (Mather et al., 2004). Behavioral findings replicated findings from the first study: In older adults, memory for positive images was relatively better than for negative images. Interestingly, whereas amygdala activation in younger and older adults was greater for both positive and negative images than for neutral images, older adults showed significantly greater activation for positive images than for negative ones (see Fig. 2). This finding suggests that positive and negative stimuli are differentially processed at a basic

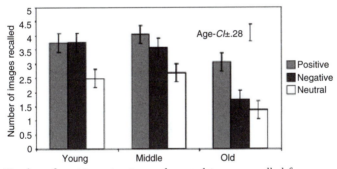

Fig. 1. Number of positive, negative, and neutral images recalled for younger adults, middle-aged adults, and older adults. From Charles, Mather, and Carstensen (2003).

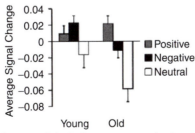

Fig. 2. Activation in the amygdala (a brain area involved in emotion processing) for younger and older adults while viewing positive, negative, and neutral images. Signal change indicates activation in the region during the task. From Mather et al. (2004).

neural level, suggesting that this age-related preference for positive information occurs in attentional as well as memorial processes.

Older people, at a subconscious or conscious level, may not attend to negative images because they are not motivated to do so. In the work described previously, participants viewed individual images one at a time on the computer screen. In another study, we examined attention to pairs of images (Mather & Carstensen, 2003). We employed a dot-probe experimental paradigm, in which pairs of faces (one neutral and one showing positive or negative emotion) are presented to participants on a computer screen simultaneously for 1000 ms, followed by a small grey dot that appears in the location where one of the photographs has been; we measured the speed at which participants identified which picture had the dot behind it. We observed that younger people responded to the dot-probes for positive and negative trials equally fast. Older adults, however, were significantly faster when the dot appeared behind the positive face than when it appeared behindthe negative face, indicating that when aneutral face was paired with a positive face, they were attending to the positive face, and that when a neutral face was paired with a negative face, they attended to the neutral face. This finding provides further evidence for the increased favoring of positive over negative material with age, even at the level of attention processing.

In one of our most recent investigations, we tested working memory for emotional images in older and younger adults (Mikels, Larkin, Reuter-Lorenz, & Carstensen, 2005). A comparison condition tested working memory for visual information. We found that older adults performed significantly poorer than younger adults on the visual working memory task. However, no age deficit emerged in working memory for emotional images. Moreover, whereas younger adults showed superior working memory for negative relative to positive emotional stimuli, older adults exhibited superior working memory for positive relative to negative emotional stimuli.

Our research team also examined the role of age and motivation in a study of autobiographical memory (Kennedy, Mather, & Carstensen, 2004). There is evidence in the literature that people remember their personal pasts more positively over time, but virtually all of the studies suffer from the inability to corroborate memories to assess accuracy. In a recent study, we were able to capitalize on a large data set collected from an order of Catholic nuns in 1987. At that time, the nuns had completed a questionnaire about physical and emotional well-being; in 2001, we had the Sisters complete the questionnaire as they remembered completing it originally. We created two quasi-experimental conditions. In one condition (emotion focus), participants were initially instructed to focus on their emotional states as they answered the questions and were periodically reminded to focus on their emotions while filling out the questionnaire. In another condition (information focus), participants were initially instructed to be as accurate as possible and then were periodically reminded to be accurate while completing the questionnaire. Findings showed that both the oldest participants and younger participants who were focused on emotional states showed a tendency to remember the past more positively than they originally reported, whereas participants focused on accuracy (whether old or young) tended to remember the past more negatively than originally reported. The differences by experimental condition make age-related neural changes an unlikely reason for the age-related positivity effect.

Although memory and attention are rarely conceptualized as self-regulatory processes, the events, people, and places that individuals attend to, hold in mind, and remember clearly influence their well-being. Memory itself is not simply "retrieval" but an elaborative process in which current goals influence constructions of the past. It appears that age-related motivational changes do not simply lead older people to prioritize emotionally meaningful goals (good or bad) but, more specifically, to prioritize the maintenance of emotional equilibrium. Older people appear to attend to, hold in mind, and remember emotionally positive information more than they do negative and neutral information.

FUTURE DIRECTIONS

The societal importance of understanding the nature of developmental changes in later life grows as the American population undergoes an unprecedented age redistribution. Cognitive functioning is integral to effective living. To date, most of the literature on cognitive aging documents areas of deterioration in functioning. Identifying areas of preserved functioning along with areas of deterioration can help to identify ways to compensate for losses. Relatively well-preserved memory for emotional material, especially positive emotional material, appears to represent one such area. Whereas negative material appears to be especially salient in youth, a shift evident in middle age and extending into old age appears to occur such that positive material is increasingly favored. We call this developmental pattern the *positivity effect*.

According to socioemotional selectivity theory, the focus on positive material to the exclusion of negative material operates in the service of emotional well-being. It is possible to speculate that the positivity effect may contribute to age differences in psychopathology. Depression and anxiety are far more prevalent in younger adults than in older adults. However, in keeping with basic principles of life-span theory, both gains and losses typically accompany any developmental change. One can easily imagine situations in which attending to positive information more than to negative information and remembering positive information better than negative information could have unfortunate consequences. For example, when decisions require that people consider negative as well as positive options, a preference for positive information could lead to poor-quality decisions (Löckenhoff & Carstensen, 2004).

Of course, many questions remain. It is possible that a reliance on feelings instead of memory for details results in better decision quality in older adults. Alternatively, because focusing on one's emotions for to-be-remembered information impairs memory for the source of that information, reliance on emotions could reduce the quality of decisions. Considerable knowledge about the aging mind has amassed in the past three decades. We suspect that the next frontier in aging research will extend beyond documentation of decline and growth and begin to identify ways both processes work in concert.

Recommended Reading

Carstensen, L.L., Mikels, J.A., & Mather, M. (in press). The intersection of cognition, motivation and emotion. In J. Birren and K.W. Schaie (Eds.), *Handbook of the Psychology of Aging*.

Mather M. (2004) Aging and emotional memory. In *Memory and Emotion* (Reisberg D. and Hertel P., eds.), pp. 272–307, Oxford University Press.

Mather, M., & Carstensen, L.L. (in press). Aging and motivated cognition: The positivity effect in attention and memory. *Trends in Cognitive Science*.

Acknowledgments—The preparation of this review was supported by National Institute on Aging research grant AG08816 to Laura L. Carstensen and Ruth L. Kirschstein National Research Service Award AG022264 to Joseph A. Mikels.

Notes

1. Address correspondence to Laura L. Carstensen, Department of Psychology, Stanford University, Jordan Hall – Building 420, Stan-ford, CA 94305-2130; e-mail: llc@psych.stanford.edu.

2. Images were from the International Affective Picture System, which contains over 700 images including positive images of babies and animals, negative images of mutilations and bugs, and neutral images of cups and mushrooms.

References

Baumeister, R.F., Bratslavsky, E., Finkenauer, C., & Vohs, K.D. (2001). Bad is stronger than good. *Review of General Psychology, 5*, 323–370.

Carstensen, L.L., & Fredrickson, B.L. (1998). Influence of HIV status and age on cognitive representations of others. *Health Psychology, 17*, 494–503.

Carstensen, L.L., Isaacowitz, D.M., & Charles, S.T. (1999). Taking time seriously: A theory of socioemotional selectivity. *American Psychologist, 54*, 165–181.

Charles, S.T., & Carstensen, L.L. (2004). A life-span view of emotional functioning in adulthood and old age. In P. Costa (Ed.), *Recent advances in psychology and aging* (Vol. 15, pp. 133–162). Amsterdam: Elsevier.

Charles, S.T., Mather, M., & Carstensen, L.L. (2003). Focusing on the positive: Age differences in memory for positive, negative, and neutral stimuli. *Journal of Experimental Psychology, 85*, 163–178.

Fung, H.H., & Carstensen, L.L. (2003). Sending memorable messages to the old: Age differences in preferences and memory for advertisements. *Journal of Personality & Social Psychology, 85*, 163–178.

Hashtroudi, S., Johnson, M.K., & Chrosniak, L.D. (1990). Aging and qualitative characteristics of memories for perceived and imagined complex events. *Psychology & Aging, 5*, 119–126.

Kahneman, D. (2003). A perspective on judgment and choice: Mapping bounded rationality. *American Psychologist, 58*, 697–720.

Kennedy, Q., Mather, M., & Carstensen, L.L. (2004). The role of motivation in the age-related positivity effect in autobiographical memory. *Psychological Science, 15*, 208–214.

Löckenhoff, C.E. & Carstensen, L.L. (2004). Socioemotional selectivity theory, aging, and health: The increasingly delicate balance between regulating emotions and making tough choices. *Journal of Personality, 72*, 1395–1424.

Mather, M., Canli, T., English, T., Whitfield, S., Wais, P., Ochsner, K., Gabrieli, J.D.E., & Carstensen, L.L. (2004). Amygdala responses to emotionally valenced stimuli in older and younger adults. *Psychological Science, 15*, 259–263.

Mather, M., & Carstensen, L.L. (2003). Aging and attentional biases for emotional faces. *Psychological Science, 14*, 409–415.

Mikels, J.A., Larkin, G.R., Reuter-Lorenz, P.A., & Carstensen, L.L. (2005). *Divergent trajectories in the aging mind: Changes in working memory for affective versus visual information with age*. Manuscript submitted for publication.

Rahhal, T.A., Hasher, L., & Colcombe, S.J. (2001). Instructional manipulations and age differences in memory: Now you see them, now you don't. *Psychology & Aging, 16*, 697–706.

Rahhal, T.A., May, C.P., & Hasher, L. (2002). Truth and character: Sources that older adults can remember. *Psychological Science, 13*, 101–105.

Critical Thinking Questions

1. What goals increase in importance with age? According to socioemotional selectivity theory, what is responsible for this increase?

2. What is the positivity effect, and how might this influence the well-being of older adults?

3. Age-related shifts in motivations may provide both advantages and risks. Give at least one example of a situation where these motivations may carry advantages in daily life, and another example where these age-related shifts may carry negative consequences.

This article has been reprinted as it originally appeared in *Current Directions in Psychological Science*. Citation information for this article as originally published appears above.

Dynamic Integration: Affect, Cognition, and the Self in Adulthood

Gisela Labouvie-Vief[1]

Department of Psychology, Wayne State University, Detroit, Michigan

Abstract

Positive self- and emotional development is often measured by optimization of happiness, but a second aspect of positive development—the ability to tolerate tension and negativity in the interest of maintaining objective representations—needs to be integrated with this hedonic emphasis. The integration of these two aspects, optimization and differentiation, reflects a dynamic balance. Such integration is possible when emotional activation or arousal is moderate, but is impaired at very high levels of activation. From youth to middle adulthood, the capacity for integration increases, but later in life, limitations or poor regulation strategies foster compensatory processes that compromise integration.

Keywords

adulthood; affect differentiation; emotional development; integration; self-development

Research on positive self- and emotional development in adulthood and aging has revealed two seemingly contradictory patterns (Labouvie-Vief & Márquez, in press). One line of research has demonstrated that older individuals' emotion regulation improves, because the balance of positive over negative affect increases into old age. However, another research tradition has pointed to regulation problems that result from later-life decline of cognitive resources (such as planning and impulse regulation) that can affect emotion regulation. How can these two aspects of emotion regulation be reconciled? The work I report here suggests that these two bodies of research reflect different approaches to research that are based on different concepts of what is "good" regulation. One of these concepts emphasizes the *optimization* of individual well-being. The other, instead, emphasizes *differentiation and complexity* as individuals coordinate feelings in the here and now with past and future feelings and synchronize them with those of other people. Thus, at times, positive feelings must be delayed and negative affect endured, at least temporarily. In the work reported here, I suggest that, as a consequence, optimal functioning involves an integration and flexible coordination of two core emotion regulation strategies or modes—optimization and differentiation. How do individuals coordinate these dual demands?

COMPLEXITY AND DIFFERENTIATION OF EMOTIONS

Since Darwin's work on affect, researchers have developed many theories focused on primary affects, emotions hardwired by evolution to secure survival through highly automated responses. However, during development such basic emotions become embedded into more complex cognitive networks that reflect the contribution of higher-order thought processes (see Metcalfe & Mischel, 1999). My work on the relationship between feelings and thinking originally was influenced by Piaget (1981), whose writings on affect anticipated the more recent interest in complex emotions by suggesting that the individual's evolving cognitive capacities alter the very dynamics of emotional life.

As children develop complex (especially linguistic) forms of representation, emotions become less tied to the here and now and more tied to an inner world of mental states shared with other people. This gives rise to new emotions—such as embarrassment, pride, or guilt—that signal awareness that one's feelings and thoughts link one to the feelings and thoughts of other people. By adolescence, individuals experience emotions about abstract ideals and norms, and they guide their behavior through complex plans that are based on an evolving identity spanning wide segments of time and place. Even so, adolescents' representational skills remain limited (Labouvie-Vief, 1994), relying on the presence of already well-structured societal and cultural systems such as political and religious ideologies. Adults, in turn, develop more complex representations that support further development.

My colleagues and I investigated such transformations in individuals aged 10 to 80 and older (Labouvie-Vief, Chiodo, Goguen, Diehl, & Orwoll, 1995; Labouvie-Vief, DeVoe, & Bulka, 1989). We coded participants' descriptions of their emotions and their selves into qualitative levels of differing *cognitive-affective complexity*. Findings showed that from adolescence to middle adulthood, individuals acquired more conscious insight into aspects of emotions that previously were unconscious, gained clearer differentiation of self from others, and blended distinct emotions, especially ones involving positive and negative contrasts (e.g., a mixture of joy and sadness). These developments allowed many (but not all) adults to carve out a renewed sense of self that was complex, was historically situated, and entailed a more distinct sense of their individuality.

These results confirmed our expectation that significant growth in affective complexity continues through middle adulthood. However, the results also contained surprises, even disappointments: Not only did growth abate in late middle adulthood (see Fig. 1), but a significant decline occurred thereafter. These findings highlight the role of middle-aged adults as the carriers of complex knowledge integrating mind and emotion (Labouvie-Vief, 1994) but suggest that problems with regulation of emotions occur with aging. Although the elderly reported the highest levels of positive affect, such as joy and interest, they also reported the lowest levels of negative affect, such as sadness and anger. Does this finding indicate increases in resilience among the elderly? We do not think so, because our notion of declining complexity implies reduced integration of negative affect so that as individuals age, they may find it more difficult to tolerate negative feelings. Indeed, our findings suggested such difficulty, because cognitive-affective complexity was uncorrelated with measures of hedonic tone such as well-being and positive affect. It was significantly positively correlated, however, with negative affect, as well as with measures of cognitive functioning. The fact that individuals of higher complexity express more negative affect goes along with our notion that affective differentiation involves coordinating positive and negative affect, but it also suggests that negative affect—but not positive

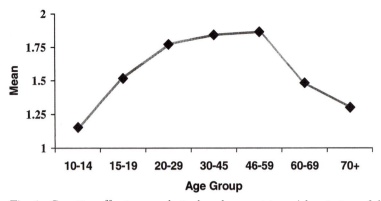

Fig. 1. Cognitive-affective complexity, based on participants' descriptions of their emotions and themselves, as a function of age.

affect—is related to cognitive functioning, perhaps because processing negative experience is more cognitively demanding. Is it possible, then, that individuals compensate for declines in cognitive-affective complexity with increases in optimization?

DYNAMIC INTEGRATION OF DIFFERENTIATION AND OPTIMIZATION

The notion that optimization and differentiation constitute quite different modes of regulating emotions is well embedded in the social-cognitive literature. Optimization is automatic and relatively effortless and involves experience that is personal and relatively ineffable or preconscious. Affect differentiation involves elaborative processing as individuals differentiate already existing knowledge. It requires more cognitive resources than optimization and is related to learning and knowledge that are relatively explicit and conscious.

To determine how the two modes interact, we (Labouvie-Vief & Márquez, in press) expanded Piaget's concept of an interplay between two core strategies of processing information (assimilation and accommodation) through a generalization of the Yerkes-Dodson law (Metcalfe & Mischel, 1999; Paulhus & Suedfeld, 1988). This law postulates a compensatory and curvilinear relationship between an individual's level of emotional activation or arousal and the degree to which complex, integrated behavior is possible (see Fig. 2). Slight elevations of activation foster integrated, well-ordered thinking and behavior. However, when activation rises to extremely high levels, it tends to disrupt or degrade integration. At high levels of activation, automated nonconscious thoughts and behavior, which are less easily disrupted by high arousal or activation, take over in an effort to maintain affect in a sufficiently positive range.

As an example, think about common reactions to a frightening event, such as the terrorist attack on September 11, 2001. The reactions to the attack involved an increase in patriotic feelings and emphasis on family values, but also increases in racial and ethnic stereotyping. This example shows that the degradation of complex thinking due to high emotional activation does not necessarily

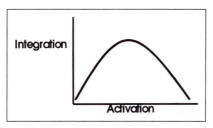

Fig. 2. Curvilinear relationship between integration (of thinking and behavior) and emotional activation. Integration is highest at moderate levels of activation and decreases at very high levels.

result in complete fragmentation, but can be relatively coherent or graceful. First, behavior becomes more automatic and schematized (Metcalfe & Mischel, 1999). Second, the ability to coordinate positive and negative aspects about self and others is disrupted, leading to a positivity bias in which attention is diverted from negative information about the self. In contrast, negative affect and information often are projected onto others, resulting in increased black-and-white thinking, stereotyping, and polarization among in-groups and out-groups (e.g., Paulhus & Lim, 1994; Paulhus & Suedfeld, 1988). Finally, individuals attempt to retreat to safe havens by reducing the range of their action and seeking refuge in close social networks. Erikson (1984) has referred to these ways of simplifying psychological complexity as pseudospeciation—the exclusion of others from the circle of humanity in which one includes oneself.

In a sense, trading off differentiation and complexity in favor of optimization makes good sense in situations that pose a threat to the well-being and survival of the self. Such situations stimulate emergency responses in which resources are focused on the self-protective task of restoring equilibrium and securing survival. However, not all individuals opt for optimization; some may attempt to maintain a differentiated and fairly objective picture of reality. They may even over-differentiate, or unsuccessfully try to reduce high levels of activation through intellectual analysis and rumination and become unable to act.

DYNAMIC INTEGRATION AND DEGRADATION OF OPTIMIZATION AND DIFFERENTIATION IN ADULT DEVELOPMENT

How does the complexity-optimization trade-off explain adult development and aging? Although the principle ideally works in a dynamic, flexible, and integrated way, two conditions can reduce flexible integration. First, normal developmental changes in cognitive resources can alter vulnerability to degradation of optimization or differentiation. As these resources grow, individuals are better able to maintain integrated behavior even when levels of activation are high. In contrast, as cognitive resources decline, individuals are more strongly affected by overactivation (Labouvie-Vief & Márquez, in press; Metcalfe & Mischel, 1999). Second, if development does not proceed in a context of relatively low and well-regulated arousal or activation, individuals are likely to develop poor strategies of affect regulation; these, in turn, should render the individuals particularly vulnerable to the degrading effects of overactivation. In our recent research, we have addressed both of these possibilities.

We began by defining two regulation modes, affect optimization and affect differentiation (Labouvie-Vief & Medler, 2002). As predicted, individuals who emphasized positive hedonic tone (high positive affect but low negative affect) displayed an optimization strategy, whereas those favoring cognitive-affective complexity adopted differentiation strategies. High optimizers were defined as individuals who minimized negative feelings; they did not engage in rich exploration of feelings and other nonrational processes (such as intuitions and dreams), and they tended to ignore unpleasant facts, but also exhibited low levels of self-doubt. High differentiators were defined as individuals who tended to analyze their emotions; they exhibited high tolerance of ambiguity and low levels of repression. Although the dimensions of optimization and differentiation were uncorrelated, they were associated with distinct patterns of additional traits. High optimizers were characterized by high ratings on self-acceptance, a sense of mastery, and purpose in life. High differentiators, in contrast, scored high on conceptual complexity, personal growth, and empathy, confirming our assumption that understanding another's perspective is a core aspect of affect complexity.

Optimizers and differentiators also reported having experienced different kinds of life events (Labouvie-Vief & Márquez, in press). Optimizers described their lives as free from major negative life events and turning points, such as emotional problems, loss of friends, experience with severe punishment or discrimination, and identity crises. In contrast, differentiators described their lives as containing major negative experiences, such as severe punishment and discrimination, and turning points, such as changes in self-concept or spiritual belief.

These results suggest that quite different pathways of development may exist in adulthood—one characterized by optimization, the other by differentiation. Do individuals develop unique styles of coordinating these modes? Through statistical analyses, we (Labouvie-Vief & Medler, 2002) identified four such styles (see Fig. 3). Following Werner (1957), we defined an *integrated* style, manifested by individuals who scored high on using both modes.

These individuals displayed the most positive development: They scored high in positive but low in negative affect; reported high well-being, empathy, and health; and indicated they had a secure relationship style. In contrast, the *dysregulated* (low differentiation, low optimization) scored lowest on all of these variables, except negative affect, on which they scored highest. The *self-protective* (low differentiation, high optimization) and the *complex* (high differentiation, low optimization) displayed more mixed patterns that were nevertheless fairly coherent. Compared with the complex, the self-protective scored low in negative affect, but the two groups were similar in positive affect, relationship security, and health. The self-protective also placed less emphasis on personal growth but more on environmental mastery than the complex; they scored higher on good impression and conformance but lower on empathy. This pattern suggests that the self-protective tend to dampen negative affect, whereas the complex amplify it. The diverging affective patterns we identified appear to indicate

Integrated	Complex
High Positive Affect	Med Negative Affect
Low Negative Affect	Med Negative Affect
High Personal Growth	High Personal Growth
High Environmental Mastery	High Environmental Mastery
High Good Impression	Med Good Impression
High Empathy	High Empathy
High Self-Related Health	Med Self-Related Health
High Relationship Security	Med Relationship Security

Self-Protective	Dysregulated
Med Positive Affect	Low Positive Affect
Low Negative Affect	High Negative Affect
Med Personal Growth	Low Personal Growth
High Environmental Mastery	Low Environmental Mastery
High Good Impression	Low Good Impression
Low Empathy	Low Empathy
Med Self-Related Health	Low Self-Related Health
Med Self-Related Security	Low Relationship Security

Fig. 3. Four regulation styles resulting from different combinations of differentiation (high in top row, low in bottom row) and optimization (high in left column, low in right column): integrated (high differentiation, high optimization), complex (high differentiation, low optimization), self-protective (low differentiation, high optimization), and dysregulated (low differentiation, low optimization). Significant differences between the styles are indicated by different qualifiers: high, medium ("med"), and low. Environmental mastery refers to having a sense of mastery over one's environment. Good impression refers to a tendency to give socially desirable responses.

different identity styles, each reflecting characteristic variations in how individuals integrate positive and negative affect (see Helson & Srivastava, 2001).

According to the principle of dynamic integration, the optimization and differentiation strategies are related in a compensatory fashion, especially among individuals, such as the elderly, who have limited resources. This is exactly what our data indicate. When we compared young, middle-aged, and old adults, our results showed that among the oldest age group, a significantly smaller than expected number of individuals fell into the complex group, whereas a disproportionately high number fell into the self-protective group: About 20% of the young and middle-aged adults (younger than 60) fell into the complex and self-protective groups, whereas only 10% of the older adults (aged 60 or older) were classified as complex, but 42% were classified as self-protective. Thus, as individuals grow older and experience declines in cognitive-affective complexity, they tend to rely more strongly on optimization strategies. This pattern was confirmed by longitudinal evidence as well: Over a 6-year interval, declines in differentiation predicted increases in optimization. On the positive side, however, our data also suggested that there were no significant declines in the number of elderly integrated individuals.

The notion of a trade-off between complexity and optimization in late life predicts not only increases in positive affect balance, but also impaired dynamic regulation of affect (i.e., degradation) in situations that require reflection to modulate emotion. Beyond our own work, much emerging experimental evidence (see Labouvie-Vief & Márquez, in press) also attests to such regulatory problems. In comparison to younger adults, older adults distort information in a positive direction, are less resistant to stereotypes, and limit their behavior to a more restricted range of tasks and goals that are directly relevant to the self (such as security); they also limit themselves to a narrower range of physical and social environments. Thus, as individuals experience reductions in cognitive-affective complexity, they can maintain a strategy of affect optimization as long as they reduce the demands made on them by their external environment.

CONCLUSIONS AND FUTURE RESEARCH

The dynamic-integration principle is able to reconcile two quite contradictory bodies of literature on adult self- and emotion regulation, one focusing on the maintenance of positive hedonic tone and the other focusing on development of cognitive-affective complexity and differentiation. Dynamic integration suggests that many elderly individuals compensate for a decrease in cognitive-affective complexity with an optimization response that involves the degradation of complex representations. The possibility of such cognitive-affective degradation means that researchers should not simply equate such concepts as well-being and positive development with positive feelings. Although the need to maintain a sufficiently positive balance of affect constrains emotional life, mature emotional development implies the ability to coordinate one's affect with that of others. This ability is widely considered a hallmark of complex emotions relating to caring, empathy, or equanimity. However, researchers still know little about the nature of those emotions. What permits some individuals to extend themselves beyond the most personal concerns with the here and now across time and to wide, perhaps unlimited, circles of others? What prevents other individuals from doing so? Researchers know little about that generation of middle-aged adults in whom these emotions come to full maturity: It is they who provide cognitive-affective scaffolding for younger generations and who, for better or for worse, regulate their development.

The concept of integration suggests that the activation of affect and the regulative function of the cognitions involved in differentiation interact in ways that can be mutually enhancing or limiting. What is the cusp that separates the two possibilities? With respect to aging, a critical threshold may be reached around the age of 60, when the capacity for conscious regulation becomes impaired. However, our data indicate that nearly half of that age group remains classified as integrated. Is it possible that many aging individuals are able to resist the degradation of complex cognitive-affective representations? If so, does a prior developmental pathway of integration differentiate them from those who embark on a less positive course?

Issues of integration extend well beyond aging, however, and raise important questions about other segments of the life span. For example, the present theory predicts that age and individual styles of regulation—with the differences in integration they imply—are important in moderating the effects of difficult and frightening events. How do individuals with different levels of cognitive-affective integration respond to a variety of emotion-activating events, both in the laboratory and in real life? Do those levels help explain why some individuals are able to grow from difficult experience, whereas others break or close down? Looking beyond behavioral data, what are the exact ways in which cognition and representation work to alter the dynamics of emotional activation? New neuro-biological studies are beginning to show that this regulative function involves setting of new higher-order circuits in the brain (see Metcalfe & Mischel, 1999) that in turn are related to reduced levels of activation, as originally suggested by Freud, Luria, and Piaget. Such research brings the exciting promise of bridging the mental operations that characterize complex affects and the biological processes by which they become embodied in the brain.

Recommended Reading

Baltes, P.B., & Baltes, M.M. (1990). Psychological perspectives on successful aging: The model of selective optimization with compensation. In P.B. Baltes & M.M. Baltes (Eds.), *Successful aging: Perspectives from the behavioral sciences* (pp. 1–34). New York: Cambridge University Press.

Labouvie-Vief, G., & Márquez, M.G. (in press). (See References)

Ryan, R.M., & Deci, E.L. (2001). On happiness and human potentials: A review of research on hedonic and eudaimonic well-being. *Annual Review of Psychology, 52,* 141–166.

Acknowledgments—This research was supported by National Institute on Aging Grant AG09203.

Note

1. Address correspondence to Gisela Labouvie-Vief, Department of Psychology, Wayne State University, Detroit, MI 48202; e-mail: gvief@sun. science.wayne.edu.

References

Erikson, E.H. (1984). *The life cycle completed.* New York: Norton.

Helson, R., & Srivastava, S. (2001). Three paths of adult development: Conservers, seekers, and achievers. *Journal of Personality and Social Psychology, 80,* 995–1010.

Labouvie-Vief, G. (1994). *Psyche and Eros: Mind and gender in the life course.* New York: Cambridge University Press.

Labouvie-Vief, G., Chiodo, L.M., Goguen, L.A., Diehl, M., & Orwoll, L. (1995). Representations of self across the life span. *Psychology and Aging, 10,* 404–415.

Labouvie-Vief, G., DeVoe, M., & Bulka, D. (1989). Speaking about feelings: Conceptions of emotion across the life span. *Psychology and Aging, 4,* 425–437.

Labouvie-Vief, G., & Márquez, M.G. (in press).Dynamic integration: Affect optimization and differentiation in development. In D.Y. Dai & R.J. Sternberg (Eds.), *Motivation, emotion, and cognition.* Mahwah, NJ: Erlbaum.

Labouvie-Vief, G., & Medler, M. (2002). Affect optimization and affect complexity: Modes and styles of regulation in adulthood. *Psychology and Aging, 17*, 571–587.

Metcalfe, J., & Mischel, W. (1999). A hot/cool-system analysis of delay of gratification: Dynamics of willpower. *Psychological Review, 106*, 3–19.

Paulhus, D.L., & Lim, D.T.K. (1994). Arousal and evaluative extremity in social judgments: A dynamic complexity model. *European Journal of Social Psychology, 24*, 89–99.

Paulhus, D.L., & Suedfeld, P. (1988). A dynamic complexity model of self-deception. In J.S. Lockard & D.L. Paulhus (Eds.), *Self-deception: An adaptive mechanism* (pp. 132–145). New York: Prentice-Hall.

Piaget, J. (1981). *Intelligence and affectivity: Their relationship during child development* (T.A. Brown & C.E. Kaegi, Trans.). Palo Alto, CA: Annual Reviews.

Werner, H. (1957). *Comparative psychology of mental development*. New York: International Universities Press.

Critical Thinking Questions

1. The dynamic balance refers to the integration of optimization and differentiation. How might each of these processes help with self-regulation?

2. Why does cognitive-complexity increase into middle-age, and why does it decline in old age?

3. What are the costs and benefits of age-related changes in optimization and differentiation?

This article has been reprinted as it originally appeared in *Current Directions in Psychological Science*. Citation information for this article as originally published appears above.

Motivated Gaze: The View From the Gazer

Derek M. Isaacowitz[1]
Brandeis University

Abstract

How does gaze relate to psychological properties of the gazer? Studies using eye tracking reveal robust group differences in gaze toward emotional information: Optimists gaze less at negative, unpleasant images than do pessimists, and older individuals look away from negative faces and toward happy faces. These group differences appear to reflect an underlying motivation to achieve and maintain good moods by directing attention to mood-facilitating stimuli. Maintaining a positive mood is only one goal-related context that influences visual attention; recent work has also suggested that other goal states can impact gaze. Gaze therefore is a tool of motivation, directing gazers toward stimuli that are consistent with their goals and away from information that will not facilitate goal achievement.

Keywords

attention; motivation; optimism; aging

References to how gaze can be used strategically abound in everyday conversation: For example, people commonly advise distressed friends to "look on the bright side" of a bad situation. Similarly, the survivor of a traumatic experience may describe having new "perspective" on life since the event. While perhaps meant figuratively, such comments may have some literal truth. Is it possible that gaze can actually be used strategically by gazers?

In this article, I propose several ways of linking gaze to psychological properties of the gazer, as a step toward developing a general model of how motivation regulates visual attention. First, gaze is linked both to individual differences in personality-related constructs and to individual development. Second, gaze is a tool for optimizing the affect of the gazer. Third, gaze serves a general motivational role, guiding people toward information that will help them achieve goals and away from stimuli that will not.

I describe results of studies using eye tracking to measure gaze directly, in nearly real time, to support these general properties of gaze. I also use research using observation of gaze, when it is available, to support eye-tracking findings. While it is possible to separate gaze from visual attention, the two are generally considered identical (Parkhurst, Law, & Niebur, 2002); thus, here I use *gaze* to refer to where an individual fixates, but it could also be called the *target of visual attention*.

GAZE IS TIED TO PERSONALITY AND DEVELOPMENT

In my lab, we have used eye tracking, a technique previously used mostly in reading research, to investigate group differences in visual attention to emotional stimuli. Participants are seated in front of a computer screen; a remote eye-tracking system records their left-eye gaze position using infrared illumination 60 times a second. Fixations are defined as gaze within a small area for at least 100 milliseconds, allowing us to distinguish between saccades (fast eye movements between fixations) and gaze meaningfully fixated on stimuli. Using fixation to emotional stimuli as the dependent variable, several robust group differences in gaze have been documented.

One eye-tracking study conducted in my lab tested for differences in gaze patterns among young adults with different levels of dispositional optimism as indicated by a self-report optimism measure (Isaacowitz, 2005, Study 1), evaluating whether some individuals can indeed look on the bright side of things. Participants' eyes were tracked as they viewed images of skin cancer, line drawings with the same shape as the cancer images, and neutral faces. Skin cancer was selected because it had been used in past work on optimism–health relations and was unpleasant as well as graphic. Relatively optimistic young adults fixated less on the skin-cancer images than their less optimistic peers did, even in a conservative test in which fixation to schematic drawings (matched for lines and shapes to the cancer images but without the actual unpleasant cancer component) was controlled. This effect of optimism was not eliminated by controlling for affect (i.e., participants' mood at the time of the test) or neuroticism, nor did a perceived-relevance index of family history and worry about skin cancer interact with optimism.

This evidence of optimists wearing "rose-colored glasses" was provocative, so I conducted a follow-up study to replicate and extend the findings (Isaacowitz, 2005, Study 2). The setup was similar, with two additions. First, participants completed self-report anxiety measures to rule out the possibility that observed effects were simply due to anxiety (as anxious individuals appear especially vigilant toward potentially threatening stimuli). Second, self-relevance was further examined through an experimental manipulation: Some participants were told that they were going to see images related to real-world health concerns and problem detection (relevance condition), whereas others were asked to "look naturally" as if at home watching television (control). The effect of optimism on visual attention to the skin cancer was replicated, and neither the relevance manipulation nor anxiety predicted gaze. Again, more optimistic young adults looked less at the skin cancer than their more pessimistic peers did. In both studies, no effect of expecting in advance to see skin-cancer images was found: Gaze patterns were similar for cancer stimuli both early and late in the presentation.

We moved even closer to real-world health-related attention in another study, when we measured the gaze of college students as they viewed text and pictorial skin-cancer information (Luo & Isaacowitz, 2006). We followed Aspinwall and Brunhart's (1996) approach of defining relevance by how much risk each participant possessed for the particular negative outcome; however, unlike the self-reported risk information used by Aspinwall, we used an objective risk-assessment tool that indexed actual risk factors for skin cancer to determine risk relevance for each participant. Results for dispositional optimism replicated the previous findings: Individuals high in dispositional optimism appeared to look less at cancer-related stimuli, even in some cases when the stimuli were objectively relevant to them.[2] These three studies therefore point consistently to individuals higher in dispositional optimism looking less at unpleasant stimuli, regardless of the self-relevance (defined in various ways) of those stimuli.

My lab has also been studying gaze and aging, pursuing theoretical work suggesting that emotional material may be particularly salient to older adults (Carstensen, Isaacowitz, & Charles, 1999). In the first eye-tracking study to investigate age-related gaze preferences for different emotional stimuli (Isaacowitz, Wadlinger, Goren, & Wilson, in press), synthetic faces displaying emotional and nonemotional expressions were used as target stimuli. These faces minimized psychophysical differences that might grab attention while simultaneously using facial geometry to create expressions of happiness, sadness, anger, and fear. Pretest ratings ensured that the faces did indeed represent the intended emotional expression and were equivalent in intensity across emotional subtypes. Participants had their eyes tracked as they "looked naturally" at images featuring a face making an emotional expression paired with the same face in a nonemotional expression. Gaze-preference scores were used to explore whether a particular age group showed a pattern of looking toward or away from the emotional faces in those pairs. Older participants (age 57–84) showed a gaze preference toward happy and away from angry faces. Younger adults' (age 18–21) only preference was toward afraid faces. An example of these gaze preferences is shown in Figure 1. This is evidence for specific attentional preferences in both young and older adults; importantly, these preferences were found in a sample in which the age groups were well matched in overall cognitive functioning, and the effects were not eliminated when statistically controlling for perceptual individual-difference variables, such as visual acuity. Older adults show gaze preferences toward positive and away from negative emotional stimuli in their environment.

GAZE IS A TOOL FOR OPTIMIZING POSITIVE AFFECT

Findings of optimists gazing less at negative images and of older adults showing gaze preferences toward positive and away from negative images suggest that gaze patterns may reflect an underlying motivation to regulate emotions and to feel good. There is theoretical rationale for a motivational basis for these "feel good" patterns of attention, at least in terms of age-related patterns. According to socioemotional selectivity theory (Carstensen et al., 1999), contexts in which time is perceived as limited (such as old age) are associated with motivation to pursue emotionally meaningful goals and to regulate emotional experience in a positive direction. The evidence presented earlier, that older individuals show gaze preferences favoring positive material, is consistent with a motivation to process information to optimize positive affect. However, such age differences may reflect more general effects of cognitive aging rather than specifically motivated processes.

Several approaches have been used to ensure that age differences in gaze reflect motivation to feel good rather than artifacts of cognitive aging. The first involves extensive perceptual and cognitive testing, then using matching or statistical controls to show that gaze patterns are not due to these more general

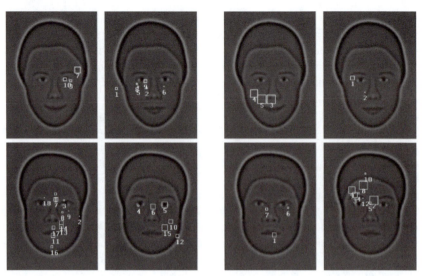

Fig. 1. Gaze-fixation patterns of a younger adult (left group of panels) and an older adult (right group of panels) to the same face images for a happy–neutral (top) and angry–neutral (bottom) pair. Numbers signify order of fixation (1 = first fixation), and box size is an index of fixation length, with larger boxes indicating a longer fixation at that location. Percent fixation within the Area of Interest (AOI) for the happy–neutral pair (top panels) was 43.21% to the happy face and 47.09% to the neutral face for the younger individual and 78.62% to the happy face and 15.18% to the neutral face for the older individual. Percent fixation within the AOI for the angry–neutral pair (bottom panels) was 54.37% to the angry face and 45.63% to the neutral face for the younger individual and 14.49% to the angry face and 85.51% to the neutral face for the older individual. From Isaacowitz, Wadlinger, Goren, and Wilson (in press).

changes in perception and cognition that occur with age (e.g., Isaacowitz et al., in press). Second, a study was conducted in my lab comparing gaze toward emotional faces in two groups that are generally comparable in cognitive functioning but vary in time perspective: first-year college students and seniors. College seniors, for whom impending graduation served to constrain time perspective, gazed less at negative stimuli than did first-year students. Consistent with gaze preferences relating to affect, the college seniors were also happier (Pruzan & Isaacowitz, 2006). Together, these findings suggest that motivational rather than cognitive factors influence observed gaze patterns.

An even more powerful demonstration that motivation to feel good can lead to observed gaze patterns comes from a recent study of young adults randomly assigned to instruction conditions mimicking motivational states before viewing emotionally valenced images (Xing & Isaacowitz, 2006). Some participants were instructed to regulate their emotions as they viewed (the instruction was to "manage how you feel as you view"), whereas others were told to gather as much information from the pictures as possible. Participants instructed to regulate emotions gazed less at negative than at positive or neutral stimuli, whereas no such differences were found among those told to gather information.

It is worth noting that a motivation to achieve and maintain positive mood by selective information processing is not unique to socioemotional selectivity theory; the hedonic contingency model (Wegener & Petty, 1994) also proposes motivated information processing in the service of positive mood maintenance. Thus, different motivational theories share the same prediction, supported by eye-tracking evidence, that gaze can work to keep the gazer in a positive mood.

GAZE IS A GENERAL TOOL OF MOTIVATION AND GOAL-DIRECTED BEHAVIOR

The above evidence suggests that gaze is a tool of optimizing affect; however, feeling good is only one goal that people may be motivated to accomplish. The final proposition of this paper is that gaze serves as a more general tool of motivation. For example, the life-span theory of control (Heckhausen & Schulz, 1995) suggests that the underlying motivation for humans is to maintain control over their environment. In the context of development, that means focusing resources on goal achievement when a goal is still possible and disengaging from goals that are no longer achievable (due to biological changes, for example). Pursuing unattainable goals might lead to unhappiness, but the theory argues that continuing engagement with goals that cannot be attained does more than just make people unhappy; it also impairs the ability to exert and maintain control in other domains. Thus, emotional ramifications are secondary to motivational and behavioral ones. My lab set out to investigate whether gaze could be linked to this theoretical perspective on motivation.

Jessica Light and I (Light & Isaacowitz, in press) adopted a paradigm from control research that examines processing of goal-relevant and goal-irrelevant stimuli in individuals who are before a developmental deadline and in those who have passed it. This was done by investigating attention among childless women who were either before or after the developmental deadline for childbearing. While technological advances have allowed some females to extend their childbearing years, there continues to be a shared perception of the age (around 40) at which having children becomes significantly less likely. We measured gaze patterns as participants viewed images of babies and pictures of puppies and kittens matched for cuteness. Post-deadline participants averted their gaze from babies faster than did predeadline women, while the groups did not differ in gaze toward non-baby stimuli. Gaze appeared to be more closely tied to goal processes than to affective outcomes, supporting the idea that gaze can reflect more general motivational processes than emotion regulation. Moreover, the life-span theory of control would argue that any affective results of motivated information processing are adaptive only if they facilitate achievement of behavioral control; gaze reflecting control motivation should therefore be oriented toward stimuli that optimize control.

Earlier work using observational methods supports the idea that gaze works in the general service of goal achievement, sometimes even at the expense of feeling good. Kleinke (1986) reviews findings in which individuals gaze more at information that will not make them feel good—such as looking more at a person who has given you negative feedback in order to determine why. Together with our work on gaze toward baby pictures, these findings suggest that gaze does not orient only to happy-making stimuli in the environment, and even when gaze is directed toward positive material, it may be working in support of longer-term general goals rather than short-term emotional ones.

Given that motivated cognition has been documented in other stages of information processing, such as reasoning (Kunda, 1990), why is another tool needed in the toolbox of motivated cognition? Successful goal pursuit likely requires multiple levels of cognitive effort, due to the number of intruding non-goal-relevant stimuli in the environment. Someone with the goal of feeling good will be assaulted with negative images on the evening news, and someone trying to get a task done may get interrupted by competing demands, such as receiving a distracting e-mail. Older adults may be at even greater risk of goal-irrelevant stimuli impinging on their thinking. Thus, multiple levels of motivated cognition are needed. Motivational influences on gaze are particularly efficient at keeping goal-irrelevant stimuli out of later processing: Gaze is highly selective, happens early in processing, and appears responsive to multiple motivational influences—from maintaining control to feeling good. Gaze is thus perhaps the most economical tool in motivation's toolbox.

FUTURE DIRECTIONS

The findings I discussed suggest important basic issues that might be investigated using gaze, such as whether the motivational effects on gaze are automatic or consciously controlled. For example, if individuals can force themselves to look on the bright side of things, can that volitional process be transformed into an automatic one with repeated intentional practice?

Time is obviously critical when it comes to interpreting gaze data. While fixations may vary from 100 to 500 milliseconds in length (or longer), it takes 150 to 175 milliseconds to execute an eye movement (Reichle, Pollatsek, Fisher, & Rayner, 1998). Millisecond-by-millisecond analyses of our gaze data are currently underway. It is nonetheless notable that the earliest effect of motivation we have found on gaze has been on duration of first fixation (the first location on the image on which the participant fixates); we have not documented any effects thus far on the very earliest aspects of gaze (such as where the first fixation falls). This pattern suggests that some visual scanning is occurring before motivated effects on gaze pattern emerge, which is reasonable given that some basic detection must take place to provide input for motivation to act on. This interpretation is supported by recent findings that older adults detect angry stimuli similarly to younger adults (Mather & Knight, 2006) but avert their gaze away from such stimuli over longer time intervals (Isaacowitz et al., in press). The search for the mechanisms underlying motivated-gaze effects will require attention to time; motivational effects are likely rapid, but not immediate.

Another future direction involves determining the behavioral effects of motivated gaze. We have started to document connections between motivation, gaze, and behavior in the health domain (Luo & Isaacowitz, 2005) and are continuing to investigate the behavioral effects of motivated gaze toward health-relevant information. Looking at looking not only provides an opportunity to link motivation, personality, development, and social psychology in the context of real-time transactions between the individual and the environment, but also has implications for designing visual stimuli (such as advertisements and health-promotion messages) intended to change behavior by grabbing people's gaze.

Recommended Reading

Isaacowitz, D.M. (2005). (See References)
Isaacowitz, D.M., et al. (in press). (See References)
Kleinke, C.L. (1986). (See References)

Notes

1. Address correspondence to Derek M. Isaacowitz, Department of Psychology, Brandeis University, MS 062, Waltham, MA 02454-9110; e-mail: dmi@brandeis.edu.

2. Aspinwall and Brunhart (1996) found that health-related optimism predicted longer latency to click off a Web page featuring self-relevant negative information. In Luo & Isaacowitz (2006), participants who were high in dispositional optimism but low in health-related optimism looked less at health-related information as self-relevance increased. This dissociation between health-specific optimism and dispositional optimism is beyond the scope of this article but warrants future research.

References

Aspinwall, L.G., & Brunhart, S.M. (1996). Distinguishing optimism from denial: Optimistic beliefs predict attention to health threats. *Personality and Social Psychology Bulletin, 22*, 993–1003.
Carstensen, L.L., Isaacowitz, D.M., & Charles, S.T. (1999). Taking time seriously: A theory of socioemotional selectivity. *American Psychologist, 54*, 165–181.
Heckhausen, J., & Schulz, R. (1995). A life-span theory of control. *Psychological Review, 102*, 284–304.
Isaacowitz, D.M. (2005). The gaze of the optimist. *Personality and Social Psychology Bulletin, 31*, 407–415.
Isaacowitz, D.M., Wadlinger, H.A., Goren, D., & Wilson, H.A. (in press). Selective preference in visual fixation to negative images in old age? An eye tracking study. *Psychology and Aging.*
Kleinke, C.L. (1986). Gaze and eye contact: A research review. *Psychological Bulletin, 100*, 78–100.
Kunda, Z. (1990). The case for motivated reasoning. *Psychological Bulletin, 108*, 480–498.
Light, J., & Isaacowitz, D.M. (in press). The effect of developmental regulation on visual attention: The example of the "Biological Clock." *Cognition and Emotion.*
Luo, J., & Isaacowitz, D.M. (2006). *How optimists face skin cancer: Risk assessment, attention, memory, and behavior.* Manuscript submitted for publication.
Mather, M., & Knight, M. (2006). Angry faces get noticed quickly: Threat detection is not impaired among older adults. *Journal of Gerontology: Psychological Sciences, 61*, P54–P57.
Parkhurst, D., Law, K., & Niebur, E. (2002). Modeling the role of salience in the allocation of overt visual attention. *Vision Research, 42*, 107–123.
Pruzan, K., & Isaacowitz, D.M. (2006). An attentional application of socioemotional selectivity theory in college students. *Social Development, 26*, 326–338.
Reichle, E.D., Pollatsek, A., Fisher, D.L., & Rayner, K. (1998). Toward a model of eye movement control in reading. *Psychological Review, 105*, 125–157.
Wegener, D.T., & Petty, R.E. (1994). Mood management across affective states: The hedonic contingency hypothesis. *Journal of Personality and Social Psychology, 66*, 1034–1048.
Xing, C., & Isaacowitz, D.M. (2006). *Aiming at happiness: How motivation affects attention to and memory for emotional images.* Manuscript submitted for publication.

Critical Thinking Questions

1. What does visual attention reveal about an individual? Provide one example from the reading.

2. How might attention to positive stimuli influence emotional experience?

3. Design a study examining age differences in visual attention. What stimuli would you use, and what would you hypothesize given your knowledge about life span development?

This article has been reprinted as it originally appeared in *Current Directions in Psychological Science*. Citation information for this article as originally published appears above.

Section 4: Psychosocial Factors of Aging

The articles in the previous section discussed how age differences in cognitive processing influences the processing of emotional information as well as provides insight into emotion-related goals of overall well-being. The current section continues the theme of well-being in the first three articles. M. Powell Lawton was one of the leaders in the field of emotion and aging, publishing some of the first papers examining age differences in the structure and mean levels of affective experience. In his article, "Emotion in later life" he reviews findings regarding age differences in physiological reactivity, behavioral response, and subjective emotional experience. He then places these findings within the current theories of aging, including theories of control, motivation, and cognition. In Daniel Mroczek's article, "Age and emotion in adulthood," he discusses the experience of positive and negative emotions changes across the adult life-span. He describes findings showing that negative affect decreases and positive affect increases across successively older age groups until around age 70, at which time age-related trajectories take on a different shape. He offers possible reasons to explain why these trajectories change in very old age, mentioning health problems and other negative events that occur at the end of the lifespan.

The influence of life events is described in the article, "Adaptation and the set-point model of subjective well-being." The author, Richard Lucas, reviews literature concerning events that occur in adulthood that influences emotional well-being. He shows that certain life events, such as widowhood, have long term effects on affective well-being. Some events, such as severe functional impairments, exert lasting effects. He also describes how other major life events do not exert such strong influences as one may think, instead showing little influence on later reports of happiness.

The next articles discuss psychological processes often related to well-being. Richard Robins and Kali Trzesniewski discuss age differences in levels of self-esteem from childhood to old age. In their article, "Self esteem development across the lifespan" they discuss how self-esteem begins high in childhood and decreases rapidly until late adolescence. Self-esteem then slowly increases, with people in their sixties highest than at any other time in adulthood. After this pinnacle, self-esteem then decreases. The authors discuss potential explanations for these rises and falls, as well as for the gender difference that is present in almost every age group with the exception of the very young and the oldest adults in the sample.

The final two articles focus on control beliefs and their relationships to affective and physical well-being. Margie Lachman discusses the importance of high levels of perceived control for an array of psychological outcomes, including affective and physical functioning. Her article, "Perceived control over aging-related declines" discusses the importance of perceived control for people of all ages, but highlights research showing how control partially explains age differences in cognitive performance among older adults. In addition, she describes findings from an intervention designed to reduce the risks of falls among older adults to exemplify how changing control beliefs can lead to changes in thoughts and behaviors related to physical health and well-being.

Carsten Wrosch, Richard Schulz, and Jutta Heckhausen authored the article, "Health stresses and depressive symptomatology in the elderly: A control-process approach." In this article, they use the life-span theory of control to explain why control strategies for modifiable events differ from those when coping with an intractable, chronic health condition. Although compensatory strategies are useful when a situation cannot be changed, active control strategies are best when a situation is under the control of the individual.

Emotion in Later Life

M. Powell Lawton[1]

Polisher Research Institute, Philadelphia Geriatric Center,
Philadelphia, Pennsylvania

Abstract

Recent research investigating emotion in old age suggests that autonomic responsiveness diminishes with age. The experiential aspects of emotion, however, show less marked age differences. Despite the health-related and social losses of old age, research findings on changes in the frequency and valence of affect in old age are inconsistent, and those studies that have reported changes have found only small ones. Studies of emotion regulation have found evidence of increasing self-regulatory skill with age. Theoretical accounts of emotional development in late life emphasize the integration of cognitive and affective processes, but differ in whether accommodative mechanisms are considered to be as effective as proactive mechanisms in reaching emotional goals.

Keywords

emotion; old age; self-regulation; positive feelings

The long period of human development and aging offers the opportunity to examine emotion in terms of two processes: the maturation and aging of the nervous system and the processes of learning and adaptation that occur over many years. Basic sensory and some cognitive processes do change in concert with the aging of the nervous system. In the history of gerontology, it has often been assumed that the declines in psychomotor speed and information processing associated with aging are paralleled by declines in other functions. Almost invariably, however, empirical testing has shown these folk-wisdom-generated assertions to be either false or true under very limited conditions. This is true of several common beliefs about emotion and aging. In this article, I review changes in emotion across the life span. My focus is on the autonomic, facial-expressive, behavioral, and subjective aspects of emotion (genetic and neural aspects are not included). I end the discussion with brief overviews of some recent theoretical contributions regarding the role of emotion in adult development.

AUTONOMIC AND FACIAL-EXPRESSIVE ASPECTS OF EMOTION

In empirical studies, psycho-physiological and facial emotion, which are linked to the biological substratum of emotion, have shown age-related changes. In one study, older and younger participants showed similar emotion-specific patterns in four physiological functions during directed facial emotion-simulating action, but the levels of autonomic activity were lower among the older adults (Levenson, Carstensen, Friesen, & Ekman, 1991). Levenson et al. viewed the two age groups' similarity in the differential autonomic configurations for anger, fear, and other emotions as evidence in favor of the continuity of emotional responsiveness over the life cycle. In another study with an experiential focus, however, older participants reported fewer autonomic symptoms accompanying typical emotion than did middle-aged and younger people (Lawton, Kleban, Rajagopal, & Dean, 1992).

Facial expression has long been identified as an intrinsic aspect of emotion with close ties to the neurology of emotion. There are two sides to facial expression: the ability to display (encode) facial expressions that can be decoded by other people, which is referred to as emotion expression, and the ability to decode other people's facial expressions, which is referred to as emotional understanding. Emotional understanding is a step further removed from brain processes than emotion expression, but both forming a facial expression and understanding the facial expression of another person are communicative acts that are subject to social learning and personal control. Empirical evidence is not consistent, but some research has found that older people are less able than younger people to encode and decode facial expressions in accord with expectations (Levenson et al., 1991; Malatesta, Izard, Culver, & Nicolich, 1987); also, elders may be better able to decode expressions of their own age-mates than those of younger people.

EMOTION, BEHAVIOR, AND SUBJECTIVE EXPERIENCE

Affect Salience

Malatesta and Kalnok (1984) used a self-response questionnaire to explore whether people of different ages differ in their perception of how central emotion in general is to their overall functioning. Young people saw emotion as more central to their lives than did middle-aged and older people, who did not differ from each other in their reports. Malatesta and Kalnok found no age differences, however, in participants' use of emotion terms in describing significant events, and similarly, no age differences were found in another study using an incidental memory task that provided an opportunity for either neutral or emotional information to be recalled (Carstensen & Turk-Charles, 1994).

Affect Frequency

Old age has often been thought of as a period of loss and decline. In fact, a steady stream of research beginning with small or unrepresentative samples but now including very large and sophisticated samples has led to the conclusion that life satisfaction is higher among older than among younger people and that the frequency of negative affect does not conform with the "age of loss" hypothesis. Cross-sectional studies suggest that young and old people do not differ in the frequency with which they experience negative affect, although positive affect appears to become less prevalent with age (see, e.g., Costa et al., 1987; Stacey & Gatz, 1991). The complexity of the relationship between emotion and age is evident in data from a recent study (Kunzmann, Little, & Smith, in press): Initial analyses indicated that negative affect was higher with age and positive affect lower, but once functional health was statistically controlled, negative affect was lower and positive affect was higher with increased age.

There is less evidence that the valence of affect changes with age when affect is measured longitudinally than when it is measured cross-sectionally. In

9-year and 14-year longitudinal studies (Costa et al., 1987; Stacey & Gatz, 1991), older people's negative affect did not change, nor did negative affect in very old samples change over 4 years (Kunzmann et al., in press). Costa et al. similarly reported no 9-year change in positive affect among older people, although Stacey and Gatz found a decrease in positive affect after 14 years for people ages 65 and older. Further, when Kunzmann et al. differentiated the very old from the oldest-old, they found a longitudinal decline in positive affect in the oldest group only.

Many uncertainties remain. The foregoing studies illustrate the dependence of some findings on the age range studied; "the aged" who are 60 to 69 years old clearly differ from those who are 80 and over. The study by Kunzmann et al. (in press) illustrates the critical position of health, yet the growing probability of poor health as age increases makes the statistical separation of age and health somewhat specious.

Affect Intensity

Given age-related changes in health, vigor, and nervous system functioning, it has seemed almost self-evident to some observers that the experienced intensity of emotion would also decline with age. A possible counteracting force, however, might come from the subjective and, possibly, self-constructing nature of the experience of intensity; felt intensity is certainly more than simple recognition of autonomic or motoric aspects of emotional arousal.

Here again, empirical evidence is very mixed. Comparisons of older and younger people's self-assessments of their experienced emotion showed that older people rated their own affects as being less intense and themselves as less moody, lower in sensation seeking, and more likely to experience a leveling of positive affect (Diener, Sandvik, & Larsen, 1985; Lawton et al., 1992). In other studies in which emotion was induced and rated on the spot, however, no age differences in intensity were reported (Levenson et al., 1991, in their relived-emotion task; Malatesta et al., 1987). Studies of observer-rated affective responses in real-life situations are clearly needed.

Emotion Regulation

The relationship of emotion to other psychological processes is acknowledged particularly well in the concept of emotion regulation, which may be defined as modification (by either active or passive means) of the eliciting conditions of emotion, its subjective experience, or the behavior associated with it in such a way as to optimize some personal goal. Regulation thus may be imposed on the neural, sensory, cognitive, behavioral, and environmental systems. Regulation in particular seems to be a skill that might change with age, as a result of learning, practice, selective reinforcement, and personal preference exercised over a life-time. Seen in this light, phenomena such as diminished autonomic arousal, less efficient facial responsiveness, and diminished intensity of affect could be inter-preted as resource-conservational moves appropriate to a time of life when bio-logical resources are diminishing. Some research has demonstrated that perceived control of emotion and affect regulation become stronger with age (Gross et al., 1997; Lawton et al., 1992).

THEORETICAL ACCOUNTS OF EMOTION IN ADULT DEVELOPMENT

In this section, I discuss four theories of emotion in adult development. They all share some recognition of the essential oneness of the psychological processes that play a role in emotion, and in particular reflect the fact that cognition is inseparable from emotion. All emphasize to some extent the individual's active shaping of emotion in the service of personal goals.

Control Theory of Late-Life Emotion

Schulz and Heckhausen (1998) have offered a control theory of late-life emotion. Their evolutionary theory is largely a cognitive-behavioral model in which achievement of primary control is the major goal at every life stage. Primary control is exerted when the environment and the self are managed actively to satisfy personal goals; in contrast, secondary control is directed toward changing thoughts and goal-seeking behaviors when primary control is not achievable. Within this framework, emotion is viewed as motivating and providing feedback on efforts toward establishing primary control. Affective goals are thus primarily means rather than end points. Specifically, counteracting negative emotions is a by-product of primary control, but diminished negative emotions and the experience of positive emotion are seen as a way of recharging "the motivational resources . . . so that other control-related goals might be pursued" (Schulz & Heckhausen, 1998, p. 192). In this framework, research demonstrating that emotion regulation becomes stronger in old age is seen as consistent with the age-related loss of primary control and compensatory efforts to preserve the self through secondary control.

Integration of Cognition and Emotion

The other three perspectives suggest late-maturing processes that are parallel to the successful striving modes of earlier life, modes that represent growth rather than retrogression. Labouvie-Vief, Hakim-Larson, DeVoe, and Schoeberlein (1989) maintained that cognitive and affective processes develop separately, and that development of both kinds of processes continues in successive stages throughout the total life span, at each step building on earlier developmental phases. The final stage of the maturing process in late middle age is characterized by complete integration of cognitive and affective functions; that is, each function has free expression within the constraints of higher-level integration with the self. In earlier phases, either cognition and emotion are incompletely controlled by the self or they are externally controlled. The achieved integration of cognitive and affective functions in later life facilitates both experienced emotion and social behaviors in ways that are more complex and realistic, but still fulfilling.

Although Labouvie-Vief's perspective puts cognitive function developmentally ahead of affect, her most mature stage reflects total equality—indeed, unity—of the two. Blanchard-Fields (1998) has also been concerned with the relationship between these spheres over the life span and with their contribution to social judgment. Older people, more than younger people, appear to utilize emotion-based judgments in social decision making, a propensity that she sees as adaptive and reflective of an increased ability to deal with uncertainty and complexity in social relationships during later life. This ability to integrate emotion and cognition gives greater range for elders to use accommodative strategies, when direct problem solving (assimilation) would prove to be a suboptimal strategy and particularly when social goals may be increasingly salient. One result is that emotion may act as an intrusive element in social decisions among developmentally immature people but as a source of differentiation among social situations for mature people.

Carstensen's socioemotional selectivity theory (1995) also focuses on emotion and cognition in the domain of social relationships. In her work, she has searched for an explanation of the decline of social activity with age, which she sees as reflecting changes in goals with age. The young value the knowledge-acquisition functions of social relationships, but as people grow older, they move toward valuing more highly the emotional rewards of social relationships. As time goes on, the present is composed more and more of short-term emotional social rewards. Social choices are made increasingly selectively with these rewards in mind, and with less emphasis on the novelty and stimulation of new social relationships. Thus, later life is characterized not by either diminution of affect or lowered intensity of affect, but rather by greater selectivity in the objects or goals toward which emotion regulation is directed.

CONCLUSION

Although evidence is sketchy now, it seems likely that age-related cognitive decline has an analogue in the domain of emotion at the levels most closely associated with the biological substratum (i.e., autonomic and facial-expressive aspects of emotion). At more complex levels of affective function, there is compelling evidence that older people continue to direct their own affective lives as they do other sectors of their lives. There is little evidence of affective loss at the subjective level, although theories differ in whether they attribute this continued high level of functioning to a new level of maturity, regulation of affect, or compensatory behavior.

Older people perceive themselves as being more effective than they were earlier in their lives in a variety of types of emotion regulation. However, because regulation has been operationalized differently in different studies, understanding of the actual processes of regulation has not been very well advanced. Until these processes are specified better and distinguished in terms of the relative contributions of passive, or accommodative, versus proactive management practices to the forms of emotion regulation, we will lack knowledge regarding a central component of the developmental psychology of affect.

Recent research on age and emotion thus contradicts stereotypes of older people as affectively blunted and particularly as depressed by illness and losses. The knowledge that older people actively construct their own socially meaningful and productive emotional worlds adds to the picture of old age as a time of continuing independence and fulfillment. Like everyone else, they experience good and bad moods, but in no way do they feel selectively powerless or defeated. Because they have purposefully achieved emotional maturity, they clearly can teach us lessons that are applicable to human development at any stage.

Theorists must find ways to incorporate better the concept of quality of life into their structural models of emotion. The dynamics of both human development and the ecology of affect now require elaboration so that we may better understand how the mix of affect states in older people can be optimized—through self-help efforts of older people themselves, interventions undertaken by professionals, and social policy.

Recommended Reading

Cumming, E., & Henry, W.E. (1961). *Growing old: The process of disengagement.* New York: Basic Books.

Frederickson, B.L., & Carstensen, L.L. (1990). Choosing a social partner: How old age and anticipated endings make people more selective. *Psychology and Aging, 5,* 335–347.

Magai, C., & McFadden, S.H. (Eds.). (1996). *Handbook of emotion, adult development, and aging.* San Diego: Academic Press.

Schaie, K.W., & Lawton, M.P. (Eds.). (1998). *Annual review of gerontology and geriatrics: Vol. 17. Emphasis on emotion and adult development.* New York: Springer.

Note

1. With deep sadness, we regret to report that M. Powell Lawton passed away on January 29, 2001.

References

Blanchard-Fields, F. (1998). The role of emotion in social cognition across the life span. In K.W. Schaie & M.P. Lawton (Eds.), *Annual review of gerontology and geriatrics: Vol. 17. Emphasis on emotion and adult development* (pp. 238–265). New York: Springer.

Carstensen, L.L. (1995). Evidence for a life-span theory of socioemotional selectivity. *Current Directions in Psychological Science, 4,* 151–156.

Carstensen, L.L., & Turk-Charles, S. (1994). The salience of emotion across the adult life span. *Psychology and Aging, 9,* 259–264.

Costa, T., Jr., Zonderman, A.B., McCrae, R., Cornoni-Huntley, J., Locke, B.Z., & Barbano, H.E. (1987). Longitudinal analyses of psychological well-being in a national sample: Stability of mean levels. *Journal of Gerontology, 42,* 50–55.

Diener, E., Sandvik, E., & Larsen, R.J. (1985). Age and sex effects for emotional intensity. *Developmental Psychology, 21,* 542–546.

Gross, J.J., Carstensen, L.L., Pasupathi, M., Tsai, J., Skorpen, C.G., & Hsu, A.Y.C. (1997). Emotion and aging: Experience, expression, and control. *Psychology and Aging, 12,* 590–599.

Kunzmann, V., Little, T.D., & Smith, J. (in press). Is subjective well-being stable in old age? *Psychology and Aging.*

Labouvie-Vief, G., Hakim-Larson, J., DeVoe, M., & Schoeberlein, S. (1989). Emotions and self-regulation: A lifespan view. *Human Development, 32 ,* 279–299.

Lawton, M.P., Kleban, M.H., Rajagopal, D., & Dean, J. (1992). The dimensions of affective experience in three age groups. *Psychology and Aging, 7,* 171–184.

Levenson, R.W., Carstensen, L.L., Friesen, W.V., & Ekman, P. (1991). Emotion, physiology, and expression in old age. *Psychology and Aging, 6,* 28–35.

Malatesta, C.Z., Izard, C.E., Culver, C., & Nicolich, M. (1987). Emotion communication skills in young, middle-aged and older women. *Psychology and Aging, 2,* 193–203.

Malatesta, C.Z., & Kalnok, M. (1984). Emotional experience in younger and older adults. *Journal of Gerontology, 39,* 301–308.

Schulz, R., & Heckhausen, J. (1998). Emotion and control: A life span perspective. In K.W. Schaie & M.P. Lawton (Eds.), *Annual review of gerontology and geriatrics: Vol. 17. Emphasis on emotion and adult development* (pp. 185–205). New York: Springer.

Stacey, C.A., & Gatz, M. (1991). Cross-sectional age differences and longitudinal change on the Bradburn Affect Balance Scale. *Journal of Gerontology: Psychological Sciences, 46,* P76–P78.

Critical Thinking Questions

1. Compared to younger adults, older adults show reduced autonomic activity in response to emotional stimuli. They report the same subjective experience of this same emotional experience. How might these two findings be reconciled? Why is older age related to less physiological reactivity but not to differences in emotional experience?

2. Given the relationship between health and emotion, how should issues of health be included, or not, in studies examining age differences in emotional processes.

3. How does the finding that younger people view emotions as more central to their life reconcile with the theories of aging reviewed in this paper?

This article has been reprinted as it originally appeared in *Current Directions in Psychological Science*. Citation information for this article as originally published appears above.

Age and Emotion in Adulthood

Daniel K. Mroczek[1]

Department of Psychology, Fordham University, New York, New York

Abstract

Evidence suggests that positive affect rises from youth through young and then older adulthood, but may decline after one's mid-70s. Negative affect appears to decrease steadily from early adulthood to older adulthood, but this decline may taper off in the oldest years. The relationship between age and affect in adulthood is further complicated by the effects of moderators, such as extraversion and marital status. Despite these complexities, recent empirical studies and current theory have furthered the understanding of age and affect in adulthood, although important questions remain.

Keywords

adult development; affect; aging; emotion; well-being

What is the relationship between age and emotion over the adult life span? Affect plays a large role in the unfolding of many phenomena that occur in early human development, such as attachment to caregivers. It is thus germane to ask how emotion is manifested in later psychological development, especially in adulthood. Further, the question is important for researchers trying to understand age-related changes in psychological well-being over the life span, as most scholars agree that affect is one of the main cornerstones of well-being. Finally, much current thought on psychological development over the life span has centered on how people's emotions change over time (Carstensen, 1995; Carstensen, Isaacowitz, & Turk-Charles, 1999; Labouvie-Vief & DeVoe, 1991). In this article, I describe recent research on the association between age and affect.

AGE AND AFFECT

Early investigations of how affect changes across the life span yielded mixed results. By the mid-1990s, many scholars had completed studies of age and emotion in adulthood, yet the collective body of literature did not draw a consistent picture with regard to either positive or negative affect (Ferring & Filipp, 1995; Malatesta & Kalnok, 1984; Rossi & Rossi, 1990; Ryff, 1989; Smith & Baltes, 1993). Some studies found that the frequency of positive and negative affect increases with age, others documented decreases in the frequency of affect with increasing age, and still others reported no association at all. Recently, Kolarz and I attempted to resolve some of these inconsistencies by addressing the question using a large national sample that would yield precise estimates of the relationship between age and affect (Mroczek & Kolarz, 1998). After analyzing data from the Midlife in the United States (MIDUS) survey, sponsored by the MacArthur Foundation Research Network on Successful Midlife Development, we concluded that older adults tend to report experiencing more positive affect and less negative affect than younger adults. Additionally, the effect for positive affect was nonlinear—it increased at an accelerating rate. The MIDUS respondents ranged in age from 25 to 74, and it would be risky to extrapolate the findings to adults who are even older. Nonetheless, over this 50-year age range, we documented discernible, but small, changes in the frequency of both positive and negative affect. Regression lines depicting these associations are displayed in Figure 1.

Further, the relationships between age and affect endured after we statistically controlled for a host of variables that are known to influence either positive or negative affect, and thus might have explained away the associations we found. Positive affect was higher for men than for women, for married people than for single people, for extraverts than for introverts, and for people in good physical health than for those in poor health; also, positive affect was inversely related to stress and neuroticism. Negative affect was higher for women than for men, for unmarried people than for married people, for individuals with high scores on measures of neuroticism than for those with low scores, and for people experiencing stress than for those with relatively stress-free lives; negative affect was lower among extraverts than among introverts and among people in good physical health than among those in poor health. Over and above the effects of this wide array of influences, older people reported more positive and less negative affect than those at midlife, who in turn expressed more positive and less negative affect than the youngest members of the sample.

This is an optimistic finding, suggesting that as people move away from the trials and vicissitudes of youth, they may increasingly experience a more pleasant balance of affect, at least up until their mid-70s. Of course, this statement rests upon the assumption that the association is an effect of the aging process and not a cohort effect (i.e., not an effect due to circumstances peculiar to this particular birth cohort). It is also generalizable only to the U.S. population from which the MIDUS sample was drawn. Nevertheless, it does fit with a body of findings collectively known as the *paradox of well-being* (Filipp, 1996; Staudinger, Fleeson, & Baltes, 1999)—the fact that the documented correlation between objective rigors and subjective happiness is small. The paradox is relevant to research on age and

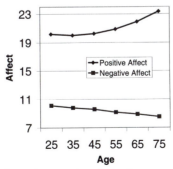

Fig. 1. Plotted regression lines showing the relation between positive affect and age (diamonds) and negative affect and age (squares). Positive and negative affect scores have a possible range of 6 to 30, with higher scores indicating higher levels of affect. The lines are based on the following equations: positive affect $= 22.38 + \text{age}(-.14) + \text{age}^2(.002)$; negative affect $= 10.94 + \text{age}(-.03)$. Adapted from Mroczek and Kolarz (1998).

well-being, for despite the cruelties of aging (e.g., worsening physical health, deaths of old friends and relatives), older adults do not report concomitant decreases in the emotional aspects of well-being.

AFFECT AMONG THE OLDEST ADULTS

No MIDUS participant was older than 74 at the time of assessment, so it is necessary to look elsewhere for data regarding the level of affect among the oldest old. Recent reports have indicated that positive affect may drop during the oldest years. In the Berlin Aging Study, positive affect declined by as much as half a standard deviation across several age categories ranging from 70–75 to 95–100 (Smith, Fleeson, Geiselmann, Settersten, & Kunzman, 1999). The same study also documented a correlation of −.22 between age and positive affect over the age range from 70 to 100 years, in contrast to an association of .10 over the age range of the MIDUS survey (25–74). The decline in positive affect in the Berlin sample prevailed even when many other factors, including nearly all those utilized in the MIDUS study, were statistically controlled (Isaacowitz & Smith, 2000).

Combining the MIDUS and Berlin results suggests that the relationship between positive affect and age is curvilinear, with frequency reports of this emotion rising from young adulthood through midlife before peaking in the earlier years of older adulthood, and then diminishing during the oldest years, when health deficits and other problems become more severe. This educated guess regarding the typical path of positive affect over the adult years is not supported by all the evidence, as one study documented a more consistent decline in positive affect, with no increase in midlife, in a sample ranging in age from 19 to 92 (Rossi & Rossi, 1990). Nevertheless, the combination of two of the largest samples brought to bear on the question of the relation between age and affect (MIDUS and Berlin) points toward a curvilinear association between age and positive affect in adulthood. Nonlinearity is likely the root of the confusion that has at times obfuscated the relationship between age and positive affect.

Less confusion surrounds the association between age and negative affect. Many investigators have reported declines in negative affect over wide age ranges (e.g., Isaacowitz & Smith, 2000; Mroczek & Kolarz, 1998; Rossi & Rossi, 1990). However, at least one study reported no relationship between age and negative affect among the oldest old (Smith et al., 1999). Thus, it is possible that negative emotion may steadily decrease through adulthood, but then the decline may taper off in the oldest years.

Again, this is a generally optimistic message, and it resonates with one of the most significant lessons of late-20th-century gerontology, namely, that gains as well as losses characterize the human aging process (Baltes & Baltes, 1990). Yet this very upbeat portrait may not characterize the very oldest members of the population. Further, it is perhaps simplistic to state that people get happier as they age (Isaacowitz & Smith, 2000). Expressing a more subtle view, Carstensen, Pasupathi, Mayr, and Nesselroade (2000) have suggested that older adults and others who are reaching end points in life may experience mixed and complex emotions. They use the term "poignancy" to describe the simultaneous experience of positive and negative affect, as well as the capacity of older adults (and others facing endings) to feel emotions in a more complex manner than younger adults. Other researchers have offered similar arguments, stating that well-being, especially among older adults, adds up to more than a maximization of positive and a minimization of negative affect (Ryff, 1989). Ultimately, the story of emotion and age may focus on greater complexity of affect in later life, and less on simple ups and downs in the frequency of positive and negative emotion.

MODERATORS OF THE AGE-AFFECT RELATIONSHIP

Adult emotional development is complex in other ways as well, for certain combinations of variables are associated with heightened or diminished levels of affect (Mroczek & Kolarz, 1998). Such interaction, or moderator, effects provide another piece of the age-affect story. For example, the analysis of positive affect in the MIDUS study showed an interaction between age and extraversion, but only among men. Specifically, the association between age and positive affect was weaker among extraverted men and stronger among introverted men. Men who were extraverted tended to have high positive affect, regardless of their age. Age made more of a difference in predicting positive affect among introverted men: Older introverted men reported higher positive affect than younger introverted men. Essentially, the effect of age was magnified if a man was an introvert, but was lessened if he was an extravert.

The analysis of negative affect in the MIDUS sample showed an interaction between age and marriage, again only for men (Mroczek & Kolarz, 1998). Among married men, there was a steep decline in negative affect from age 25 to age 74. Unmarried men, in contrast, reported high negative affect across the full age range. Basically, young men, married or not, admitted high levels of negative affect. However, midlife and older men (especially the latter) reported much less negative affect if they were married. This could be a cohort effect, but it could also indicate that one of the benefits of marriage for men is that it helps to diminish negative emotion once middle and older age arrive.

Earlier, I noted that the effects of age on the frequency of positive and negative affect are small. However, regardless of the size of these effects, age also appears to interact with other variables in determining the frequency of emotion.

CONCLUSION

Several research questions in the area of adult emotion require answers. First, although most studies have reported a decline in negative affect (with perhaps an upturn in very late life), many investigators are in disagreement about the trajectory of positive affect. It is clear that future research must resolve this issue by studying people across a broad range of ages, from the youngest adults to the oldest old. Second, and more important, research needs to ascertain whether these age differences in affect are due to aging or cohort effects. To fully answer this question, investigators will need to conduct longitudinal studies, and in particular, longitudinal studies that also contain a broad cross-section of age cohorts.

Such studies (cross-sequential designs) would make it possible to tease apart how much change in affect is due to cohort influences, and how much is due to the effects of aging regardless of cohort membership.

Fortunately, there are thoughtful theories of life-span emotional development that can guide investigators in answering these questions (e.g., Baltes & Baltes, 1990; Carstensen et al., 1999; Labouvie-Vief & DeVoe, 1991). As a result of these theories and the empirical studies discussed in this article, psychologists now have a stronger grasp than ever before on the issues surrounding the relationship between age and emotion over the adult portion of the life span. The coming years will bring an even firmer understanding.

Recommended Reading

Carstensen, L.L., Isaacowitz, D.M., & Turk-Charles, S. (1999). (See References)
Filipp, S.-H. (1996). (See References)
Labouvie-Vief, G., & DeVoe, M. (1991). (See References)
Mroczek, D.K., & Kolarz, C.M. (1998). (See References)
Smith, J., Fleeson, W., Geiselmann, B., Settersten, R.A., & Kunzman, U. (1999). (See References)

Acknowledgments—The author acknowledges the support of the John D. and Catherine T. MacArthur Foundation Research Network on Successful Midlife Development and the National Institute on Aging (R03-AG16054).

Note

1. Address correspondence to Dan Mroczek, Fordham University, Department of Psychology, Dealy Hall, Bronx, NY 10458-5198; e-mail: mroczek@ fordham.edu.

References

Baltes, P.B., & Baltes, M.M. (1990). Psychological perspectives on successful aging: The model of selective optimization with compensation. In P.B. Baltes & M.M. Baltes (Eds.), *Successful aging: Perspectives from the behavioral sciences* (pp. 1–34). Cambridge, England: Cambridge University Press.

Carstensen, L.L. (1995). Evidence for a life-span theory of socioemotional selectivity. *Current Directions in Psychological Science, 4*, 151–155.

Carstensen, L.L., Isaacowitz, D.M., & Turk-Charles, S. (1999). Taking time seriously: A theory of socioemotional selectivity. *American Psychologist, 54*, 165–181.

Carstensen, L.L., Pasupathi, M., Mayr, U., & Nesselroade, J.R. (2000). Emotional experience in everyday life across the adult life span. *Journal of Personality and Social Psychology, 79*, 644–655.

Ferring, D., & Filipp, S.-H. (1995). The structure of subjective well-being in the elderly: A test of different models by structural equation modeling. *European Journal of Psychological Assessment, 11*, 32.

Filipp, S.-H. (1996). Motivation and emotion. In J.E. Birren & K.W. Schaie (Eds.), *Handbook of the psychology of aging* (4th ed., pp. 218–235). San Diego: Academic Press.

Isaacowitz, D.M., & Smith, J. (2000). *Positive and negative affect in very old age: A reply to Mroczek & Kolarz (1998).* Unpublished manuscript, Max Planck Institute for Human Development, Berlin, Germany.

Labouvie-Vief, G., & DeVoe, M. (1991). Emotional regulation in adulthood and later life: A developmental view. In K.W. Schaie (Ed.), *Annual review of gerontology and geriatrics* (pp. 172–194). New York: Springer.

Malatesta, C.Z., & Kalnok, M. (1984). Emotional experience in younger and older adults. *Journal of Gerontology, 39*, 301–308.

Mroczek, D.K., & Kolarz, C.M. (1998). The effect of age on positive and negative affect: A developmental perspective on happiness. *Journal of Personality and Social Psychology, 75*, 1333–1349.

Rossi, A.S., & Rossi, P.H. (1990). *Of human bonding: Parent-child relations across the life course.* New York: Aldine de Gruyter.

Ryff, C.D. (1989). Happiness is everything, or is it? Explorations on the meaning of psychological well-being. *Journal of Personality and Social Psychology, 57*, 1069–1081.

Smith, J., & Baltes, P.B. (1993). Differential psychological aging: Profiles of the old and very old. *Ageing and Society, 13*, 551–587.

Smith, J., Fleeson, W., Geiselmann, B., Settersten, R.A., & Kunzman, U. (1999). Sources of well-being in very old age. In P.B. Baltes & K.U. Mayer (Eds.), *The Berlin Aging Study: Aging from 70 to 100* (pp. 450–471). Cambridge, En-gland: Cambridge University Press.

Staudinger, U.M., Fleeson, W., & Baltes, P.B. (1999). Predictors of subjective physical health and global well-being: Similarities between the United States and Germany. *Journal of Personality and Social Psychology, 79*, 305–319.

Critical Thinking Questions

1. Mroczek and Kolarz (1998) found that positive affect was higher among older adults than younger adults in a sample ranging from 25 to 74 years-old. What could be some reasons for this age-related pattern?

2. How do patterns of positive and negative affect vary for people aged 70 to 100?

3. What role does personality have in the study of age differences in positive and negative affect?

This article has been reprinted as it originally appeared in *Current Directions in Psychological Science*. Citation information for this article as originally published appears above.

Adaptation and the Set-Point Model of Subjective Well-Being: Does Happiness Change After Major Life Events?

Richard E. Lucas[1]
Michigan State University and German Institute for Economic Research, Berlin

Abstract

Hedonic adaptation refers to the process by which individuals return to baseline levels of happiness following a change in life circumstances. Dominant models of subjective well-being (SWB) suggest that people can adapt to almost any life event and that happiness levels fluctuate around a biologically determined set point that rarely changes. Recent evidence from large-scale panel studies challenges aspects of this conclusion. Although inborn factors certainly matter and some adaptation does occur, events such as divorce, death of a spouse, unemployment, and disability are associated with lasting changes in SWB. These recent studies also show that there are considerable individual differences in the extent to which people adapt. Thus, happiness levels do change, and adaptation is not inevitable.

Keywords

happiness; subjective well-being; adaptation; set-point theory

People's greatest hopes and fears often center on the possible occurrence of rare but important life events. People may dread the possibility of losing a loved one or becoming disabled, and they may go to great lengths to find true love or to increase their chances of winning the lottery. In many cases, people strive to attain or avoid these outcomes because of the outcomes' presumed effect on happiness. But do these major life events really affect long-term levels of subjective well-being (SWB)? Dominant models of SWB suggest that after experiencing major life events, people inevitably adapt. More specifically, set-point theorists posit that inborn personality factors cause an inevitable return to genetically determined happiness set points. However, recent evidence from large-scale longitudinal studies challenges some of the stronger conclusions from these models.

ADAPTATION RESEARCH AND THEORY

Although the thought that levels of happiness cannot change may distress some people, researchers believe that adaptation processes serve important functions (Frederick & Loewenstein, 1999). For one thing, these processes protect people from potentially dangerous psychological and physiological consequences of prolonged emotional states. In addition, because adaptation processes allow unchanging stimuli to fade into the attentional background, these processes ensure that change in the environment receives extra attention. Attention to environmental change is advantageous because threats that have existed for prolonged periods of time are likely to be less dangerous than novel threats. Similarly, because rewards that have persisted are less likely to disappear quickly than are novel rewards, it will often be advantageous to attend and react more strongly to these novel rewards. Finally, by reducing emotional reactions over time, adaptation processes allow individuals to disengage from goals that have little chance of success. Thus, adaptation can be beneficial, and some amount of adaptation to life circumstances surely occurs.

Yet many questions about the strength and ubiquity of adaptation effects remain, partly because of the types of evidence that have been used to support adaptation theories. In many cases, adaptation is not directly observed. Instead, it must be inferred from indirect evidence. For instance, psychologists often cite the low correlation between happiness and life circumstances as evidence for adaptation effects. Factors such as income, age, health, marital status, and number of friends account for only a small percentage of the variance in SWB (Diener, Suh, Lucas, & Smith, 1999). One explanation that has been offered for this counterintuitive finding is that these factors initially have an impact but that people adapt over time. However, the weak associations between life circumstances and SWB themselves provide only suggestive evidence for this explanation.

Additional indirect support for the set-point model comes from research that takes a personality perspective on SWB. Three pieces of evidence are relevant (Lucas, in press-b). First, SWB exhibits moderate stability even over very long periods of time and even in the face of changing life circumstances. Recent reviews suggest that approximately 30 to 40% of the variance in life-satisfaction measures is stable over periods as long as 20 years. Second, a number of studies have shown that well-being variables are about 40 to 50% heritable. These heritability estimates appear to be even higher (about 80%) for long-term levels of happiness (Lykken & Tellegen, 1996). Finally, personality variables like extroversion and neuroticism are relatively strong predictors of happiness, at least when compared to the predictive power of external factors. The explanation for this set of findings is that events can influence short-term levels of happiness, but personality-based adaptation processes inevitably move people back to their genetically determined set point after a relatively short period of time.

More direct evidence for hedonic adaptation comes from studies that examine the well-being of individuals who have experienced important life events. However, even these studies can be somewhat equivocal. For instance, one of the most famous studies is that of Brickman, Coates, and Janoff-Bulman (1978) comparing lottery winners and patients with spinal-cord injuries to people in a control group. Brickman et al. showed that lottery winners were not significantly happier than the control-group participants and that individuals with spinal-cord injuries "did not appear nearly as unhappy as might be expected" (p. 921). This study appears to show adaptation to even the most extreme events imaginable. What is often not mentioned, however, is that although the participants with spinal-cord injuries were above neutral on the happiness scale (which is what led Brickman et al. to conclude that they were happier than might be expected), they were significantly less happy than the people in the control group, and the difference between the groups was actually quite large. Individuals with spinal-cord injuries were more than three quarters of a standard deviation below the mean of the control group. This means that the average participant from the control group was happier than approximately 78% of participants with spinal-cord injuries. This result has now been replicated quite often—most existing studies show relatively large differences between individuals with spinal-cord injuries and healthy participants in control groups (Dijkers, 1997).

In addition to problems that result from the interpretation of effect sizes, methodological limitations restrict the conclusions that can be drawn from many existing studies of adaptation. Most studies are not longitudinal, and even fewer are prospective (though there are some notable exceptions; see e.g., Bonanno, 2004; Caspi et al., 2003). Because participants' pre-event levels of SWB are not known, it is always possible that individuals who experienced an event were more or less happy than average before the event occurred. Certain people may be predisposed to experience life events, and these predisposing factors may be responsible for their happiness levels being lower than average. For instance, in a review of the literature examining the well-being of children who had lost limbs from various causes, Tyc (1992) suggested that those who lost limbs due to accidents tended to have higher levels of premorbid psychological disorders than did those who lost limbs due to disease. Thus, simply comparing the well-being of children who lost limbs to those who did not might overestimate the effect of the injury. Psychologists have demonstrated that level of happiness predicts the occurrence of a variety of events and outcomes (Lyubomirsky, King, & Diener, 2005), and therefore, studies that compare individuals who have experienced a particular event with those who have not but that do not take into account previous happiness level must be interpreted cautiously.

A second methodological concern relates to what are known as demand characteristics. When researchers recruit participants specifically because they have experienced a given life event, participants may over- or underreport SWB. These reports may occur because people believe the life event should have an impact, because they want to appear well-adjusted, or simply because the context of the study makes the event more salient. For instance, Smith, Schwarz, Roberts, and Ubel (2006) showed that patients with Parkinson's disease reported lower life satisfaction when the study instructions indicated that Parkinson's disease was a focus than when the instructions indicated that the study focused on the general population.

USING LARGE-SCALE PANEL STUDIES TO ASSESS ADAPTATION TO LIFE EVENTS

Recently, my colleagues and I have turned to archival data analysis using large, nationally representative panel studies to address questions about adaptation to life events. These studies have a number of advantages over alternative designs. First, they are prospective, which means that pre-event levels of SWB are known. Second, they are longitudinal, which means that change over time can be accurately modeled. Third, very large samples are often involved, which means that even rare events are sampled. Finally, because designers of these studies often recruit nationally representative samples, and because the questionnaires often focus on a variety of issues, demand characteristics are unlikely to have much of an effect.

We have used two such panel studies—the German Socioeconomic Panel Study (GSOEP) and the British Household Panel Study (BHPS)—to examine the amount of adaptation that occurs following major life events. The GSOEP includes almost 40,000 individuals living in Germany who have been assessed yearly for up to 21 years. The BHPS includes more than 27,000 individuals living in Great Britain who have been assessed yearly for up to 14 years. We have used these data sets to examine the extent to which people adapt to events such as marital transitions (Lucas, 2005; Lucas, Clark, Georgellis, & Diener, 2003), bouts of unemployment (Lucas, Clark, Georgellis, & Diener, 2004), and the onset of a disability (Lucas, in press-a). At least three important findings have emerged (see Diener, Lucas, & Scollon, 2006, for a more detailed review).

First, long-term levels of SWB do change, and adaptation is not inevitable. In fact, these studies show that there is no single answer to the question of whether people adapt to life events. Instead, the pattern of adaptation varies across different events. Figure 1 shows the average within-person trajectories for life satisfaction before and after various life events. These data show that although the average person adapts to marriage (and this adaptation tends to occur within just a couple of years; Lucas et al., 2003), adaptation to other events is often very slow or incomplete. Widows and widowers return very close (within about .15 points) to the level of life satisfaction that they reported before their spouse died, but this process of adaptation takes approximately 7 years (Lucas et al., 2003). Individuals who get divorced or experience unemployment report what appear to be permanent changes in life satisfaction following these events (Lucas, 2005; Lucas et al., 2004). Furthermore, these changes can sometimes be very large. Individuals who acquire a severe disability report life-satisfaction levels that are more than a full standard deviation below their baseline levels, and these levels do not appear to rebound over time (Lucas, in press-a).

A second important finding is that, for all events we have studied, there are large individual differences in the amount of adaptation that occurs. To demonstrate, it is possible to calculate the variability in within-person change that occurs

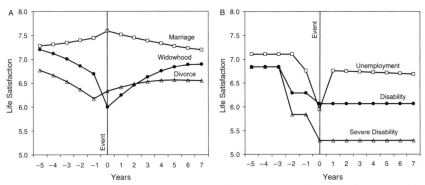

Fig. 1. Average within-person trajectories for life satisfaction before and after various life events. Panel A shows reaction and adaptation to marriage, death of a spouse, and divorce. Panel B shows reaction and adaptation to unemployment and the onset of varying degrees of disability. Adapted from Lucas (2005), Lucas (in press-a), Lucas, Clark, Georgellis, and Diener (2003), and Lucas, Clark, Georgellis, and Diener (2007).

before and after the event. In the case of marriage, very little change occurs on average. However, the standard deviation for the amount of change that occurs was approximately 1.0 (for responses derived from an 11-point scale). This means that approximately 30% of participants reported lasting changes in satisfaction of between a half and a full point, and an additional 32% reported lasting changes of more than a full point. These effects are quite large in relation to the amount of variance that exists in baseline levels of well-being. A participant who began the study with an average level of life satisfaction but experienced a change that was one standard deviation above the mean change would move to the 74th percentile overall in level of life satisfaction. Similarly, someone who experienced a change that was one standard deviation below the mean would move to the 26th percentile overall. These individual differences in reaction and adaptation likely result both from variability in the nature of the event (some marriages are better than others) and from variability in people's reactions to similar events. In either case, the average trajectory does not tell the whole story about the potential for life events to have a major impact on people's long-term levels of SWB.

A third major finding is that people who will eventually experience a major life event often differ from people who will not, even before the event occurs. Therefore prospective longitudinal studies are necessary to separate pre-existing differences from longitudinal change. For instance, cross-sectional studies have consistently shown that married people are happier than single, divorced, or widowed people; yet our studies showed that marriage was not associated with lasting increases in happiness. Instead, people who eventually married were happier than average (or at least happier than those who married and then divorced) even more than 5 years before the marriage (Lucas, 2005; Lucas et al., 2003). People who eventually divorced, on the other hand, started out with lower levels of well-being than those who did not divorce, and they reported lasting changes following this event. These findings are illustrated in Figure 2, in which levels of life satisfaction before and after marriage are plotted for participants who eventually divorced and for those who stayed married. These results suggest that about half of the difference that is typically found between married and divorced individuals in cross-sectional studies is the result of selection effects, and half is the result of lasting changes that follow divorce.

FUTURE DIRECTIONS

Although large-scale, nationally representative panel studies are an important tool for answering questions about adaptation, they are not without limitations. The set of psychological variables that has been assessed thus far is relatively limited. This lack of information about psychological characteristics means that moderators and process variables cannot be examined. Future research on adaptation should focus on achieving the following three goals.

First, sophisticated methodologies to assess adaptation to a wide variety of events must be used, so that researchers can develop a clear picture of the events to which people can and cannot adapt. As these events are catalogued, hypotheses about the characteristics that distinguish these events can be formulated and

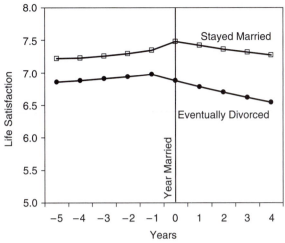

Fig. 2. Trajectories of life satisfaction before and after marriage for individuals who remain married and those who eventually divorce. Adapted from Lucas (2005).

tested. For instance, Frederick and Loewenstein (1999) suggested that people may be able to adapt to one-time events like the loss of a spouse or the onset of an unchanging medical condition but may be less able to adapt to conditions that change or worsen over time.

A second goal is that programmatic research should lead to greater insight into the processes that underlie hedonic adaptation. Adaptation may result from physiological processes that reduce emotional reactivity to constant stimuli, or it could result from psychological processes that change the way people think about events that have occurred in their lives. For instance, adaptation effects may emerge when people disengage from goals that have become unattainable and set new goals toward which they can strive, or it may occur as people develop strengths or acquire new skills that enable them to deal more effectively with less-than-ideal life circumstances.

A third research goal is to clarify the individual-level characteristics that promote or prevent adaptation. Our studies (Lucas, 2005, in press-a; Lucas et al., 2003, 2004) show that there are considerable individual differences in the amount of adaptation that occurs. One fruitful avenue for understanding these individual differences is to look for personality variables that moderate adaptation effects over time. For instance, Bonanno and colleagues have identified distinct trajectories of distress following major traumatic life events like the loss of a spouse or a child (Bonanno, 2004). Notably, characteristics including hardiness, self-enhancement, and positive emotions have been shown to be associated with the most resilient pattern of reactions. In addition, Caspi and colleagues have shown that interactions between stressful life events and specific genes predict the onset of depression (Caspi et al., 2003). It is possible that similar gene-by-environment interactions would also affect reaction and adaptation to life events. Future research must identify additional demographic, social, and personality factors that promote positive reactions to major life events.

147

IS THERE A HAPPINESS SET POINT?

The studies reviewed in this paper do not refute the set-point model of happiness. Instead, they put the empirical findings that have emerged from that model in a broader context. What does it mean to an individual that happiness is 50% or even 80% heritable? What does it mean that 35% of the variance in well-being is stable over time? Do these empirical facts mean that long-term levels of happiness do not change? The results reviewed in this paper show that the answer to this question is no. They confirm that although happiness levels are moderately stable over time, this stability does not preclude large and lasting changes. Happiness levels do change, adaptation is not inevitable, and life events do matter.

Recommended Reading

Bonanno, G. (2004). (See References)
Diener, E., Lucas, R.E., & Scollon, C.N. (2006). (See References)
Frederick, S., & Loewenstein, G. (1999). (See References)

Note

1. Address correspondence to Richard E. Lucas, Department of Psychology, Michigan State University, East Lansing, MI 48823; e-mail: lucasri@msu.edu.

References

Bonanno, G.A. (2004). Loss, trauma, and human resilience: Have we underestimated the human capacity to thrive after extremely aversive events? *American Psychologist, 59,* 20–28.

Brickman, P., Coates, D., & Janoff-Bulman, R. (1978). Lottery winners and accident victims: Is happiness relative? *Journal of Personality & Social Psychology, 36,* 917–927.

Caspi, A., Sugden, K., Moffitt, T.E., Taylor, A., Craig, I.W., Harrington, H., et al. (2003). Influence of life stress on depression: Moderation by a polymorphism in the 5-HTT gene. *Science, 301,* 386–389.

Diener, E., Lucas, R.E., & Scollon, C. (2006). Beyond the hedonic treadmill: Revising the adaptation theory of well-being. *American Psychologist, 61,* 305–314.

Diener, E., Suh, E.M., Lucas, R.E., & Smith, H.L. (1999). Subjective well-being: Three decades of progress. *Psychological Bulletin, 125,* 276–302.

Dijkers, M. (1997). Quality of life after spinal cord injury: A meta analysis of the effects of disablement components. *Spinal Cord, 35,* 829–840.

Frederick, S., & Loewenstein, G. (1999). Hedonic adaptation. In D. Kahneman, E. Diener, & N. Schwarz (Eds.), *Well-being: The foundations of hedonic psychology* (pp. 302–329). New York: Sage.

Lucas, R.E. (2005). Time does not heal all wounds: A longitudinal study of reaction and adaptation to divorce. *Psychological Science, 16,* 945–950.

Lucas, R.E. (in press-a). Long-term disability is associated with lasting changes in subjective well-being: Evidence from two nationally representative longitudinal studies. *Journal of Personality and Social Psychology.*

Lucas, R.E. (in press-b). Personality and subjective well-being. In M. Eid & R.J. Larsen (Eds.), *The science of subjective well-being.* New York: Guilford.

Lucas, R.E., Clark, A.E., Georgellis, Y., & Diener, E. (2003). Reexamining adaptation and the set point model of happiness: Reactions to changes in marital status. *Journal of Personality & Social Psychology, 84,* 527–539.

Lucas, R.E., Clark, A.E., Georgellis, Y., & Diener, E. (2004). Unemployment alters the set point for life satisfaction. *Psychological Science, 15,* 8–13.

Lykken, D., & Tellegen, A. (1996). Happiness is a stochastic phenomenon. *Psychological Science, 7*, 186–189.

Lyubomirsky, S., King, L., & Diener, E. (2005). The benefits of frequent positive affect: Does happiness lead to success? *Psychological Bulletin, 131*, 803–855.

Smith, D.M., Schwarz, N., Roberts, T.R., & Ubel, P.A. (2006). Why are you calling me? How study introductions change response patterns. *Quality of Life Research, 15*, 621–630.

Tyc, V.L. (1992). Psychosocial adaptation of children and adolescents with limb deficiencies: A review. *Clinical Psychology Review, 2*, 275–291.

Critical Thinking Questions

1. What situations cause long-lasting changes to well-being?

2. What is adaptation, and what aspects of a life event would make adaptation easier or more difficult?

3. How would selection effects influence the study of life events and well-being?

This article has been reprinted as it originally appeared in *Current Directions in Psychological Science*. Citation information for this article as originally published appears above.

Self-Esteem Development Across the Lifespan

Richard W. Robins[1]
Department of Psychology, University of California, Davis

Kali H. Trzesniewski
Institute of Psychiatry, King's College, London, United Kingdom

Abstract

After decades of debate, a consensus is emerging about the way self-esteem develops across the lifespan. On average, self-esteem is relatively high in childhood, drops during adolescence (particularly for girls), rises gradually throughout adulthood, and then declines sharply in old age. Despite these general age differences, individuals tend to maintain their ordering relative to one another: Individuals who have relatively high self-esteem at one point in time tend to have relatively high self-esteem years later. This type of stability (i.e., rank-order stability) is somewhat lower during childhood and old age than during adulthood, but the overall level of stability is comparable to that found for other personality characteristics. Directions for further research include (a) replication of the basic trajectory using more sophisticated longitudinal designs, (b) identification of the mediating mechanisms underlying self-esteem change, (c) the development of an integrative theoretical model of the life-course trajectory of self-esteem.

Keywords

self-esteem; development; change; stability

As he was nearing the end of his life, Michelangelo began working on what many people believe to be his most important work, the Florentine Pietà. After working intensely for almost a decade, he entered his studio one day and took a sledgehammer to the sculpture. He broke away the hands and legs and nearly shattered the work before his assistants dragged him away. Why did Michelangelo attempt to destroy one of his greatest creations, a statue that has been described as among the finest works of the Renaissance? Disillusioned and isolated in the last decades of his life, Michelangelo had a heightened sense of perfectionism that was exacerbated by his failure to live up to the expectations of his father, who viewed being a sculptor as akin to being a manual laborer. Michelangelo, it seems, had self-esteem issues. Was Michelangelo's low self-esteem normative for someone his age? Was he likely to have been plagued by self-doubts throughout his life? An emerging body of evidence is beginning to offer answers to these kinds of questions.

In this article, we review the current state of scientific evidence regarding the development of self-esteem across the lifespan.[2] After decades of debate, a consensus is emerging about the way self-esteem changes from childhood to old age. We focus here on two forms of change: (a) normative changes in self-esteem, which reflect whether individuals, on average, increase or decrease over time (assessed by mean differences in self-esteem across age groups); and (b) the stability of individual differences in self-esteem, which reflect the degree to which the relative ordering of individuals is maintained over time (assessed by correlations between self-esteem scores across two time points, i.e., test–retest correlations).[3]

THE NORMATIVE TRAJECTORY OF SELF-ESTEEM ACROSS THE LIFESPAN

As we go through life, our self-esteem inevitably waxes and wanes. These fluctuations in self-esteem reflect changes in our social environment as well as maturational changes such as puberty and cognitive declines in old age. When these changes are experienced by most individuals at about the same age and influence individuals in a similar manner, they will produce normative shifts in self-esteem across developmental periods.

The findings from three recent studies—a meta-analysis of 86 published articles (Trzesniewski, Donnellan, & Robins, 2001; see also Twenge & Campbell, 2001); a large, cross-sectional study of individuals aged 9 to 90 (Robins, Trzesniewski, Tracy, Gosling, & Potter, 2002); and a cohort-sequential longitudinal study of individuals aged 25 to 96 (Trzesniewski & Robins, 2004)—paint a portrait of the normative trajectory of self-esteem across the lifespan (see Fig. 1). Below, we summarize the major changes that occur from childhood to old age.

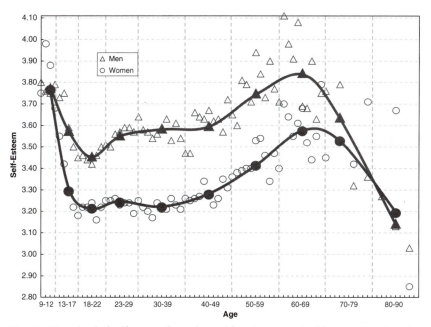

Fig. 1. Mean level of self-esteem for males and females across the lifespan. Also plotted are year-by-year means, separately for males (open triangles) and females (open circles). From "Global Self-Esteem Across the Lifespan," by R.W. Robins, K.H. Trzesniewski, J.L. Tracy, S.D. Gosling, and J. Potter, 2002, *Psychology and Aging, 17*, p. 428. Copyright 2002 by the American Psychological Association. Reprinted with permisson.

Childhood

Young children have relatively high self-esteem, which gradually declines over the course of childhood. Researchers have speculated that children have high self-esteem because their self-views are unrealistically positive. As children develop cognitively, they begin to base their self-evaluations on external feedback and social comparisons, and thus form a more balanced and accurate appraisal of their academic competence, social skills, attractiveness, and other personal characteristics. For example, as children move from preschool to elementary school they receive more negative feedback from teachers, parents, and peers, and their self-evaluations correspondingly become more negative.

Adolescence

Self-esteem continues to decline during adolescence. Researchers have attributed the adolescent decline to body image and other problems associated with puberty, the emerging capacity to think abstractly about one's self and one's future and therefore to acknowledge missed opportunities and failed expectations, and the transition from grade school to the more academically challenging and socially complex context of junior high school.

Adulthood

Self-esteem increases gradually throughout adulthood, peaking sometime around the late 60s. Over the course of adulthood, individuals increasingly occupy positions of power and status, which might promote feelings of self-worth. Many lifespan theorists have suggested that midlife is characterized by peaks in achievement, mastery, and control over self and environment (e.g., Erikson, 1985). Consistent with these theoretical speculations, the personality changes that occur during adulthood tend to reflect increasing levels of maturity and adjustment, as indicated by higher levels of conscientiousness and emotional stability (Trzesniewski, Robins, Roberts, & Caspi, 2004).

Old Age

Self-esteem declines in old age. The few studies of self-esteem in old age suggest that self-esteem begins to drop around age 70 (about the age when Michelangelo began working on the Florentine Pietà). This decline may be due to the dramatic confluence of changes that occur in old age, including changes in roles (e.g., retirement), relationships (e.g., the loss of a spouse), and physical functioning (e.g., health problems), as well as a drop in socioeconomic status. The old-age decline may also reflect a shift toward a more modest, humble, and balanced view of the self in old age (Erikson, 1985). That is, older individuals may maintain a deep-seated sense of their own worth, but their self-esteem scores drop because they are increasingly willing to acknowledge their faults and limitations and have a diminished need to present themselves in a positive light to others. Consistent with this interpretation, narcissism tends to decline with age (Foster, Campbell, & Twenge, 2003).

Gender Differences

Overall, males and females follow essentially the same trajectory: For both genders, self-esteem is relatively high in childhood, drops during adolescence, rises gradually throughout adulthood, and then declines in old age. Nonetheless, there are some interesting gender divergences. Although boys and girls report similar levels of self-esteem during childhood, a gender gap emerges by adolescence, such that adolescent boys have higher self-esteem than adolescent girls (Kling, Hyde, Showers, & Buswell, 1999; Robins et al., 2002). This gender gap persists throughout adulthood, and then narrows and perhaps even disappears in old age (Kling et al., 1999; Robins et al., 2002). Researchers have offered numerous explanations for the gender difference, ranging from maturational changes associated with puberty to social-contextual factors associated with the differential treatment of boys and girls in the classroom or gender differences in body image ideals. However, no generally accepted integrative theoretical model exists.

RANK-ORDER STABILITY OF SELF-ESTEEM

Over the past several decades, researchers have debated the degree to which self-esteem should be thought of as a trait-like construct that remains relatively stable over time or as a state-like process that continually fluctuates in response to environmental and situational stimuli. If self-esteem is more state-like over the long term than other personality characteristics, then it may not be a useful predictor of important real-world outcomes.

The findings of a recent meta-analysis support the claim that self-esteem is a stable, trait-like construct (Trzesniewski, Don-nellan, & Robins, 2003). The stability of self-esteem across all age groups, as determined by test-retest correlations, is comparable to that of the major dimensions of personality, including Extraversion, Agreeableness, Conscientiousness, Neuroticism, and Openness to Experience (Roberts & DelVecchio, 2000). Thus, individuals who have relatively high self-esteem at one point in time tend to have high self-esteem years later; likewise those with low self-esteem earlier in life tend to have low self-esteem later.

However, self-esteem is more stable in some periods of life than in others. Stability is relatively low during early childhood, increases throughout adolescence and early adulthood, and then declines during midlife and old age. This curvilinear trend holds for men and women, for U.S. and non-U.S. participants, and for different self-esteem scales.

The lower levels of stability found during childhood and old age may reflect the dramatic life changes, shifting social circumstances, and relatively rapid maturational changes that characterize both the beginning and end of life. For example, during old age, important life events such as retirement and becoming a grandparent may transform one's sense of self, producing higher levels of self-esteem in some individuals and lower levels in others. These life events can lead to lower levels of self-esteem stability if they are experienced at different ages (e.g., some people retire earlier than others) or differentially affect individuals (e.g., only some retirees decline in self-esteem). Moreover, Erikson (1985) noted that as individuals grow older they begin to review their lifelong accomplishments and experiences, leading in some cases to more critical self-appraisals (ego despair) and in other cases to increased self-acceptance (ego integrity). Thus, a developmental shift toward greater self-reflection in old age may produce increases in self-esteem for some individuals but decreases for others.

IMPLICATIONS

Until recently, the self-esteem literature had been caught in a quagmire of conflicting findings and there was little agreement about the way self-esteem develops. The research reviewed in this article will hopefully move the field toward consensus, and help address questions such as: When in the lifespan is self-esteem relatively high or low? Is self-esteem more like a state (relatively transitory) or more like a trait (relatively unchanging)?

Understanding the trajectory of self-esteem may provide insights into the underlying processes that shape self-esteem development. For example, the fact that self-esteem drops during both adolescence and old age suggests that there might be something common to both periods (e.g., the confluence of multiple social and physical changes) that negatively affects self-esteem.

Knowledge about self-esteem development also has implications for the timing of interventions. For example, the normative trajectory of self-esteem across the lifespan suggests that interventions should be timed for pre- or early adolescence because by late adolescence much of the drop in self-esteem has already occurred. Moreover, developmental periods during which rank-order stability is relatively low may be ideal targets of intervention programs because self-esteem may be particularly malleable during these times of relative upheaval in the self-concept.

CONCLUSIONS AND FUTURE DIRECTIONS

Research accumulating over the past several years paints an increasingly clear picture of the trajectory of self-esteem across the lifespan. Self-esteem shows remarkable continuity given the vast array of experiences that impinge upon a lived life. At the same time, self-esteem also shows systematic changes that are meaningfully connected to age-related life experiences and contexts. These normative changes illustrate the role of the self as an organizing psychological construct that influences how individuals orient their behavior to meet new demands in their environment and new developmental challenges.

Several difficult but tractable issues remain. First, some of the findings reported here require further replication and exploration. In particular, relatively few studies have documented the decline in self-esteem during old age. Establishing the robustness of this effect is important given inconsistent findings in the literature about whether emotional well-being and other aspects of adjustment drop during old age (Mroczek, 2001). In addition, a more fine-grained analysis of age trends might reveal important fluctuations (e.g., changes from early to late adulthood) that were obscured in the present studies.

Second, although the methodological quality of self-esteem research has increased dramatically over the past decade, there is still room for improvement. Greater attention should be paid to measurement issues, including analyses of whether self-esteem scales show different forms of measurement invariance (e.g., does the meaning of self-esteem items vary across age groups?). The use of more representative samples would increase the generalizability of the findings and allow for a deeper exploration into the potential moderating effects of gender, race, ethnicity, and social class. Sophisticated statistical models should be used to better understand dynamic, reciprocal causal influences (e.g., is self-esteem a cause or consequence of important life experiences; e.g., Ferrer & McArdle, 2003). Cohort-sequential longitudinal studies, in which individuals from different age groups are followed over time, are needed to tease apart aging and cohort effects (e.g., will all older individuals develop lower self-esteem or just the particular cohort of individuals who experienced the Great Depression and other life events unique to that cohort?). Finally, genetically informed designs are needed to explore the mutual influence of nature and nurture on self-esteem development; researchers have yet to appreciate the profound implications of the finding that global self-esteem, like most traits, has a genetic basis (e.g., McGuire et al., 1999).

Third, research is needed on the mediating mechanisms underlying self-esteem change. Chronological age has no causal force per se. We need to understand what else changes with age that might produce changes in self-esteem at different developmental periods. One approach is to document the social-contextual factors associated with chronological age, such as the key social roles and events that define and shape one's position in the life course. However, it is important to recognize that such factors can only influence self-esteem through intrapsychic mechanisms, such as perceptions of control and agency and feelings of pride and shame, which shape the way people react to and internalize the events that occur in their lives. In our view, the best way to understand self-esteem development is to understand the self-evaluative mechanisms that drive the self system—that is, the cognitive and affective processes presumed to play a role in how self-evaluations are formed, maintained, and changed. Although experimental studies have linked a number of self-evaluative processes to short-term changes in self-evaluation, we know little about the influence of such processes on self-esteem change over long periods of time. Lifespan research on the self should draw on this experimental work to develop hypotheses about long-term change in self-esteem and explore how self-evaluative processes documented in the lab play out in real-world contexts.

Finally, the literature on self-esteem development lacks an overarching theoretical framework. Most past theoretical work has focused on particular developmental periods (e.g., the transition to adolescence) and particular life domains (e.g., work). Consequently, although the literature has generated a laundry list of possible reasons why self-esteem might drop during adolescence (and why this might be particularly true for girls), there is no integrative model of how the various proposed processes work together to shape self-esteem development. We also do not know whether these same processes can be invoked to account for the drop in self-esteem during old age. Given the complexity of self-esteem development, such a model would necessarily incorporate biological, social, and psychological factors; account for reciprocal and dynamic causal influences; and include mechanisms of continuity as well as change (e.g., various forms of person–environment interaction). Our hope is that, by examining patterns of findings across developmental contexts (childhood to old age) and across life domains (work, relationships, health), the field will move toward an overarching theory of the life-course trajectory of self-esteem.

Recommended Reading

Harter, S.(1999). The construction of the self: A developmental perspective. New York: Guilford.

Robins, R.W., Trzesniewski, K.H., Tracy, J.L., Gosling, S.D., & Potter, J. (2002). (See References)

Trzesniewski, K.H., Donnellan, M.B., & Robins, R.W. (2003). (See References)

Acknowledgments—This research was supported by Grant AG022057 from the National Institute of Aging.

Notes

1. Address correspondence to Richard W. Robins, Department of Psychology, University of California, Davis, CA 95616-8686; e-mail: rwrobins@ucdavis.edu.

2. The focus of this article is on explicit (i.e., conscious) global evaluations of self-worth, not implicit (i.e., unconscious) or domain-specific (e.g., math ability) self-evaluations.

3. These two forms of change are conceptually and statistically distinct. Individuals in a sample could increase substantially in self-esteem but the rank ordering of individuals would be maintained if everyone increased by the same amount. Similarly, the rank ordering of individuals could change substantially over time without producing any aggregate increases or decreases (e.g., if the number of people who decreased offset the number of people who increased).

References

Erikson, E.H. (1985). *The life cycle completed: A review.* New York: W.W. Norton.

Ferrer, E., & McArdle, J.J. (2003). Alternative structural models for multivariate longitudinal data analysis. *Structural Equation Modeling, 10,* 493–524.

Foster, J.D., Campbell, W.K., & Twenge, J.M. (2003). Individual differences in narcissism: Inflated self-views across the lifespan and around the world. *Journal of Research in Personality, 37,* 469–486.

Kling, K.C., Hyde, J.S., Showers, C.J., & Buswell, B.N. (1999). Gender differences in self-esteem: A meta-analysis. *Psychological Bulletin, 125,* 470–500.

McGuire, S., Manke, B., Saudino, K., Reiss, D., Hetherington, E.M., & Plomin, R. (1999). Perceived competence and self-worth during adolescence: A longitudinal behavioral genetic study. *Child Development, 70,* 1283–1296.

Mroczek, D.K. (2001). Age and emotion in adulthood. *Current Directions in Psychological Science, 10,* 87–90.

Roberts, B.W., & DelVecchio, W.F. (2000). The rank-order consistency of personality from childhood to old age: A quantitative review of longitudinal studies. *Psychological Bulletin, 126,* 3–25.

Robins, R.W., Trzesniewski, K.H., Tracy, J.L., Gosling, S.D., & Potter, J. (2002). Global self-esteem across the lifespan. *Psychology and Aging, 17,* 423–434.

Trzesniewski, K.H., Donnellan, M.B., & Robins, R.W. (2001, April). *Self-esteem across the life span: A meta-analysis.* Poster session presented at the biennial meeting of the Society for Research on Child Development, Minneapolis, MN.

Trzesniewski, K.H., Donnellan, M.B., & Robins, R.W. (2003). Stability of self-esteem across the lifespan. *Journal of Personality and Social Psychology, 84,* 205–220.

Trzesniewski, K.H., & Robins, R.W. (2004). *A cohort-sequential study of self-esteem from age 25 to 96.* Poster presented at the Society for Personality and Social Psychology. Austin, Texas.

Trzesniewski, K.H., Robins, R.W., Roberts, B.W., & Caspi, A. (2004). Personality and self-esteem development across the lifespan. In P.T. Costa, Jr. & I.C. Siegler (Eds), *Recent advances in psychology and aging* (pp. 163–185). Amsterdam, the Netherlands: Elsevier.

Twenge, J.M., & Campbell, W.K. (2001). Age and birth cohort differences in self-esteem: A cross-temporal meta-analysis. *Personality and Social Psychology Review,* 5, 321–344.

Critical Thinking Questions

1. Why do you think the gender differences in self-esteem disappear in old age?

2. What aspects of the self do you think are important in forming self-esteem, and how might these aspects vary according to age?

3. If you were planning in intervention to reduce the decline in self-esteem with age, what life domains would you target? What would your intervention include?

This article has been reprinted as it originally appeared in *Current Directions in Psychological Science.* Citation information for this article as originally published appears above.

Perceived Control Over Aging-Related Declines: Adaptive Beliefs and Behaviors

Margie E. Lachman[1]

Brandeis University

Abstract

The belief that people are in control of desired outcomes, including those associated with aging, is a hallmark of American culture. Nevertheless, older adults are less likely than the young to believe there are things that can be done to control aging-related declines in areas such as memory. Within age groups, individual differences in control beliefs are related to cognitive performance, health, and well-being. Mechanisms linking perceived control and positive outcomes include adaptive behaviors such as strategy use and physical activity. There is some evidence that control beliefs can be modified in later life, as illustrated in an intervention for fear of falling. Further work is needed to examine the antecedents of perceived control in later life and the implications of control beliefs in other aging-related domains.

Keywords

control beliefs; sense of control; aging; memory; physical health

More so than citizens of any other country, Americans believe that they are in control of outcomes in their lives. A 2002 Pew Center poll of 38,000 people in 44 countries presented a typical control-belief item: "Success in life is pretty much determined by forces outside our control" (Leland, 2004). In the United States, about 65% disagreed with the statement, as did 60% in Canada. In other countries, disagreement ranged from about 10% (Bangladesh) to 50% (Japan).

A majority of Americans believe they have control over many aspects of life, and aging is one such aspect. A survey conducted by *Parade* magazine and Research America (2006) asked, "Do you think there is anything you can do to stay healthy as you grow older, or do you think the way you age is basically outside your control?" The results revealed that 84% of Americans believe there are things they can do to control the aging process. The $40 billion-a-year anti-aging industry, which offers products and treatments designed to prevent, slow, reverse, or compensate for aging-related changes in the face, body, and mind, depends on this prevalent belief that there are things we can do to take control of aging-related changes.

Control over the aging process is heralded not only in popular culture but also in professional journals and books such as *Successful Aging* by Rowe and Kahn (1998). A key message conveyed is that although aging is influenced to some degree by genetic factors, there is a large component that is determined by lifestyle choices and behavioral factors—that is, the nature of aging is to some extent under one's own control.

AGE DIFFERENCES IN CONTROL BELIEFS

Although there is a widespread belief that we can control aspects of aging, there is also strong evidence, based on both cross-sectional and longitudinal studies, that the sense of control decreases, on average, with age (Krause & Shaw, 2003; Lachman & Firth, 2004; Mirowsky, 1995). In the 1995 John D. and Catherine T. MacArthur Foundation National Survey of Midlife in the United States (MIDUS), we administered an item similar to the one in the Pew Center Poll to a national probability sample of 4,242 Americans, aged 25 to 75 (Lachman & Firth, 2004). Respondents were asked to agree or disagree with the statement, "What happens in my life is often beyond my control." Overall, we found results similar to the Pew results in that 70% disagreed with this statement. We also examined demographic factors (age, sex, education, income, religion, race, marital status) in relation to agreement or disagreement with this control item, and we found the largest variations by age. Almost 80% of the young (ages 25–39) said they are in control (i.e., disagreed with the statement), whereas it was 71% for the middle aged (40–59), and only 62% for the older adults (60–75). These age-group differences were not due to group variations in education, income, or health, although control beliefs were also related to socioeconomic status and health (Lachman & Firth, 2004).

Those who score higher in sense of control strongly believe there are things they can do to bring about desired outcomes. The primary focus of our research program is on perceptions of control especially in relation to declines associated with aging, including beliefs about prevention, remediation, and compensation. These expectancies for control, or lack thereof, have implications for affect and action whether or not they are veridical (Thompson, 1999).

Older adults seem to maintain their overall sense of mastery (beliefs about one's ability or self-efficacy), perhaps because they adjust the salient domains or the standards that they use to define their competence. With aging, we see mainly a loss of control associated with an increasing acknowledgment of the constraints and limitations due to uncontrollable factors or to reduced contingency between actions and outcomes (Lachman & Firth, 2004).

CONTROL AND WELL-BEING IN LATER LIFE

Although a majority in the United States may believe that the decrements associated with aging are preventable or modifiable, there are many, especially in later life, who believe declines are largely inevitable or irreversible. There is a great deal of evidence that such individual differences in control beliefs are associated with key aging outcomes (Rowe & Kahn, 1998). It is consistently found that a high sense of control is associated with being happy, healthy, wealthy, and wise. In the MIDUS sample, those with a higher sense of control had greater life satisfaction and a more optimistic view of adulthood; they reported that things were going well and expected them to either stay that way or even to get better in the future (see Lachman & Firth, 2004). We also have found that those with higher control are less depressed and have better self-rated health, fewer chronic conditions, and less-severe functional limitations.

Control beliefs moderate the well-known relationship between socioeconomic status (SES) and health. Those with lower incomes typically have a lower sense of control and poorer health. This likely reflects, at least in part, the reality of conditions tied to economic circumstances. Differences by countries in control beliefs such as those found in the Pew Center study cited above may mirror economic circumstances and public health conditions, or religious and cultural ideologies. In the United States, we found that although, on average, lower-income groups reported less control, there were individual differences within groups and the distribution of control beliefs overlapped across SES groups. Those with lower incomes who managed to develop and maintain a high sense of control had health similar to that of the higher-income groups (Lachman & Weaver, 1998). Thus, control beliefs buffer the negative health consequences of lower SES.

In the cognitive domain, the sense of control is tied to better memory and greater intellectual functioning, especially among older adults. Although much of the work has been cross-sectional and correlational, there is longitudinal evidence that those who have higher control beliefs improve more on cognitive tests with practice and also are less likely to show aging-related declines in cognitive functioning over time (Caplan & Schooler, 2003).

HOW ARE CONTROL BELIEFS ADAPTIVE?

Although relationships between control beliefs and positive outcomes such as good memory, health, and well-being are fairly well established, there is little work examining the processes linking control beliefs with outcomes in these domains. To guide our work, we have used a conceptual model of the role of adaptive beliefs (e.g., control) and behaviors (e.g., strategy use, physical activity) in relation to aging-related changes, derived from cognitive-behavioral theory (Bandura, 1997). This model (see Fig. 1) shows a multidirectional process in which control beliefs are influenced by prior performance outcomes and beliefs about control also have an influence on subsequent performance and outcomes through their impact on behavior, motivation, and affect. For example, older adults who experience memory lapses or declines in physical strength may respond with a lowered sense of control in these domains, especially if these changes are attributed to uncontrollable factors. Such beliefs in low control can be detrimental if they are associated with distress, anxiety, inactivity, and giving up without expending the effort or using the strategies needed to support optimal outcomes.

We have examined possible affective, behavioral, motivational, and physiological mechanisms, including anxiety, effort, compensatory strategies, and physical activity, that link control beliefs and outcomes. In the health domain, for example, we found that those who have a higher sense of control are more likely to exercise regularly and also to have better health (Lachman & Firth, 2004).

We also have investigated mechanisms linking control beliefs to memory, a domain that typically shows age-related declines. In a study of 335 adults aged 20 to 85, we asked participants to recall a list of 30 categorizable words such as types of fruit and flowers (Lachman & Andreoletti, 2006). We found that control beliefs were positively related to effective strategy use and to recall performance for middle-aged and older adults, but not for young adults. These age differences in the pattern of correlations for beliefs with effective strategy use and memory

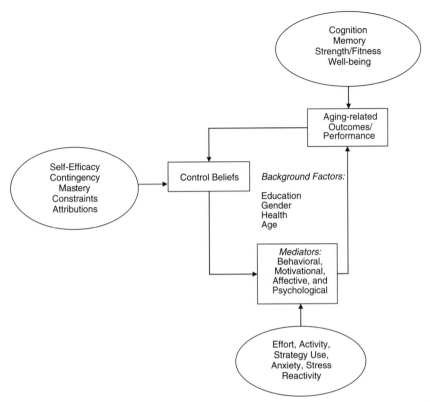

Fig. 1. Conceptual model of the relationship between control beliefs and aging-related performance outcomes with postulated mediators, based on cognitive-behavioral theory.

are shown in Figure 2. Moreover, the relationship between control beliefs and recall was mediated by strategy use for the middle aged and partially mediated for older adults. Those who had a higher sense of control were more likely to use an effective strategy, in this case categorizing the words, and they in turn had better recall. Although the directional relationship cannot be confirmed given the correlational design, we tested alternative directional models and this mediational model provided the best fit.

CONTROL INTERVENTIONS

Given the apparent benefits of control beliefs and the likelihood of declines in sense of control in later life, we were interested in whether we could modify control beliefs among older adults and if this would affect outcomes in a given domain. Many older adults assume they are too old to improve performance or functioning or to make up for losses in areas such as memory or physical ability. Using the model in Figure 1 as a guide, we have conducted interventions that all have in common a joint focus on modifying control beliefs and behaviors (Lachman, 2000). We assumed that enduring behavior change is unlikely without first instilling confidence that aging-related declines can be controlled.

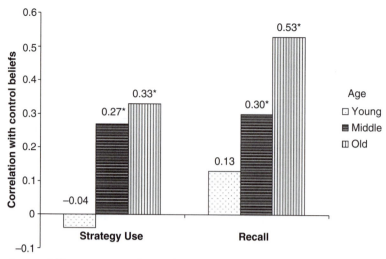

Fig. 2. Age differences in correlations between control beliefs, strategy use, and recall, based on data from Lachman & Andreoletti (2006).

A fear of falling is relatively common among older adults. This is typically manifested as a low sense of efficacy for engaging in activities without falling and a sense that falling is uncontrollable (Tennstedt et al., 1998). Consistent with our cognitive-behavioral conceptual model, the best predictor of self-efficacy and control with respect to falling is previous fall status, and low falls self-efficacy is subsequently associated with maladaptive behavioral changes such as activity restriction, which can lead to increased risk of falling through muscle atrophy and deconditioning.

Our multifaceted intervention targeted beliefs about control over falls with 434 older adults who reported fear of falling and were randomly assigned to an intervention or a contact control condition (Tennstedt et al., 1998). We used cognitive-restructuring strategies to reframe control beliefs. This entailed analysis and challenge of maladaptive beliefs (e.g., I can't do this; I am too old; it won't do any good; I will get hurt) and information that efforts (e.g., using fall-prevention strategies; engaging in strength and balance exercises, which were also taught to participants) can make a difference for outcomes. The contact control group was given information about risk factors for falls and saw a video about ways to minimize the risk of falls. Those who completed the treatment increased their falls self-efficacy, sense of control over falls, level of intended activity, and physical mobility functioning significantly more than the control group did. Although the fear-of-falling intervention did not target falls reduction directly, greater mobility and increased activity should lead to a decrease in falls due to better physical conditioning. However, if intervention participants increased their activity levels as indicated by their intentions, they might also have inadvertently increased their risk of falls due to greater exposure. There were no significant differences between intervention and control subjects in the number of falls for up to 12 months (Tennstedt et al., 1998), which suggests, at least, that the intervention did not have unintended side effects.

IS A SENSE OF CONTROL ALWAYS ADAPTIVE?

Most of the work exploring a sense of control in relation to age-related well-being has focused on types of performance and situations that are to some extent controllable. There is some evidence that in uncontrollable situations, those with lower control beliefs do better, at least over the short run. For example, Bisconti, Bergeman, and Boker (2006) found recent widows with greater levels of perceived control over their social support had poorer overall adjustment across the first 4 months of widowhood. Longitudinal studies over longer periods are needed to investigate whether a high sense of control may be more beneficial for resilience and coping over the long run. Those who have a strong sense of control would be expected to be better at finding ways to cope with uncontrollable events or unattainable goals or outcomes by using secondary (change the self) rather than primary (change the situation) control strategies (Wrosch, Heckhausen, & Lachman, 2006).

CONCLUSIONS AND FUTURE DIRECTIONS

Adults with a low sense of control over aging-related declines may be vulnerable to memory problems and physical disabilities in later life, in part, because they are not likely to use compensatory strategies or adopt preventative or remedial behaviors. There is the potential to reduce declines in cognition and physical functioning by instilling more adaptive beliefs about controllability over aspects of the aging process in conjunction with training in adaptive behaviors.

Although to some extent people may be able to prevent, postpone, or compensate for aging-related declines, it is rare to be able to influence diseases, illnesses, injuries, loss of loved ones, and ultimately when and how one's own aging process comes to an end. Thus, to some extent a belief in control over aging has an illusory quality (Thompson, 1999). Nevertheless, for domains in which efforts do make a difference, there is consistent evidence that those who believe they can control aging-related outcomes do better.

We found some evidence for the mediational role of strategy use and activity, and we are currently exploring anxiety and stress reactivity as potential mediators of the relationship between control beliefs and memory. With regard to areas with aging-related declines, we find that control beliefs make more of a difference for middle-aged and older adults even though on average their control beliefs are lower (Lachman & Andreoletti, 2006). More work is needed to examine whether control beliefs play similar roles for change outcomes at younger ages and in other domains as well as in other cultures. We have focused mainly on the domains of memory and physical health, and we are now looking at control in relation to hearing loss.

Previous research has looked primarily at the consequences of control beliefs. In future work we will explore the sources of control beliefs and address issues of causal direction. We have just completed collecting 10-year longitudinal data with the MIDUS sample, which will enable us to examine biopsychosocial antecedents of changes in control beliefs. We will examine the impact of changes in health and disability and identify those who are most vulnerable to losses in the sense of control.

Recommended Reading

Lachman, M.E., & Firth, K.M. (2004). (See References)
Thompson, S.C. (1999). (See References)
Wrosch, C., Heckhausen, J., & Lachman, M.E. (2006). (See References)

Acknowledgments—This article is dedicated to Paul B. Baltes, my extraordinary mentor and wonderful friend, who passed away on November 7, 2006. I would like to express my appreciation for financial support for this research from the John D. and Catherine T. MacArthur Foundation Research Network on Successful Midlife Development and the National Institute on Aging: Grants R01 AG 17920, AG 11669, and PO1 AG 20166. In addition, I would like to acknowledge the many contributions from my collaborators: Carrie Andreoletti, Kimberly Firth, Jonathan Howland, Alan Jette, Shevaun Neupert, Ann Pearman, Ron Spiro, Sharon Tennstedt, Suzanne Weaver, and Stacey Whitbourne.

Note

1. Address correspondence to Margie E. Lachman, Department of Psychology, MS062, Brandeis University, Waltham, MA 02454-9110; e-mail: lachman@brandeis.edu.

References

Bandura, A. (1997). *Self-efficacy: The exercise of control*. New York: Freeman.

Bisconti, T.L., Bergeman, C.S., & Boker, S.M. (2006). Social support as a predictor of variability: An examination of the adjustment trajectories of recent widows. *Psychology and Aging, 21*, 590–599.

Caplan, L.J., & Schooler, C. (2003). The roles of fatalism, self-confidence, and intellectual resources in the disablement process in older adults. *Psychology and Aging, 18*, 551–561.

Krause, N., & Shaw, B.A. (2003). Role-specific control, personal meaning, and health in late life. *Research on Aging, 25*, 559–586.

Lachman, M.E. (2000). Promoting a sense of control over memory aging. In R.D. Hill, L. Backman, & A.S. Neely (Eds.), *Cognitive rehabilitation in old age* (pp. 106–120). New York: Oxford University Press.

Lachman, M.E., & Andreoletti, C. (2006). Strategy use mediates the relationship between control beliefs and memory performance for middle-aged and older adults. *Journals of Gerontology: Psychological Sciences, 61B*, P88–P94.

Lachman, M.E., & Firth, K.M. (2004). The adaptive value of feeling in control during midlife. In O.G. Brim, C.D. Ryff, & R. Kessler (Eds.), *How healthy are we?: A national study of well-being at midlife* (pp. 320–349). Chicago: University of Chicago Press.

Lachman, M.E., & Weaver, S.L. (1998). The sense of control as a moderator of social class differences in health and well-being. *Journal of Personality and Social Psychology, 74*, 763–773.

Leland, J. (2004, June 13). Faith in the future: Why Americans see the silver lining. *The New York Times*, Section 4, p. 1.

Mirowsky, J. (1995). Age and the sense of control. *Social Psychology Quarterly, 58*, 31–43.

Rowe, J.W., & Kahn, R.L. (1998). *Successful aging*. New York: Pantheon Books.

Research America (2006). Taking our pulse: The PARADE/Research!America Health Poll. Alexandria, VA: Charlton Research Company. Downloaded February 8, 2006, from http://www.researchamerica.org

Tennstedt, S., Howland, J., Lachman, M., Peterson, E.W., Kasten, L., & Jette, A. (1998). A randomized, controlled trial of a group intervention to reduce fear of falling and associated activity restriction in older adults. *The Journals of Gerontology: Psychological Sciences, 53B*, 384–392.

Thompson, S.C. (1999). Illusions of control: How we overestimate our personal influence. *Current Directions in Psychological Science, 8*, 187–190.

Wrosch, C., Heckhausen, J., & Lachman, M.E. (2006). Goal management across adulthood and old age: The adaptive value of primary and secondary control. In D. Mroczek & T. Little (Eds.), *Handbook of personality development* (pp. 399–421). Mahwah, NJ: Erlbaum.

Critical Thinking Questions

1. Name some of the correlates of self-reported control, and give an example of how high levels of control may offset, or buffer, an adverse situation.

2. What types of cognitive strategies are related to higher perceived control?

3. What common age-related changes may benefit from interventions designed to enhanced control efficacy among older adults?

This article has been reprinted as it originally appeared in *Current Directions in Psychological Science*. Citation information for this article as originally published appears above.

Health Stresses and Depressive Symptomatology in the Elderly: A Control-Process Approach

Carsten Wrosch[1]

Department of Psychology and Centre for Research in Human Development, Concordia University, Montreal, Quebec, Canada;

Richard Schulz

Department of Psychiatry and University Center for Social and Urban Research, University of Pittsburgh;

Jutta Heckhausen

Department of Psychology and Social Behavior, School of Social Ecology, University of California at Irvine

Abstract

The social and life sciences need to examine pathways of successful aging to master the consequences of increased longevity and physical vulnerability of the elderly population. One of older adults' well-known problems relates to the fact that their quality of life can be threatened by physical health stresses and associated depressive symptomatology. Common health problems among older adults often contribute to depressive symptomatology, and, in turn, depressive symptoms may further compromise older adults' health. It is thus an important task to discover factors that can protect older adults from experiencing the negative emotional consequences of health stresses. Using ideas from the life-span theory of control, we show how to adaptively manage the negative consequences of health problems in the elderly. Active investments in overcoming health problems that are controllable should result in positive outcomes. In contrast, it may be beneficial for older adults to disengage from health goals that are unattainable. By adjusting their control-related behaviors to the controllability of specific health stresses, older adults can maintain their psychological and physical health.

Keywords

aging; control; depression; disengagement; health

More human beings live to old age today than ever before. However, the increased longevity comes at a price. Many older adults experience physical illness and disability, such as arthritis, heart disease, or diabetes. In addition, it is widely recognized that physical disease and depressive symptomatology are positively associated in the elderly, and may reciprocally influence each other. From a psychological point of view, it is thus important to understand how older individuals manage the challenges associated with physical disease and to identify processes that enhance and maintain their psychological and physical health.

In this article, we examine the link between physical disease and depressive symptomatology, and identify adaptive processes for managing physical disease (i.e., control strategies) in the elderly. These processes may prevent older adults from experiencing the negative emotional consequences of health stresses. At the most general level, we argue that adaptive management of health stresses requires older adults to adjust their control strategies to the type of health stressor encountered. Whereas some health stresses are potentially controllable in old age (e.g., pain) and can be overcome when active control processes are used, the controllability of other health stresses is often sharply reduced (e.g., functional disabilities, such as difficulty using the toilet, dressing, or preparing meals) and may require older adults to adjust their health-related goals. The use of control processes that are functionally adjusted to the controllability of specific health stresses may alleviate the negative emotional consequences of health problems and thereby contribute to maintaining physical and psychological health.

HEALTH STRESSES AND DEPRESSIVE SYMPTOMATOLOGY IN THE ELDERLY

One of the most robust findings in the literature is the relation between physical declines and depressive symptomatology in the elderly (Lenze et al., 2001). Indeed, the fact that many older individuals suffer from physical illness and disability places them at risk for clinical depression. For example, depressive symptomatology has been shown to be particularly high among elderly individuals with specific medical conditions, such as rheumatoid arthritis or osteoarthritis, Parkinson's disease, advanced cardiovascular disease, or stroke. Studies that focus on the functional consequences of chronic health problems (e.g., limitations in activities of daily living) also report high levels of depressive symptoms.

The relationship between health and depression is complex. First, poor health can directly influence depressive symptomatology. Those older adults who confront physical health problems are often more likely than their healthier peers to develop subsequent depressive symptoms. Second, depression may contribute to further health problems, either directly or indirectly (Schulz, Martire, Beach, & Scheier, 2000). For example, depression has been shown to contribute to mortality in older adults. In addition, depressive symptomatology can be associated with changes in motivational, behavioral, and biological factors, thereby affecting further health declines. The reciprocal relations between depression and disease suggest that a substantial proportion of older adults is at risk of developing both physical and psychological problems.

HOW TO MANAGE HEALTH STRESSES IN THE ELDERLY

Given the link between health stresses and depressive symptoms in older adults, it is important to explore potential moderators of this relationship. Identifying protective factors may contribute to a better understanding of the relation between health and depression and can be a tool for improving older adults' quality of life. The life-span theory of control (Heckhausen & Schulz, 1995; Schulz & Heckhausen, 1996) provides a conceptual framework for examining psychological and behavioral mechanisms that may help older adults to manage their experience of health threats. This theory distinguishes between primary and secondary control strategies that can be activated to realize important objectives and to manage failure and unattainable goals. Primary control targets the external world and involves attempts to achieve effects in the immediate environment external to the individual. In contrast, secondary control targets the self and is aimed at optimizing the individual's motivation and emotion, which are, in turn, essential resources for further primary control.

One of the important functions that primary and secondary control strategies fulfill is facilitating goal attainment. In particular, three types of control strategies support the attainment of personal goals: actively investing effort and time (i.e., selective primary control), seeking advice and help from other people (i.e., compensatory primary control), and strengthening motivational commitment for goal attainment (i.e., selective secondary control). Control strategies aimed at realizing personal goals should be particularly adaptive if they are used when the circumstances seem to favor goal attainment. Another important function of individuals' control strategies relates to the management of failure and unattainable goals. If it is not possible to realize important life goals, disengagement from them and self-protective secondary control strategies (e.g., attributing failures to external causes or comparing oneself with others who are worse off) may save control resources for attainable goals and help a person to maintain a positive view of the self.

Research examining the adaptive role of control strategies across a wide range of different life domains (e.g., intimate relationships, childbearing, financial issues) has confirmed that the use of control strategies that are adjusted to the controllability of personal goals facilitates a good quality of life. In addition, evidence from a large U.S. study (Midlife Development in the United States, or MIDUS) has demonstrated that self-protective secondary control is particularly strongly associated with subjective well-being among older adults who confront a high number of health problems (Wrosch, Heckhausen, & Lachman, 2000). These findings strongly support a basic tenet of the life-span theory of control: Given that with advancing age people confront decreasing opportunities for overcoming health problems (and achieving other goals), the adaptive value of control strategies that are aimed at goal disengagement and self-protection increases in the elderly.

Figure 1 illustrates a highly simplified model of the relation between physical illness and depression and can be used to conceptualize the adaptive role of control processes in managing health stresses. One pathway in the figure addresses the direct association between physical disease and depression in the elderly. Recent work has suggested that physical illness can directly contribute to depression by causing neuroanatomical and biochemical changes (e.g., disregulated neurotransmission). The other pathway from physical illness to depressive symptomatology emphasizes symptom-related consequences of physical illness. Physical illness, such as arthritis, hypertension, or heart disease, may affect older individuals' lives in at least two ways. First, these conditions often result in functional disabilities that limit people's abilities to carry out normal daily activities. Second, many illnesses generate acute symptoms, such as pain and difficulty breathing, which may further compromise quality of life. In turn, both types of health stresses may increase an older person's risk of experiencing depressive symptoms (e.g., Williamson, Shaffer, & Parmelee, 2000). According to the model in Figure 1, however, this is not necessarily always the case. In particular, we

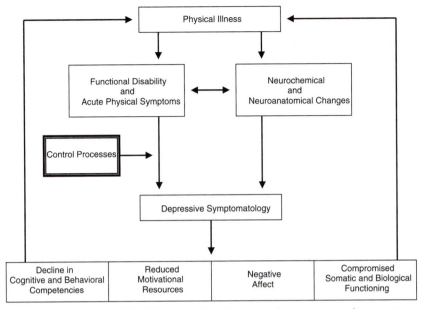

Fig. 1. Conceptual model of the role played by control processes in the association between physical illness and depressive symptomatology in the elderly.

suggest that depressive symptomatology emerges in the elderly when control strategies are unable to adequately address health threats and losses. Thus, the influence of health stresses on depression can be attenuated or even rendered minimal if appropriate control strategies are used.

To identify specific control strategies involved in the adaptive management of health stresses among the elderly, it is necessary to consider that some health stresses are more controllable than others, and that adaptive management of health threats may require older adults to adjust their control processes to the specific opportunities for overcoming each problem. In this regard, an important implication can be drawn from the distinction between functional disabilities and acute physical problems. Functional disabilities are often relatively intractable, and a person's active efforts to overcome them may not be successful. In contrast, in many cases, the acute physical symptoms associated with disease and disability (e.g., pain) are potentially controllable. Thus, active efforts to counteract acute physical symptoms are likely to alleviate disease symptoms and reduce their negative emotional consequences.

A corollary of this proposition is that the use of control strategies that are adjusted to the controllability of specific health stresses may enhance elderly individuals' feelings of well-being in the face of age-related loss. In particular, we suggest that investment in control strategies aimed at overcoming acute physical symptoms should moderate the relation between acute physical symptoms and depressive symptomatology. Such control strategies should facilitate the achievement of those health goals that are still attainable. Older adults who have more intractable functional disabilities, by contrast, may need to activate control strategies that facilitate disengagement from unattainable health goals and protect the self. In situations in which a health problem cannot be overcome, disengagement and self-protection may alleviate distress deriving from trying to attain the unattainable, and free personal resources that can be invested in the pursuit of other meaningful and more attainable goals. In short, elderly individuals should be able to reduce their depressive symptomatology by using control strategies that are appropriate to whether the health stresses they confront are tractable or not.

Finally, it is important to note that the model presented in Figure 1 also includes several feedback loops and thus addresses the reciprocal pathways between depressive symptomatology and disease. Depression can result in declines of cognitive and behavioral competencies, reduced motivation, increased negative affect, and compromised biological functioning, thereby contributing to further health declines. A relevant implication of the proposed feedback loops is that older adults who do not succeed in adaptively controlling their acute physical symptoms and functional disabilities are at risk not only of developing high levels of depression, but also of experiencing further health declines as a consequence of their depression.

Recent research designed to test some of the predictions we have discussed has lent support to this model of health stresses, depression, and control in the elderly. In a recent study, we demonstrated that control strategies aimed at attaining health goals were associated with low levels of depressive symptoms only among older adults who reported high levels of acute physical symptoms (Wrosch, Schulz, & Heckhausen, 2002). In particular, older adults who experienced acute physical symptoms and did not activate strategies targeted at controlling those symptoms experienced elevated levels of depression. Moreover, a follow-up study showed that high levels of health-related control strategies were associated with reduced depression over time, and that high levels of depressive symptoms resulted in reduced active attempts to attain important health goals. These results support our theoretical model by demonstrating that control strategies aimed at attaining health goals are a significant moderator of the association between acute physical symptoms and depressive symptomatology. In addition, the findings point to the conclusion that depressive symptomatology can reduce a person's motivation to actively try to attain potentially controllable health goals, and thereby may compromise older adults' physical and psychological health.

CONCLUSION

The theoretical model and empirical research we have discussed were designed to explore the adaptive functions of control strategies among older adults who experience different types of physical health stresses. In support of the theoretical model, the research suggests that activation of appropriate control strategies may protect older adults from experiencing the negative emotional consequences of health threats. However, other parts of the model need to be tested, and more research is needed to illuminate the complex relations between physical declines, control behaviors, and depressive symptomatology in the elderly.

First, researchers need to examine in more detail how older adults can adaptively manage their functional disabilities and unattainable health goals. The proposed model suggests that self-protective control strategies and goal disengagement could reduce depression among older adults who confront functional disabilities. However, disengagement may have negative consequences under some circumstances. If older adults disengage from unattainable goals and have no alternative goals to pursue, they may feel aimless and empty. A recent study supports this argument: Levels of emotional well-being were compromised among older adults who were able to let go of unattainable goals but reported difficulties with finding new, meaningful activities to pursue (Wrosch, Scheier, Miller, Schulz, & Carver, 2003). Thus, disengagement from unattainable health goals may be adaptive only if it leads to taking up new goals and keeps a person engaged in the pursuit of meaningful and important activities.

Second, as noted earlier, the life-span theory of control proposes three different types of control strategies that are functionally related to attaining important life goals. The research we have discussed did not differentiate among these types. However, future research on the management of health stresses in the elderly should take a more fine-grained approach to assessing the adaptive value of different control strategies across different phases of the disease and treatment process. For example, in the early stages of a potentially curable health problem, strategies related to seeking help or advice from a health expert may be particularly important. Increased motivational commitment for overcoming a health problem, by contrast, may be particularly important when individuals are confronted with a long-lasting or painful treatment process.

Third, research is needed to clarify the mechanisms linking older adults' control behaviors, depressive symptoms, and physical health. In this regard, the activation of control strategies may influence not only depression, but also other variables that play an important role in the causal link between depressive symptomatology and disease. As discussed earlier, depressive symptomatology may further compromise a person's health through behavioral, motivational, and biological processes. Our theoretical framework suggests that control-related management of health stresses influences the biological and psychological consequences of depressive symptomatology and thereby may affect older adults' health.

Finally, an important implication for future research concerns the design of interventions for elderly populations. The control strategies identified by our model could be taught to individuals confronting various health challenges. Indeed, it can be argued that some therapies (e.g., problem-solving therapy) operate on this principle, because they are designed to help the individual identify problems, think through solutions, and then act on them. In addition, it may be beneficial for older adults to learn to recognize that specific health conditions are not controllable, so that they invest their efforts in maintaining a certain level of functioning despite their uncontrollable health conditions. Moreover, disengagement and self-protection may enable them to avoid the negative emotional consequences of illnesses by refocusing their resources on the pursuit of other meaningful and more attainable goals. In sum, by enabling elderly individuals to avoid a downward spiral characterized by high levels of health stresses, maladaptive control behaviors, and depressive symptomatology, intervention programs may contribute to increasing older adults' psychological and physical health and significantly reducing the costs for public health services.

Recommended Reading

Williamson, G.M., Shaffer, D.R., & Parmelee, P.A. (Eds.). (2000). (See References)
Wrosch, C., Schulz, R., & Heckhausen, J. (2002). (See References)

Note

1. Address correspondence to Carsten Wrosch, Concordia University, Department of Psychology, 7141 Sherbrooke St. West, Montreal, Quebec H4B 1R6, Canada; e-mail: wrosch@vax2.concordia.ca.

References

Heckhausen, J., & Schulz, R. (1995). A life-span theory of control. *Psychological Review, 102,* 284–304.
Lenze, E.J., Rogers, J.C., Martire, L.M., Mulsant, B.H., Rollman, B.L., Dew, M.A., Schulz, R., & Reynolds, C. F., III. (2001). The association of late-life depression and anxiety with physical disability: A review of the literature and prospectus for future research. *American Journal of Geriatric Psychiatry, 9,* 113–135.
Schulz, R., & Heckhausen, J. (1996). A life span model of successful aging. *American Psychologist, 51,* 702–714.
Schulz, R., Martire, L.M., Beach, S.R., & Scheier, M.F. (2000). Depression and mortality in the elderly. *Current Directions in Psychological Science, 9,* 204–208.
Williamson, G.M., Shaffer, D.R., & Parmelee, P.A. (Eds.). (2000). *Physical illness and depression in older adults: A handbook of theory, research, and practice.* New York: Kluwer Academic/Plenum Publishers.
Wrosch, C., Heckhausen, J., & Lachman, M.E. (2000). Primary and secondary control strategies for managing health and financial stress across adulthood. *Psychology and Aging, 15,* 387–399.
Wrosch, C., Scheier, M.F., Miller, G.E., Schulz, R., & Carver, C.S. (2003). Adaptive self-regulation of unattainable goals: Goal disengagement, goal reengagement, and subjective well-being. *Personality and Social Psychology Bulletin, 29,* 1494–1508.
Wrosch, C., Schulz, R., & Heckhausen, J. (2002). Health stresses and depressive symptomatology in the elderly: The importance of health engagement control strategies. *Health Psychology, 21,* 340–348.

Critical Thinking Questions

1. Describe primary and secondary control as well as their sub-classifications.

2. What control strategies are associated with advanced age, and what type of health conditions particularly benefit from these control strategies?

3. Describe several ways that depression can influence physical health.

This article has been reprinted as it originally appeared in *Current Directions in Psychological Science.* Citation information for this article as originally published appears above.

Section 5: Physical Health

Although not caused by age, health conditions and health-related problems increase in prevalence across the adult life-span. The study of health and aging encompasses the effects of a lifetime of behaviors resulting in accumulated risk and resilience factors in old age. In addition, reductions in reserve capacity and general physiological declines make older adults particularly vulnerable to threats on their physical health. This series of studies cover a range of topics concerning health and aging. For example, risk factors influencing health in old age can appear even before birth.

The first article by Margaret Gatz is titled, "Genetics, dementia, and the elderly." This article examines the influence of both genetic and environmental effects on the likelihood of developing Alzheimer's disease in later life. The author discusses the different genes that have been associated with this type of dementia as well as the possible pathways explaining these associations. She also discusses the need to examine interactions among different genes and interactions between genes and the environment when studying the etiology of this disease.

In the next article, M. Christopher Newland and Erin Rasmussen discuss how the effects of exposure to toxins in utero are related to functional disabilities that only reveal themselves in adulthood. The article, "Behavior in adulthood and during aging is affected by contaminant exposure in utero" discusses the results of methylmercury exposure on humans and animals. This study reveals the lifelong consequences of events occurring early in life.

The following article discusses how characteristics expressed very early in life may also be related to positive outcomes in old age. Linda Gottfredson and Ian Dreary's article , "Intelligence predicts health and longevity, but why?" describes how intelligence assessed in childhood is related to physical health and mortality in late life. They mention behaviors that may partially explain these relationships, including the role of education, socioeconomic status, and specific health behaviors such as smoking history.

In "Resilience and vulnerability to daily stressors assessed via diary methods," David Almeida discusses the potentially pernicious effects of acute and chronic stressors on physical and mental well-being. He states that daily stressors influence affective well-being both at the moment they occur as well as across time as a result of their aggregated effects. He emphasizes the use of daily diary methods for capturing the influences of daily life experiences and describes age differences in both exposure and reactivity to daily stressors.

In the last article of the series, Peter Vitaliano, Heather Young, and Jian-ping Zhang discuss the costs of caregiving in their article, "Is caregiving a risk factor for illness." They mention the current findings in the article, but temper these findings with a discussion of the methodological difficulties that arise when studying the complex issue of the effects of caregiving on physical and mental health.

Genetics, Dementia, and the Elderly

Margaret Gatz[1]
University of Southern California

Abstract

Whether or not an individual develops dementia is powerfully influenced by genes. For Alzheimer's disease, the most common type of dementia, one susceptibility gene with major effects has been identified, but progress finding other susceptibility genes has stalled. Twin studies have revealed that nongenetic risk also plays an important role, as there are many monozygotic twin pairs in which only one individual has dementia. Scientists have argued that gene-by-environment interactions will be key to understanding vulnerability to Alzheimer's disease; but to date, few substantial gene-by-environment interactions have been replicated. Often, too, the nongenetic or lifestyle factor appears to have a protective effect only for those individuals not carrying the risky version of the gene, not for those individuals who are at genetic risk.

Keywords

dementia; Alzheimer's disease; genetic risk; twins

Whether one's future includes dementia is a concern for many middle-aged adults and, now, aging Baby Boomers. Ordinary memory lapses have assumed the status of "senior moments." People play Sudoku as a form of mental exercise in the hopes that it will stave off decline. Jokes about memory are traded by e-mail:

Two elderly couples were enjoying friendly conversation when one of the men asked the other, "Fred, how was the memory clinic you went to last month?"
"Outstanding," Fred replied. "They taught us all the latest psychological techniques: visualization, association, etc. It was great."
"Sounds terrific! What was the name of the clinic?"
Fred went blank. He thought and thought, but couldn't remember.
Then a smile broke across his face and he asked, "What do you call that flower with the long stem and thorns?"
"You mean a rose?"
"Yes, that's it!"
He turned to his wife, "Rose, what was the name of that memory clinic?" (Helpguide, 2005)

A recent survey conducted by Harris Interactive for MetLife Foundation found that, among Americans aged 55 and older, Alzheimer's disease (AD) was the most feared on a list of diseases (chosen by 31% of respondents, compared to 27% choosing cancer and 20% choosing stroke; Harris Interactive, 2006). Fear for one's own cognitive future is especially strong among those who watch their own parents develop dementia.

Such a fear is not entirely misplaced. Among 65-year-olds, lifetime risk of developing any dementia has been estimated to be 11% for men and 19% for women (Seshadri et al., 1997). Rates of dementia increase exponentially with age.

The consensus among expert scholars is that 30% of North Americans aged 85 and older are living with dementia (Ferri et al., 2005). Prevalence rates generally appear to be higher for African Americans than for Whites.

A number of investigators have addressed risk of AD in first-degree relatives of AD patients, with estimates ranging from 24% to 49%. In other words, lifetime risk of developing AD is 1.8 to 4.0 times higher for those with a family history of the disorder than for those without. Proportional increase in risk associated with being a first-degree relative of an AD patient is similar for African Americans and for Whites (Green et al., 2002). At the same time, only a quarter of those with late-onset AD have had a close relative with dementia (Bird, 2005).

TYPES OF DEMENTIA

Dementia refers to a group of diseases that have their onset in old age and in which there is progressive loss of cognitive functioning that eventually affects all aspects of self-care. Few dementias are reversible, although treatable factors that might contribute to cognitive decrements—for example, vitamin B12 deficiency, hypothyroidism, depression, or dehydration accompanying acute illnesses such as influenza—are important to assess and address.

The most common type of dementia is AD, accounting for up to two thirds of all cases of dementia. The cause of AD is not established, although how it originates can be described. A key feature is the formation in the brain of deposits of a protein called beta-amyloid ($A\beta$); these deposits are called amyloid plaques. It is hypothesized that these plaques cause oxidative injury (damage due to release of free radicals during cellular metabolism), inflammation, and alterations in neurotransmitters, eventually resulting in the death of neurons. AD is notable for its insidious onset. Clinically, impairment is typically observed in episodic memory— due to either problems with learning or failures of retention. There are also deficits in language, visuospatial abilities, and executive function—with judgment and problem solving often joining memory as the earliest reported symptoms.

Other major types of dementia include dementia with Lewy bodies (DLB), vascular dementia (VaD), and frontotemporal dementia. DLB is now considered the second most common form of dementia, accounting for 15 to 20% of all cases. The key feature is aggregations of a protein called alpha-synuclein in subcortical and cortical areas of the brain; these deposits are called Lewy bodies. Parkinsonism (e.g., slowness, muscular rigidity, tremor, and impaired motor control) is observed in people with this form of dementia, along with falls, visual hallucinations, poor response to antipsychotic medications, disturbed sleep, fluctuating attention, and executive dysfunction (e.g., impaired judgment and problem solving). Autopsy results suggest that Lewy-related pathology and AD-type pathology often occur together.

VaD is characterized by cerebral infarcts (destruction of brain tissue due to blockage of blood supply) or other evidence of cerebrovascular disease. VaD often has an abrupt onset and progresses in a stepwise fashion. Most notably, VaD is found to impair executive functioning and psychomotor speed while leaving episodic memory relatively intact. Estimated prevalence of this type of dementia depends greatly on which diagnostic criteria are used. Autopsy studies suggest that prevalence of mixed AD with VaD is underestimated. With increased attention to vascular risk factors for AD, there is also recognition of common mechanisms in how these two forms of dementia originate.

Frontotemporal dementia entails loss of social awareness, disinhibition, changes in eating habits, and changes in speech output, but not a pronounced memory deficit. Neuropathologically, there may be aggregations in the brain of a protein called tau. This type of dementia typically emerges at a younger age than other dementias.

ESTIMATING GENETIC EFFECTS

Twin studies are a useful tool in estimating the importance of genetic factors in the emergence of dementia. Monozygotic (MZ) twin pairs (i.e., who come from a single egg) are regarded as being the same genetically. Dizygotic (DZ) twin pairs (i.e., from two eggs) share in principle half of their genetic makeup; effectively, they are siblings of the same age. The proportion of twin partners of affected twins who also have a disorder is called probandwise concordance. Probandwise concordance provides an indication of genetic risk. The magnitude of concordance rates for MZ twin pairs and the difference in concordance between MZ and DZ twin pairs both suggest the extent of genetic influence. And when MZ concordance is less than 100%, it indicates that environmental influences or chance processes play a role.

We recently reported concordance rates for all dementia and for AD in twins from the Swedish Twin Registry (Gatz et al., 2006). These results are shown in Figure 1. Probandwise concordance for all dementias in men was 44% for MZ pairs and 25% for DZ pairs, and in women it was 58% for MZ pairs and 45% for DZ pairs. However, concordance rates are influenced by length of life—and hence, opportunity to develop dementia. Thus, although rates are higher for women than for men, once the age of the women was taken into account in quantitative genetic models there was no significant difference in genetic influence by sex.

Because dementia is age related, there is some chance that any two older adults of equivalent age can both be expected to be affected, independent of any shared genetic influences. From the same data, we created artificial pairs in which each individual was randomly coupled with an unrelated individual born in the same year. Converging results from thirty repetitions of this procedure are shown in Figure 1. Concordance was 12% and 21% respectively for male and female unrelated pairs matched by birth year. The comparison of concordance rates for MZ twins, DZ twins, and unrelated individuals highlights the influence of genetic factors for dementia vulnerability.

SPECIFIC GENES

A great deal of research attention has been devoted to identifying the genes underlying dementia (summarized by Tsuang & Bird, 2002). There are two kinds of genes—causative genes that follow an autosomal dominant pattern of inheritance, and susceptibility genes. Autosomal dominant means that the risk to each child of an affected parent is 50% and that inheriting one copy of the mutation is sufficient to develop the disease. Susceptibility genes alter an individual's chances of developing a disease or the age at onset of a disease but are not in

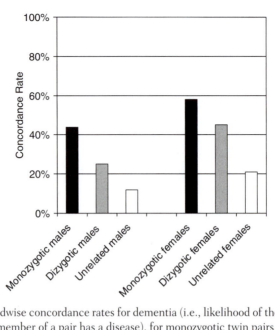

Fig. 1. Probandwise concordance rates for dementia (i.e., likelihood of the partner being affected if one member of a pair has a disease), for monozygotic twin pairs, dizygotic twin pairs, and unrelated pairs sharing the same year of birth, by sex. The number of pairs represented by the columns are 428, 679, 1547, 655, 1009, and 1569, respectively.

themselves sufficient to cause the disease. Late-onset complex diseases such as AD are rarely due to a single causative gene, and susceptibility genes account for more of the genetic risk than do causative genes.

Three genes have been identified (see Table 1) in which particular mutations cause AD following an autosomal dominant pattern of inheritance, typically with an early age of onset. Mutations in these genes explain up to half of what is often called familial AD. However, because familial AD is so rare, these three established gene mutations account for under 2% of all cases of AD.

Genetic influences on AD are believed largely to stem from predisposing rather than causative genes. The major susceptibility gene identified to date is the apolipoprotein E gene (APOE). The ApoE protein is involved in the transport of cholesterol during neuronal growth and after injury and in the deposition of Aβ. The APOE gene has three versions or alleles—ε2, ε3, and ε4. Those who inherit an ε4 allele from one parent have greater risk of developing AD. There is a dose effect, with two ε4 alleles being more unfavorable than one. Some studies find that the ε2 allele is protective.

There is a higher occurrence of the ε4 allele in African Americans than in Whites. However, surprisingly, most reports find that APOE ε4 is not a significant genetic risk factor for African Americans.

Even including APOE, identified genes at best explain half of AD cases. It is estimated that there may be six or more additional susceptibility genes with major effects on risk of disease occurrence and age at onset (Bird, 2005). Susceptibility genes may each add quantitatively to an individual's personal risk. The more promising of these susceptibility genes are shown in Table 1. All of them relate to some

Table 1 *Mutations and Susceptibility Genes Associated With Dementia, Their Locations, and Possible Pathways by Which Susceptibility Genes Might Influence Risk of Alzheimer's Disease (AD)*

Gene	Chromosome	Possible pathway to AD susceptibility
AD mutations		
Amyloid precursor protein gene (APP)	21	—
Presenilin 1 (PS1)	14	—
Presenilin 2 (PS2)	1	—
AD susceptibility genes		
Apolipoprotein E (APOE)	19	Regulates beta-amyloid (Aβ) deposition
α2-Macroglobulin (α2M)	12	Plays a role in clearing Aβ from the brain
Low density lipoprotein receptor-related protein (LRP)	12	Serves as receptor for ApoE
Insulin degrading enzyme (IDE)	10	Regulates levels of insulin and degrades Aβ
Angiotension I converting enzyme (ACE)	17	Plays a role in regulation of arterial blood pressure and in Aβ clearance
Interleukin 1 receptor alpha (IL-1α)	2	Regulates levels of proinflammatory protein
Adenosine triphosphate (ATP)-binding cassette transporter 1 (ABCA1)	9	Mediates cellular cholesterol
Ubiquilin 1 (UBQLN1)	9	Regulates protein degradation
Sortilin-related receptor (SORL1)	11	Regulates generation of Aβ
Dementia with Lewy Bodies mutations		
a-Synuclein	4	—
Vascular dementia mutations		
Notch3	19	—
Fronto-temporal dementia mutations		
Tau	17	—

Note. See Tsuang Bird (2002) and Bertram, McQueen, Blacker, and Tanzi (2007). The Bertram et al. article includes meta-analysis and a linko to the AlzGene Web site (http://www.alzforum.org/res/com/gen/alzgene/defualt.asp), where complete results from all available studies of each susceptibility gene are reported.

aspect of how AD originates, as described earlier in this paper, lending plausibility to how each might contribute to increasing disease risk. A number of these genes have been investigated with Swedish twin data—including, for example, the gene for insulin-degrading enzyme (Prince et al., 2003). Research to date, however, is characterized by many failures to replicate findings across studies.

For other types of dementia, some specific mutations, also shown in Table 1, have been implicated, but only in rare forms of these conditions. As for AD, there are familial cases not explained by genetic discoveries to date.

The question of genetic testing for dementia sometimes arises. Genetic testing along with genetic counseling would be recommended in families in which one of the specific mutations is suspected. But at present, potential misuses of testing for susceptibility genes may outweigh the information gained.

GENE-BY-GENE AND GENE-BY-ENVIRONMENT INTERACTIONS

Most scholars believe that dementia results from a combination of several genes acting together (gene-by-gene interactions) and interactions between genes and multiple environmental factors (gene-by-environment interactions). In testing for gene-by-environment interactions, the environment term encompasses anything to which an individual is exposed—hypertension or education, for example—that might affect risk of dementia, although clearly these factors might themselves be influenced by other genes.

Gene-by-gene interactions have most often been examined by testing APOE ε4 carrier status in concert with some other susceptibility gene findings have generally not shown consistent evidence of interaction. The ability to find reliable results and to test complex interactions among multiple genes should become possible with larger databases and more sophisticated analytic approaches (Bertram, McQueen, Mullin, Blacker, & Tanzi, 2007).

Finding gene-by-environment interactions has proved elusive. Where there have been significant results, they have not always been intuitive. In African American participants from the Indianapolis-Ibadan Dementia Project, for example, lower total serum cholesterol was related to reduced risk of AD only in those who carried no ε4 alleles (Evans et al., 2000). In Cardiovascular Health Study participants, it was found that estrogen replacement therapy (ERT) was related to lower risk of becoming cognitively impaired, but only among women who carried no ε4 alleles (Yaffe, Haan, Byers, Tangen, & Kuller, 2000), and that physical exercise was significantly associated with reduced risk of subsequently developing dementia, but, again, only among ε4 noncarriers (Podewils et al., 2005). In analyses of MZ twins from Sweden, intrapair differences in depressive symptoms were associated with intrapair differences in cognitive decline. However, for both estrogen receptor alpha (ESR1) and APOE, the association between depressive symptoms and cognitive decline was found only for noncarriers of the risk alleles (Reynolds, Gatz, Berg, & Pedersen, in press).

Thus, although individuals who have a positive family history for AD are particularly interested in what steps they might be able to take to reduce their chances of developing dementia, the preponderance of findings suggests that lifestyle factors—such as diet, ERT, physical exercise, and exposure to depression-evoking contexts—may be more important for those who are not at genetic risk than for those who are. People with a positive family history or who know that they are ε4 carriers are still left with remarkably little reliable guidance about what might be protective.

For vascular dementia, health habits related to preventing stroke—e.g., avoiding smoking, obesity, and hypertension—are relevant to prevention. Further advances in understanding genetic risk and potential gene-by-environment interactions are likely to arise from identifying genes that make brain tissue more or less susceptible to vascular injury.

CONCLUSIONS AND FUTURE DIRECTIONS

Taken together, twin studies and molecular-genetic studies indicate that genetic factors are clearly important in dementia, especially AD. A major new effort called the AD Genetics Initiative, funded by the National Institute on Aging, is being undertaken to identify these genes. Yet, equally evident is that genetic factors are only part of the picture, and finding the causes of dementia must entail more than a search for genes.

Clinical trials and experimental studies, including animal studies and neuroimaging work, will be useful complements to epidemiological studies in obtaining evidence about the gene-by-environment interactions. Future research might also build on twin studies—for example, focusing on MZ pairs who share particular susceptibility genes but in which only one of the pair has dementia.

Finally, epigenetic phenomena may play a key role in explaining dementia. Epigenetic differences refer to changes in genetic material that arise during development. These could be seen as chance events during DNA replication that do not alter the DNA sequence but change whether a particular gene is active or not. Twin studies are an important tool because identical twins can accumulate differences between them due to epigenetic modifications (Wong, Gottesman, & Petronis, 2005). Discordance for dementia among monozygotic twin pairs could be explained by epigenetic differences arising by chance, differences in environmental influences, or environmental factors that have a long-term influence on epigenetic modifications.

Recommended Reading

Cummings, J.L., & Cole, G. (2002). Alzheimer disease. *JAMA: The Journal of the American Medical Association, 287,* 2335–2338.

Gatz, M., & Brommelhoff, J. (in press). The implications of genetic testing for Alzheimer's disease in an aging society. In C.Y. Read, R.C. Green, & M.A. Smyer (Eds.), *Aging, Biotechnology, & the Future.* Baltimore: Johns Hopkins University Press.

Gatz, M., Prescott, C.A., & Pedersen, N.L. (2006). Lifestyle risk and delaying factors. *Alzheimer Disease & Associated Disorders, 20* (Suppl. 2), S84–S88.

Read, C.Y., Roberts, J.S., Linnenbringer, E., & Green, R.C. (in press). Genetic testing for Alzheimer's disease: The REVEAL Study. In C.Y. Read, R.C. Green, & M.A. Smyer (Eds.), *Aging, Biotechnology, & the Future.* Baltimore: Johns Hopkins University Press.

Acknowledgments—Research described in this article was supported in part by National Institute on Aging Grant R01AG08724. I am grateful for comments by Malcolm Klein, Chandra Reynolds, and Martha Storandt.

Note

1. Address correspondence to Margaret Gatz, Department of Psychology, University of Southern California, 3620 McClintock Avenue, Los Angeles CA 90089-1061; e-mail: gatz@usc.edu.

References

Bertram, L., McQueen, M.B., Mullin, K., Blacker, D., & Tanzi, R.E. (2007). Systematic meta-analyses of Alzheimer disease genetic association studies: The AlzGene database. *Nature Genetics, 39*, 17–23.

Bird, T.D. (2005). Genetic factors in Alzheimer's disease. *New England Journal of Medicine, 352*, 862–864.

Evans, R.M., Emsley, C.L., Gao, S., Sahota, A., Hall, K.S., Farlow, M.R., & Hendrie, H. (2000). Serum cholesterol, APOE genotype, and the risk of Alzheimer's disease: A population-based study of African Americans. *Neurology, 54*, 240–242.

Ferri, C.P., Prince, M., Brayne, C., Brodaty, H., Fratiglioni, L., Ganguli, M., et al. (2005). Global prevalence of dementia: A Delphi consensus study. *Lancet, 366*, 2112–2117.

Gatz. M., Reynolds, C.A, Fratiglioni, L., Johansson, B., Mortimer, J.A., Berg, S., et al. (2006). The role of genes and environments for explaining Alzheimer's disease. *Archives of General Psychiatry, 63*, 168–174.

Green, R.C., Cupples, L.A., Go, R., Benke, K.S., Edeki, T., Griffith, P.A., et al. (2002). Risk of dementia among White and African American relatives of patients with Alzheimer disease. *JAMA: The Journal of the American Medical Association, 287*, 329–336.

Harris Interactive. (2006, May 11). MetLife Foundation Alzheimer's survey: What America thinks. Retrieved June 30, 2006, from http://www.metlife.com/WPSAssets/205382964211-47208330V1F AlzheimersSurvey.pdf.

Helpguide. (2005, October). Jokes to make you laugh. Retrieved July 2, 2006, from http://www.helpguide.org/life/jokes/oct_05.htm.

Podewils, L.J., Guallar, E., Kuller, L.H., Fried, L.P., Lopez, O.L., Carlson, M., & Lyketsos, C.G. (2005). Physical activity, APOE genotype, and dementia risk: Findings from the cardiovascular health cognition study. *American Journal of Epidemiology, 161*, 639–651.

Prince, J.A., Feuk, L., Gu, H.F., Johansson, B., Gatz, M., Blennow, K., & Brookes, A.J. (2003). Genetic variation in a haplotype block spanning IDE influences Alzheimer disease. *Human Mutation, 22*, 363–371.

Reynolds, C.A., Gatz, M., Berg, S., & Pedersen, N.L. (in press). Genotype–environment interactions: Cognitive aging and social factors. *Twin Research and Human Genetics*.

Seshadri, S., Wolf, P.A., Beiser, A., Au, R., McNulty, K., White, R., & D'Agostino, R.B. (1997). Lifetime risk of dementia and Alzheimer's disease. The impact of mortality on risk estimates in the Framingham Study. *Neurology, 49*, 1498–1504.

Tsuang, D.W., & Bird, T.D. (2002). Genetics of dementia. *Medical Clinics of North America, 86*, 591–614.

Wong, A.H., Gottesman, I.I., & Petronis, A. (2005). Phenotypic differences in genetically identical organisms: The epigenetic perspective. *Human Molecular Genetics, 14* (Supp. 1), R11–R18.

Yaffe, K., Haan, M., Byers, A., Tangen, C., & Kuller, L. (2000). Estrogen use, APOE, and cognitive decline: Evidence of gene–environment interaction. *Neurology, 54*, 1949–1954.

Critical Thinking Questions

1. Your friend has a grandmother who is 90 years old and was just diagnosed with Alzheimer's disease. Your friend is worried that, because her grandma has Alzheimer's Disease, she will also be diagnosed with this disease when she is older. Based on this reading, what do you tell her in response to her concerns?

2. Is Alzheimer's disease another name for dementia? What is the difference between these two terms?

3. Describe several of the hypothesized pathways through which gene mutations may increase susceptibility to an Alzheimer's disease diagnosis.

This article has been reprinted as it originally appeared in *Current Directions in Psychological Science*. Citation information for this article as originally published appears above.

Behavior in Adulthood and During Aging Is Affected by Contaminant Exposure in Utero

M. Christopher Newland[1]

Department of Psychology, Auburn University, Auburn, Alabama (M.C.N.)

Erin B. Rasmussen

Department of Psychology, College of Charleston, Charleston, South Carolina (E.B.R.)

Abstract

Environmental contaminants can alter the course of neural development, with consequences that appear in behavior. Such effects extend into adulthood and sometimes accelerate the rate of aging, even when exposure ceases by birth. The neurotoxicant methylmercury provides an interesting case study that reveals much about how disrupted neural development has lifelong consequences. Methylmercury also provides an example of the assessment and management of risks associated with exposure to developmental neurotoxicants.

Keywords

methylmercury; behavioral toxicology; delayed neurotoxicity; development and aging

In April of 1956, two sisters entered the pediatrics department of a hospital in southern Japan. Previously bright, verbal, and active, suddenly they could not walk, their speech was incoherent, and they were delirious. Eventually a number of children from the same neighborhood entered the hospital with nearly identical complaints (Smith & Smith, 1975).

This was the beginning of a major industrial disaster caused by tons of mercury that were being dumped into Minamata Bay. Adults became blind, and children were born with cerebral palsy and mental retardation. By 1993, 2,256 children and adults were diagnosed with Minamata disease in the fishing village that gave methylmercury poisoning its name (Harada, 1995). Methylmercury-contaminated fish were identified as the cause of the disease only after an all-too-familiar practice of blaming the victims for negligence, sinfulness, or drug abuse (Smith & Smith, 1975). (The pattern by which this and other disasters often unfold is captured closely in the fictional allegory *The Plague*, by Camus, 1947/1972.) The events in Minamata led researchers to recognize that developmental disorders can have environmental sources. Now these events are showing that disorders associated with aging may be related to contamination, too. Beginning at about 50 years of age, Minamata residents exposed to methylmercury as adults reported difficulties with such simple activities as buttoning a shirt or toileting themselves without assistance (Kinjo, Higashi, Nakano, Sakamoto, & Sakai, 1993), and this decline in function accelerated with age. Interestingly, death rates in exposed populations were no different from those in nearby villages, so the functional deficits are not necessarily linked to mortality.

In this article, we examine methylmercury neurotoxicity as a case study to illustrate the role that environmental contaminants can play over the course of a life span. We also hope to show how controlled studies can shed light on neural and behavioral mechanisms by which methylmercury has its effects. Such understanding can inform the development of guidelines regarding exposure to neurotoxic substances.

LABORATORY MODELS OF MINAMATA DISEASE

With methylmercury, as with many other chemicals, epidemiological evidence from human populations is correlational and cannot demonstrate causality or identify mechanisms of action. There are simply too many confounding influences. Controlled experimental studies with animals are necessary, especially with neurotoxic substances, because the effects are often irreversible and deliberate human exposure would be reprehensible.

Laboratory investigators have used nonhuman primates and rodents to study methylmercury's toxicity. Investigations with nonhuman primates reproduced the essential features of methylmercury exposure during neural development, resulting in a far better understanding of visual, auditory, and sensorimotor deficits associated with methylmercury and the exposure conditions required to produce them (Rice, 1996). Some primate studies also yielded intriguing evidence that animals that were exposed developmentally and appeared normal as adults showed deficits as they aged, but the sample sizes of these studies were small. Rodent studies had larger sample sizes but usually were less revealing about methylmercury's neurotoxicity. Sometimes no effects could be identified, or they occurred only at very high exposure levels. This discrepancy between primates and rodents sometimes led to suggestions that rats and mice are inappropriate models of human neurotoxicity of methylmercury (and sometimes of other chemicals as well).

We disagree. The difficulties with rodent studies were related to dosing regimens and the behavioral measures employed. Primate studies entailed chronic, low-level exposure regimens and sophisticated behavioral procedures designed to identify subtle effects of exposure. Rodent studies often incorporated acute, high-level exposure that could only result in wildly changing methylmercury concentrations in the brain, so the methylmercury concentration at certain crucial developmental periods could not be ascertained. Sometimes these studies used behavioral measures that are better suited to demonstrating the effects of high exposure levels than to identifying subtle impairments associated with chronic, low-level exposure (Newland & Paletz, 2000).

With appropriate experimental design, the rodent can be an excellent model of human mercury exposure, however. Stable mercury concentrations comparable to those seen in primate studies can be produced in the rodent brain by adjusting methylmercury intake to overcome the exceptionally high levels of mercury-binding hemoglobin in rat blood (because mercury binds readily to sulfur, found in hemoglobin, relatively less mercury is available for transport to the brain in rats than in other mammalian species) and by beginning exposure weeks before mating, to allow for the long time required for methylmercury levels to stabilize. In our studies (Newland & Reile, 1999), female rats consume water containing 0, 0.5, or 6 ppm of mercury (as methylmercury), resulting in intakes averaging about 0, 40, and 500 µg/kg/day, respectively, before mating. The resulting brain concentrations (about 0, 0.5, and 9 ppm) are in a range considered to be low to moderate (Burbacher, Rodier, & Weiss, 1990) in mammalian species. These levels are quite stable because of the protracted dosing regimen. Our observations confirm that these are not high exposure levels. It would be impossible to identify rats exposed under our protocol using cage-side observations, even if one were looking specifically for methylmercury-related signs.

PUZZLING ABOUT LEARNING AND MEMORY

Epidemiological studies have correlated methylmercury exposure with mental retardation at high exposure levels (Harada, 1995) and with subtle changes in language and attention tasks at lower levels (Grandjean, Weihe, White, & Debes, 1998). Paradoxically, methylmercury exposure in rats or monkeys has not affected performance on tasks commonly associated with "cognition." Performance is not impaired on discrimination tasks in which one stimulus (an S+) signals the availability of reinforcement and another (an S−) signals that reinforcement is not available. Nor do effects appear after the S+ and S− are reversed and a new discrimination must be acquired. Memory is not impaired either; methylmercury may even have increased delays at which monkeys' performance on a delayed discrimination task began to deteriorate (reviewed in Newland & Paletz, 2000, and Rice, 1996). These tasks emphasize the contextual control of behavior, and they appear to be insensitive to methylmercury. A procedure that emphasizes the selection of behavior by reinforcing events, described shortly, appears to be quite sensitive to methylmercury. A crucial distinction exists here, and it draws from the insight that operant behavior (essentially all voluntary behavior) can be understood by reducing it to a three-term contingency of reinforcement, in which a response-reinforcer relationship is viewed as acting in a stimulus context. First noted more than half a century ago by Skinner, the ability of this dynamic interplay among stimuli, responses, and consequences to account for the formation of impressively complex behavior is among the most widely replicated empirical phenomena in all of psychology.

Experiments can be designed to examine different terms, even if these terms cannot be completely isolated. In a discrimination task, the experimenter changes something about the stimuli that signal which response to perform. Thus, a red light may signal that pressing the left lever produces food, and a green light may signal that pressing the right lever produces food. In a memory task, the stimuli are removed before the opportunity to respond is made available. The response-reinforcer relationship is invariant—one lever press always produces food, for example. Accuracy is often used to measure contextual control over behavior (synonyms include *stimulus control* or *discrimination*).

To emphasize the response-reinforcer relationship, researchers hold the stimulus context constant, but the relative rate of reinforcement available from different response devices changes. In this case, behavior change has little to do with context because that remains constant. Instead, behavior change reflects different response-reinforcer relationships. For example, two levers may both produce food twice a minute for a few sessions, but then one lever produces food four times per minute and the other produces food once per minute. Context still exists (the levers are, after all, different), but its role is deemphasized relative to the role played by the specific response requirements. This thinking has been applied to methylmercury's neurotoxicity as follows (Newland & Paletz, 2000).

Figure 1 illustrates the effect of in utero methylmercury exposure on behavior of squirrel monkeys in a procedure that examines continuous choice under reinforcement contingencies that change occasionally (Newland, Yezhou, Logdberg, & Berlin, 1994). In this experiment, a squirrel monkey faced a panel containing two levers. In the first phase, pressing the left lever produced food intermittently

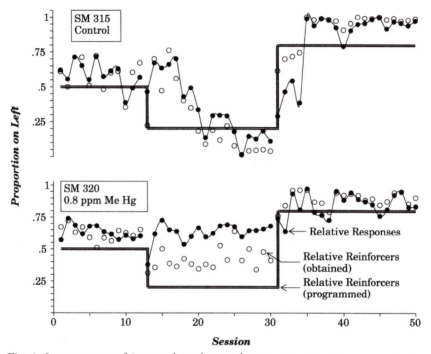

Fig. 1. Lever pressing of 2 squirrel monkeys undergoing transitions in concurrent reinforcement schedules. Initially, one half of the food reinforcers derived from the left lever and one half derived from the right lever. Beginning with the 13th session, only 20% of the reinforcers derived from the left lever, and beginning in the 31st session, 80% of the reinforcers derived from the left lever. Each datum represents a single, 30-min session. The double lines show the proportion of reinforcers programmed to derive from the left lever. Open circles show the proportion of reinforcers obtained from that lever. Closed circles show the proportion of responses made on that lever. Results are shown for a control monkey (top panel) and a monkey exposed in utero to methylmercury (Me Hg; bottom panel). Adapted from "Prolonged Behavioral Effects of in Utero Exposure to Lead or Methyl Mercury: Reduced Sensitivity to Changes in Reinforcement Contingencies During Behavioral Transitions and in Steady State," by M.C. Newland, S. Yezhou, B. Logdberg, & M. Berlin, 1994, *Toxicology and Applied Pharmacology*, 126, p. 8. Copyright 1994 by Academic Press.

but unpredictably once a minute. Pressing the right lever produced food under the same schedule of reinforcement. By switching between the two levers, the monkey could receive an average of two reinforcers per minute. (This is called a concurrent schedule of food reinforcement.)

Reinforcement rates changed abruptly at the beginning of the 13th session; the left lever produced food at one quarter the rate of the right lever (one vs. four reinforcers per minute). The behavior of the control monkey, which was not exposed to methylmercury, gradually shifted until the proportion of its responses on the left lever approximated the low proportion of reinforcers delivered by that lever. This steady-state performance in which the relative allocation of behavior approximates the relative availability of reinforcement is called matching and is commonly observed in studies of animals (Davison & McCarthy, 1988) and humans (Kollins, Newland, & Critchfield, 1997).

In contrast, the behavior of the methylmercury-exposed monkey was unperturbed by the new reinforcement rates. This insensitivity also occurred in later transitions, including the one beginning at Session 31 in Figure 1. In behavior therapy interventions (results not shown in the figure), 99% of the reinforcers were programmed to come from one lever, an extreme discrepancy that finally caused exposed monkeys' behavior to change. Three methylmercury-exposed monkeys, and many lead-exposed monkeys, exhibited retarded transitions repeatedly with this procedure; that is, they required many more reinforcers to complete the transition than did unexposed monkeys. These results have been replicated with rodents in as-yet unpublished data.

In this type of study, it is common practice to correlate the relative number of responses on a lever to the relative reinforcement rate obtained from that lever. However, the monkey study just described (Newland et al., 1994) emphasized programmed reinforcement rates instead. An extreme example exemplifies the difference between programmed and obtained reinforcement rates. The experimenter may arrange for (program) one quarter of the reinforcers to derive from the left lever, but if no responses occur on that lever, then 0% of reinforcers are obtained from that lever. Programmed reinforcement rate is a more appropriate variable because (a) the goal is to examine how neurotoxicants alter the way in which structure in behavior reflects structure in the environment and (b) obtained reinforcement proportions are not independent variables, anyway. To see the latter point, note that during the first transition for the methylmercury-exposed monkey (Fig. 1), obtained reinforcement rates lay between programmed rates and response proportions. Obtained reinforcement rates depended on both programmed reinforcement rate and behavior and cannot be considered independent.

METHYLMERCURY EXPOSURE IN UTERO INFLUENCES THE COURSE OF AGING

We now shift from young monkeys to old rats. We followed rats exposed to methylmercury during gestation (as described earlier) throughout life to examine very long-term consequences of such exposure (Newland & Rasmussen, 2000). When the rats were 4 to 6 months of age, we trained them to press a lever nine times within 4 s. (This is referred to as differential reinforcement of high rate, meaning that high response rates, including those that make up response bursts, are selectively reinforced with food.) We focused on the number of nine-response bursts that met the high-response-rate criterion, as well as on the age at which performance declined to 50% of the levels seen when the rats were young adults.

Aging exerted its own toll on this behavior. Most 2-year-old control rats performed at about 80% of the baseline established when they were young adults, but 1 crossed the 50% threshold (Fig. 2). As the figure illustrates, in utero exposure to methylmercury caused many rats to cross the threshold at a younger age, and the higher the exposure, the younger the age. The exposed animals had not had methylmercury since weaning and probably not since birth because little methylmercury is available in milk (Newland & Reile, 1999). Figure 2 also illustrates the phenomenon known as individual susceptibility, a common finding in behavioral toxicology. In each exposure group, at least 1 rat completed the study without crossing the 50% threshold, and at least 1 rat crossed this threshold; the number showing performance deficits increased with methylmercury dose. Thus, it is not the case that in utero methylmercury exposure shifted the whole population equally. Instead, it appears that some rats are susceptible to showing functional declines as they age, and methylmercury exposure in utero amplified this susceptibility. Incidentally, mortality in these rats was unrelated to exposure, as in Minamata.

DRUG CHALLENGES AND NEUROCHEMICAL MECHANISMS

Can a behavioral mechanism such as reinforcement insensitivity be related to neurotransmitter function? By observing a contaminant's effects in vitro (i.e., on

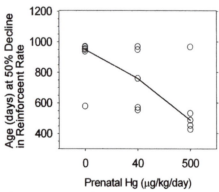

Fig. 2. Decline in reinforcement rates of rats trained to execute response bursts of nine lever presses within 4 s in order to receive food reinforcement. The graph shows the age at which each rat's performance (number of bursts meeting the criterion) declined to 50% of a baseline established when the rat was a young adult. If the rat completed the experiment without experiencing such a decline, a value of 950 days was entered. Results are shown for rats exposed to methylmercury in utero and control rats with no exposure. Adapted from "Aging Unmasks Adverse Effects of Gestational Exposure to Methylmercury in Rats," by M.C. Newland & E.B. Rasmussen, 2000, *Neurotoxicology and Teratology, 22,* p. 825. Copyright 2000 by Elsevier Science, Inc.

isolated neural tissue), researchers form hypotheses about its neurochemical mechanisms of action. To be meaningful, these hypotheses must be tested with drug challenges, in which a drug with known, specific effects is administered to animals engaging in a behavioral task. Early, and somewhat limited, studies suggested that exposure to methylmercury during development increases sensitivity to d amphetamine, a drug that promotes the activity of dopamine and norepinephrine neurotransmitter systems. We expanded on these studies by including drugs representing several drug classes, selected according to their effects on tissue; by examining a full range of doses; and by using fully adult animals (Rasmussen & Newland, 2001).

We conducted these drug challenges with the same rats described in the previous section; their lever pressing was maintained under the same differential-reinforcement-of-high-rate schedule of reinforcement as in that study. The drug challenges were conducted when the rats were between 6 months and 1 year old. To determine a drug's effect, we injected it before an experimental session and compared the resulting response rates with those seen in control sessions in which either there was no injection or an inert solution was injected. Multiple doses were used. To rule out non-specific effects of the injection process itself, we occasionally injected only the vehicle, the fluid in which the drug was dissolved. Compared with unexposed rats, methylmercury-exposed rats were up to twice as sensitive to d amphetamine; that is, the dose that significantly lowered responding in the methylmercury-exposed rats was one half the dose with the same effect in the unexposed rats. Exposed rats were less sensitive to pentobarbital, which promotes the activity of an inhibitory transmitter called GABA (gamma amino butyric acid). Equally important is the fact that the study demonstrated specificity: Methylmercury-exposed rats showed no differential sensitivity to other drugs tested.

There is substantial evidence that midbrain dopamine, and perhaps norepinephrine, pathways play a role in reinforcement and choice. The methylmercury-exposed rats' sensitivity to amphetamine might indicate that their diminished sensitivity to reinforcing consequences, illustrated in Figure 1, is related to actions of these neurotransmitter systems. In other words, it appears that a behavioral effect of methylmercury exposure, sensitivity to reinforcement, can be linked to a specific neural mechanism, alteration in the dopamine system. Many gaps remain to be filled, including relating d amphetamine's behavioral effects to altered behavioral transitions (illustrated in Fig. 1) before this can be verified.

In a similar vein, pentobarbital's actions might be viewed in light of observations that compounds that promote GABA, like alcohol, pentobarbital, and many tranquilizers, can cause selective amnesia. The diminished sensitivity to pentobarbital associated with methylmercury exposure might be related to reports that methylmercury does not disrupt performance on tasks that tax memory. At present, however, this idea is only speculation.

LINKING ANIMAL AND HUMAN EXPOSURES TO ASSESS RISK

The episode at Minamata showed not only that methylmercury is a hazard, but also that it is found in fish. It is now known that fish is the major source, close to the only source, of human methylmercury exposure worldwide. Therefore, advice about consuming methylmercury will influence the consumption of fish, an excellent source of nutrients important to neural development and cardiovascular health. It is crucial to understand how methylmercury acts, and at what doses, to ensure that advisories are not drawn so cautiously that they reduce fish consumption inappropriately. Laboratory studies are a necessary component of the process of identifying acceptable exposure levels. In our studies, and in some others, the duration, magnitude, and route of exposure were selected after considering the biology underlying methylmercury intake and elimination. However, the studies also model human exposures and therefore can contribute to evaluations of risk. Effects that are dose related, reproducible, and linked to mechanisms of action can be combined with epidemiological studies to arrive at estimates of a *reference dose,* a level of intake that is unlikely to be harmful.

Creativity and skillful application of principles of conditioning in designing behavioral procedures are key to identifying the subtle effects of low-level exposure, and the effects of low doses receive considerable attention in policymaking regarding the even lower exposure levels that people might experience. Even under the best of circumstances, it is necessary to extrapolate to doses lower than those used in laboratories. Studies with economically feasible sample sizes will not detect effects seen in fewer than 10% of subjects, but a 10% prevalence would be a disaster in a human population. The solution to this problem is beyond the scope of this article, but readers might be interested in seeing the creative approaches taken to conducting such extrapolations (Glowa & MacPhail, 1995). These approaches exploit the quantitative sophistication of well-designed behavioral experiments.

After reviewing the scientific literature, the U.S. Environmental Protection Agency (EPA) recently set the reference ("safe") dose for methylmercury at 0.1 μg/kg/day, or about one can of tuna per week, for pregnant women. The fetus was the primary concern because it was felt to be the most sensitive to methylmercury's effects. Effects associated with aging might extend concern to the elderly.

The value of 40 μg/kg/day that caused impairments in our rats might seem far removed from the reference dose, but in light of how risk assessment is actually conducted, it may be quite close. Risk assessors acknowledge that there are uncertainties embedded in extrapolating from small, relatively normal, and otherwise healthy rats to a diverse array of people. To accommodate these uncertainties, they simply divide the exposure level used in a laboratory study by one or several powers of 10 to estimate tolerable human exposures. The point of departure for conducting a risk assessment beginning with rats might be 4 and not 40 μg/kg/ day, because of the high concentration of hemoglobin in rat blood, but it is not clear how to incorporate this peculiarity of rat blood into risk assessment. Thus, the intake experienced by our animals could be uncomfortably close, by risk-assessment standards, to the level considered unlikely to cause harm in humans.

EPA's reference dose aroused considerable debate because of how it might influence fish consumption. Setting reference doses too low or communicating a message so confusing that it dissuades people from eating fish would be counterproductive. As a state risk assessor told us, "If I tell people to avoid *certain* fish, then they will simply avoid *all* fish and eat burgers and fries instead!"

Fish differ widely in mercury content and in nutrients. For example, swordfish and shark may contain 10 to 40 times the mercury found in tuna, and ocean salmon may have 10 times less. So only large, long-lived predators (mercury accumulates in the food chain and in long-lived fish) should be avoided. Health agencies recommend avoiding shark, king mackerel, tilefish ("golden bass," "golden snapper"), swordfish, and fish from contaminated waters, but these recommendations are confusing and widely ignored. Swordfish is found on many restaurant menus, and few people know what is contained in processed fish. Perhaps people would be better served if hazards were simply removed from the food supply, so consumers could be assured that the fish they do purchase will not cause harm.

CLOSING COMMENTS

Psychology can make a significant contribution to the environmental health sciences. The experimental analysis of behavior, by applying well-grounded principles of conditioning, already has. Experimental psychology has more than a century's experience in grappling with the difficult problem of studying behavior systematically. This experience has yielded many successes in identifying fundamental behavioral principles and in linking these to nervous system activity. In addition, experimentalists have developed many creative methods for examining behavior in exquisite detail. Clinical psychology, when it draws from science, can contribute to treatment, assessment, and the application of principles. All of this expertise can be used in ways that matter to science and to policy.

Recommended Reading

Clarkson, T.W. (2002). The three modern faces of mercury. *Environmental Health Perspectives, 110*(Suppl. 1), 11–23.

Committee on the Toxicological Effects of Methylmercury, National Research Council. (2000). *Toxicological effects of methylmercury.* Washington, DC: National Academy Press.

Cranmer, J.S. (Ed.). (1996). Neurotoxicity of methylmercury: Indicators and effects of low-level exposure [Special issue]. *Neurotoxicology, 17*(1).

Newland, M.C., & Reile, P.A. (1999). Learning and behavior change as neurotoxic endpoints. In H.A. Tilson & J. Harry (Eds.), *Target organ series: Neurotoxicology* (pp. 311–338). New York: Raven Press.

Weiss, B., Clarkson, T.W., & Simon, W. (2002). Silent latency periods in methylmercury poisoning and in neurodegenerative disease. *Environmental Health Perspectives, 110*(Suppl. 5), 851–854.

Acknowledgments—M.C. Newland wishes to acknowledge support by Grant ES-10865 from the National Institute of Environmental Sciences.

Note

1. Address correspondence to M. Christopher Newland, Experimental Psychology, Auburn University, AL 36849; e-mail: newlamc@auburn.edu.

References

Burbacher, T.M., Rodier, P.M., & Weiss, B. (1990). Methylmercury developmental neurotoxicity: A comparison of effects in humans and animals. *Neurotoxicology and Teratology, 12*, 191–202.

Camus, A. (1972). *The plague* (S. Gilbert, Trans.). New York: Vintage Books. (Original work published 1947)

Davison, M., & McCarthy, D. (1988). *The matching law: A research review*. Hillsdale, NJ: Erlbaum.

Glowa, J.R., & MacPhail, R.C. (1995). Quantitative approaches to risk assessment in neurotoxicology. In L.W. Chang & W. Slikker (Eds.), *Neurotoxicology: Approaches and methods* (pp. 777–787). San Diego, CA: Academic Press.

Grandjean, P., Weihe, P., White, R.F., & Debes, F. (1998). Cognitive performance of children prenatally exposed to "safe" levels of methylmercury. *Environmental Research, 77*, 165–172.

Harada, M. (1995). Minamata disease: Methylmercury poisoning in Japan caused by environmental pollution. *Critical Reviews in Toxicology, 25*, 1–24.

Kinjo, Y., Higashi, H., Nakano, A., Sakamoto, M., & Sakai, R. (1993). Profile of subjective complaints and activities of daily living among current patients with Minamata disease after 3 decades. *Environmental Research, 63*, 241–251.

Kollins, S.H., Newland, M.C., & Critchfield, T.S. (1997). Human sensitivity to reinforcement in operant choice: How much do consequences matter? *Psychonomic Bulletin & Review, 4*, 208–220.

Newland, M.C., & Paletz, E.M. (2000). Animal studies of methylmercury and PCBs: What do they tell us about expected effects in humans? *Neurotoxicology, 21*, 1003–1027.

Newland, M.C., & Rasmussen, E.B. (2000). Aging unmasks adverse effects of gestational exposure to methylmercury in rats. *Neurotoxicology and Teratology, 22*, 819–828.

Newland, M.C., & Reile, P.A. (1999). Blood and brain mercury levels after chronic gestational exposure to methylmercury in rats. *Toxicological Sciences, 50*, 106–116.

Newland, M.C., Yezhou, S., Logdberg, B., & Berlin, M. (1994). Prolonged behavioral effects of in utero exposure to lead or methyl mercury: Reduced sensitivity to changes in reinforcement contingencies during behavioral transitions and in steady state. *Toxicology and Applied Pharmacology, 126*, 6–15.

Rasmussen, E.B., & Newland, M.C. (2001). Developmental exposure to methylmercury alters behavioral sensitivity to *d* amphetamine and pentobarbital in adult rats. *Neurotoxicology and Teratology, 23*, 45–55.

Rice, D.C. (1996). Sensory and cognitive effects of developmental methylmercury exposure in monkeys, and a comparison to effects in rodents. *Neurotoxicology, 17*, 139–154.

Smith, W.E., & Smith, A.M. (1975). *Minamata*. New York: Holt, Rinehart, and Winston.

Critical Thinking Questions

1. Sometimes, exposure to a toxin in utero, childhood or early adulthood not show effects until old age. What might explain the delay between exposure and the observed changes?

2. Did methlymercury exposure in utero effect all rats in the same way?

3. How did the reinforcement response among the monkeys exposed to methymercury vary from the response of their non-exposed counterparts?

This article has been reprinted as it originally appeared in *Current Directions in Psychological Science*. Citation information for this article as originally published appears above.

Intelligence Predicts Health and Longevity, but Why?

Linda S. Gottfredson[1]
School of Education, University of Delaware

Ian J. Deary
Department of Psychology, University of Edinburgh, Edinburgh, Scotland, United Kingdom

Abstract

Large epidemiological studies of almost an entire population in Scotland have found that intelligence (as measured by an IQ-type test) in childhood predicts substantial differences in adult morbidity and mortality, including deaths from cancers and cardiovascular diseases. These relations remain significant after controlling for socioeconomic variables. One possible, partial explanation of these results is that intelligence enhances individuals' care of their own health because it represents learning, reasoning, and problem-solving skills useful in preventing chronic disease and accidental injury and in adhering to complex treatment regimens.

Keywords

intelligence; health; longevity

Health psychologists examine the impact of volition on health, but might not competence matter too? Managing one's physical health is, after all, one of life's jobs, and personnel psychology has established that psychometric intelligence, that is, intelligence as measured by IQ tests, is the best single predictor of job performance. Indeed, intelligence is the best single predictor of major socioeconomic outcomes, both favorable (good education, occupation, income) and unfavorable (adult poverty, incarceration, chronic welfare use; Gottfredson, 2002).

HOW WELL DOES EARLY INTELLIGENCE PREDICT LATER HEALTH AND LONGEVITY?

Intelligence has been linked with various health behaviors and outcomes. On the positive side, physical fitness, a preference for low-sugar and low-fat diets, and longevity increase with higher intelligence; on the negative side, alcoholism, infant mortality, smoking, and obesity increase with lower intelligence (Gottfredson, in press). Especially informative are two epidemiological studies correlating IQ in childhood to adult morbidity and mortality.

Australian Veterans Health Studies

O'Toole and Stankov (1992) used IQ at induction into the military, along with 56 other psychological, behavioral, health, and demographic variables, to predict noncombat deaths by age 40 among 2,309 Australian veterans. When all other variables were statistically controlled, each additional IQ point predicted a 1% decrease in risk of death. Also, IQ was the best predictor of the major cause of death, motor vehicle accidents. Vehicular death rates doubled and then tripled at successively lower IQ ranges (100–115, 85–100, 80–85; O'Toole, 1990).

Scottish Mental Survey 1932 (SMS1932)

To date, Scotland is the only country to have conducted IQ testing on almost a whole year-of-birth cohort. This took place in the remarkable Scottish Mental Survey of 1932 (SMS1932). On June 1, 1932, a version of the Moray House Test (MHT) was administered to almost all children born in 1921 and attending schools in Scotland on that day (N = 87,498). The MHT is a well-validated intelligence test that has a high correlation (about .8) with the Stanford Binet. Recent follow-up studies of the SMS1932 (Deary, Whiteman, Starr, Whalley, & Fox, in press) provide novel findings on what intelligence differences during childhood portend for health in the rest of life.

Health data for subsets of the SMS1932 participants were collected in later decades. In one such follow-up study, Whalley and Deary (2001) identified the 2,792 children from the city of Aberdeen who participated in the SMS1932, and searched the Register of Deaths from 1932 to 1997 for whether they were alive or dead on January 1, 1997. Subjects not found were then sought in the Scottish Community Health Index, which records people who are registered with a general medical practitioner (more than 99% of the population). Many women were still untraced, mostly because they had married and changed their surname. Therefore, the Register of Marriages in Scotland was searched from 1937 onward. When a woman was traced to a marriage, the prior searches were repeated. Subjects still untraced were sought using computer and hand searches of the United Kingdom National Health Service Central Register.

Using these procedures, the researchers traced 2,230 (79.9%) of those children who took the MHT in Aberdeen: 1,084 were dead, 1,101 were alive, and 45 had moved away from Scotland. In addition, 562 were untraced. IQ at age 11 had a significant association with survival to about age 76. On average, individuals who were at a 1-standard-deviation (15-point) disadvantage in IQ relative to other participants were only 79% as likely to live to age 76. The effect of IQ was stronger for women (71%) than for men (83%), partly because men who died in active service during World War II had relatively high mean IQ scores. Further analyses of the Aberdeen subjects found that a drop of 1 standard deviation in IQ was associated with a 27% increase in cancer deaths among men and a 40% increase in cancer deaths among women (Deary, Whalley, & Starr, 2003). The effect was especially pronounced for stomach and lung cancers, which are specifically associated with low socioeconomic status (SES) in childhood.

Additional data for many SMS1932 participants are available in the Midspan studies, which began in the 1970s in the western and central areas of Scotland and are still ongoing. These studies investigated cardiovascular and respiratory diseases and their risk factors in the community. The participants were adults who completed a questionnaire and underwent physical examinations. Their social class—based on occupation at midlife—was recorded, as was the degree of deprivation or affluence of the area where they resided. The Midspan studies continue to follow participants, tracking their hospital admissions and the dates and causes of their deaths. Of the 1,251 Midspan participants born in 1921, 1,032 (82.5%) were matched to people in the SMS1932 ledgers, and 938 had an MHT score (Hart, Deary, et al., 2003). Higher IQ in 1932 had strong correlations with both higher social class and greater affluence of the area of residence at the time of Midspan participation. The risk of dying in the 25 years since participation in the Midspan studies increased 17% for each drop of 1 standard deviation in IQ at age 11 (Hart, Taylor, et al., 2003). Controlling for social class and deprivation recorded in the 1970s, when people were about 50 years old, reduced this figure to 12%.

IQ and deprivation interacted, such that the increase in mortality associated with deprivation was greatest in the lowest IQ quartile; put another way, IQ had a larger effect on mortality among people living in deprived areas than among people living in affluent areas at about age 50. Age-11 IQ had a small indirect effect on mortality from all causes combined, through its effects on adult social class and deprivation; however, the direct effects of age-11 IQ on mortality were stronger. Investigating specific causes of death among the Midspan participants, Hart, Taylor, et al. (2003) found that lower age-11 IQ predicted a significantly higher likelihood of dying from cardiovascular disease in general, coronary heart disease, and lung cancer.

Higher intelligence might lower mortality from all causes and from specific causes partly by affecting known risk factors for disease, such as smoking. In the combined SMS1932-Midspan database, there was no significant childhood IQ difference between participants who had ever smoked and those who had never smoked (Taylor, Hart, et al., 2003). However, at the time of the Midspan studies, participants who were current smokers had significantly lower childhood IQs than ex-smokers. For each standard deviation increase in IQ, there was a 33% increased rate of quitting smoking. Adjusting for social class reduced this rate only mildly, to 25%. Thus, childhood IQ was not associated with starting smoking (mostly in the 1930s, when the public were not aware of health risks), but was associated with giving up smoking as health risks became evident.

WHY DOES EARLY INTELLIGENCE PREDICT LATER HEALTH?

Health epidemiologists tend to ascribe inequalities in health to inequalities in socioeconomic resources, and then presume that intelligence is a product of such resources, and thus related to health because it is a proxy for privilege. Do differences in socioeconomic advantage explain the influence of intelligence on health?

Is Intelligence a Proxy for Material Resources?

A robust relation between childhood IQ and late-life morbidity and mortality remains after analyses control statistically for deprived living conditions. Residual confounding is possible, which means that social factors measured to date might not reliably assess all relevant aspects of social disadvantage. However, health inequalities tend to *increase* when health resources become more available to everyone (Gottfredson, in press). That is, increased availability of health resources improves health overall, but the improvements are smaller for people who are poorly educated and have low incomes than for people with more education and better incomes. Compared with people in high-SES groups, people with low SES seek more but not necessarily appropriate care when cost is no barrier; adhere less often to treatment regimens; learn and understand less about how to protect their health; seek less preventive care, even when it is free; and less often practice the healthy behaviors so important for preventing or slowing the progression of chronic diseases, the major killers and disablers in developed nations today.

Yet social class correlates with virtually every indicator of health, health behavior, and health knowledge. The link between SES and health transcends the particulars of material advantage, decade, nation, health system, social change, or disease, regardless of its treatability. Health scientists view the pervasiveness and finely graded nature of this relationship between SES and health as a paradox, leading them to speculate that SES creates health inequality via some yet-to-be-identified, highly generalizable "fundamental cause" (Gottfredson, in press). The socioeconomic measures that best predict health inequality also correlate most with intelligence (education best, then occupation, then income). This means that instead of IQ being a proxy for SES in health matters, SES measures might be operating primarily as rough proxies for social-class differences in mental rather than material resources.

Does Intelligence Provide Health-Enhancing Mental Resources?

Psychometric intelligence is manifested in generic thinking skills such as efficient learning, reasoning, problem solving, and abstract thinking. High intelligence is a useful tool in any life domain, but especially when tasks are novel, untutored, or complex and situations are ambiguous, changing, or unpredictable (Gottfredson, 1997).

Dealing with the novel, ever-changing, and complex is what health self-care demands. Preventive information proliferates, and new treatments often require regular self-monitoring and complicated self-medication. Good health depends as much on preventing as on ameliorating illness, injury, and disability. Preventing some aspects of chronic disease is arguably no less cognitive a process than preventing accidents, the fourth leading cause of death in the United States, behind cancer, heart disease, and stroke (Gottfredson, in press). Preventing both illness and accidents requires anticipating the unexpected and "driving defensively," in a well-informed way, through life. The cognitive demands of preventing illness and accidents are comparable—remain vigilant for hazards and recognize them when present, remove or evade them in a timely manner, contain incidents to prevent or limit damage, and modify behavior and environments to prevent reoccurrence. Health workers can diagnose and treat incubating problems, such as high blood pressure or diabetes, but only when people seek preventive screening and follow treatment regimens. Many do not. In fact, perhaps a third of all prescription medications are taken in a manner that jeopardizes the patient's health. Nonadherence to prescribed treatment regimens doubles the risk of death among heart patients (Gallagher, Viscoli, & Horwitz, 1993). For better or worse, people are substantially their own primary health care providers.

Researchers have concluded that high rates of noncompliance reflect many patients' inability, not unwillingness, to understand and implement the treatments their physicians recommend, especially as regimens become more complex. Many people are unable to perform some fundamental tasks in the "job" of patient, and some researchers have studied this issue using health literacy tests. Although these tests focus specifically on health content, they mimic IQ tests in assessing the same general ability to learn, reason, and solve problems. For instance, one study (Williams et al., 1995) found that, overall, 26% of the outpatients at two urban hospitals were unable to determine from an appointment slip when their next appointment was scheduled, and 42% did not understand directions for taking medicine on an empty stomach. The percentages specifically among outpatients with "inadequate" literacy were worse: 40% and 65%, respectively. In comparison, the percentages were 5% and 24% among outpatients with "adequate" literacy.

In another study (Williams, Baker, Parker, & Nurss, 1998), many insulin-dependent diabetics did not understand fundamental facts for maintaining daily control of their disease: Among those classified as having inadequate literacy, about half did not know the signs of very low or very high blood sugar, and 60% did not know the corrective actions they needed to take if their blood sugar was too low or too high. Among diabetics, intelligence at time of diagnosis correlates significantly (.36) with diabetes knowledge measured 1 year later (Taylor, Frier, et al., 2003). Like hypertension and many other chronic illnesses, diabetes requires self-monitoring and frequent judgments to keep physiological processes within safe limits. In general, low functional health literacy is linked to more illnesses, greater severity of illnesses, worse self-rated health, far higher medical costs, and (prospectively) more frequent hospitalization (Gottfredson, in press).

Most new information about health diffuses through the public media. Like improved access to health care, greater access to health information does not necessarily lead to greater equality. Rather, knowledge gaps tend to grow. When more knowledge about health risks (e.g., smoking) and new diagnostic options (e.g., Pap smears) infuse into the public sphere, already-informed persons learn the most and act on the new information more often than people who started out relatively uninformed (Gottfredson, in press). This might explain why IQ was related to smoking cessation in the SMS1932.

CONCLUSION

The SMS1932 studies have established that psychometric intelligence is an important factor in public health. Major challenges for future research are to identify the causal mechanisms for the relation between IQ and health and to capitalize on the findings to develop programs that will provide more effective health education and health care.

Correlations Have Causes

Four possible mechanisms relating childhood IQ to longevity (Whalley & Deary, 2001) provide a partial research agenda for the field. IQ at age 11 might be (a) an "archaeological record" of prior (e.g., perinatal and childhood) insults, (b) a record of the integrity of the body as a whole, (c) a predictor of healthy behaviors (e.g., avoid injuries, do not smoke), and (d) a predictor of entry into healthy environments (e.g., nonhazardous occupations). In the present article, we have focused on examining the third possibility, conceptualizing health self-care as a job, and cognitive competence as a correlate of performance in that job. However, none of these possibilities is exclusive of the others, and all four need to be considered.

A possible example of IQ as a record of prior insults is that cognitive differences, and risk of illnesses such as diabetes and cardiovascular disease later in life, are correlated with fetal development and birth weight. Investigating the second possibility requires clearly conceptualizing the construct of integrity. For example, oxidative stress (involving the generation of damaging free radicals in the body) is a factor in bodily aging and health. Perhaps people who have low levels of oxidative stress and good antioxidant defenses have better health and cognitive functions in later life than do people with more oxidative stress and poorer antioxidant defenses. Earlier in the article, we noted a confirmatory example of the third possibility: In the SMS1932-Midspan studies, people who gave up smoking between the 1930s and the 1970s tended to have had higher mental test scores at age 11 than people who continued to smoke. However, men with higher IQs were more likely to die in active service in World War II than were men with lower IQs: The association between higher IQ and longer life is not immutable.

With regard to exposure to safe versus healthy environments, the fourth possibility, many social scientists think that inequities in social structures, and perhaps education, are the fundamental causal influences that explain why IQ is related to health. The SMS1932-Midspan studies found that adjusting for occupational social class attenuated the effects of IQ on morbidity and mortality somewhat, but the effects remained significant and substantial. In the same studies, the finding of an interaction between childhood IQ and deprivation on later health attests to the importance of both intellectual and social factors. However, the fact that SES-health correlations have sometimes disfavored higher-SES groups but then reversed direction in a matter of decades (Gottfredson, in press), as groups differentially sought, understood, and acted upon new health discoveries, speaks against purely socioeconomic (or, indeed, body-integrity) explanations for some of the IQ-health relations found in the Scottish epidemiological studies. It implicates psychometric intelligence as a significant influence on effective health self-care. A key test of the influence of social background will be to examine whether siblings who have dissimilar IQs but are reared in the same family have discordant health and longevity.

Health Education and Health Care

The epidemiological studies we have discussed suggest that health care policy and practice will be more effective if they take into account how cognitive competence influences health and survival. One possibility we have raised is that the cognitive complexities of health self-care exceed the learning and reasoning capabilities of many individuals. Health educators already advocate that health materials be written at no higher than the fifth-grade reading level. However, many aspects of health self-care—for example, self-monitoring and self-medicating among individuals with chronic disease—are inherently complex and perhaps cannot be simplified without rendering care less effective. Health care workers can use this knowledge to help all patients attain optimal levels of skill and knowledge.

Recommended Reading

Deary, I.J. (2001). *Intelligence: A very short introduction*. Oxford, England: Oxford University Press.

Gottfredson, L.S. (1998). The general intelligence factor. *Scientific American Presents, 9*, 24–29.

Acknowledgments—Ian Deary is the recipient of a Royal Society-Wolfson Research Merit Award.

Note

1. Address correspondence to Linda S. Gottfredson, School of Education, University of Delaware, Newark, DE 19716.

References

Deary, I.J., Whalley, L.J., & Starr, J.M. (2003). IQ at age 11 and longevity: Results from a follow up of the Scottish Mental Survey 1932. In C.E. Finch, J.-M. Robine, & Y. Christen (Eds.), *Brain and longevity: Perspectives in longevity* (pp. 153–164). Berlin, Germany: Springer.

Deary, I.J., Whiteman, M.C., Starr, J.M., Whalley, L.J., & Fox, H.C. (in press). The impact of childhood intelligence on later life: Following up the Scottish Mental Surveys of 1932 and 1947. *Journal of Personality and Social Psychology.*

Gallagher, E.J., Viscoli, C.M., & Horwitz, R.I. (1993). The relationship of treatment adherence to the risk of death after myocardial infarction in women. *Journal of the American Medical Association, 270*, 742–744.

Gottfredson, L.S. (1997). Why g matters: The complexity of everyday life. *Intelligence, 24*, 79–132.

Gottfredson, L.S. (2002). g: Highly general and highly practical. In R.J. Sternberg & E.L. Grigorenko (Eds.), *The general factor of intelligence: How general is it?* (pp. 331–380). Mahwah, NJ: Erlbaum.

Gottfredson, L.S. (in press). Intelligence: Is it the epidemiologists' elusive "fundamental cause" of social class inequalities in health? *Journal of Personality and Social Psychology.*

Hart, C.L., Deary, I.J., Taylor, M.D., MacKinnon, P.L., Davey Smith, G., Whalley, L.J., Wilson, V., Hole, D.J., & Starr, J.M. (2003). The Scottish Mental Survey 1932 linked to the Midspan studies: A prospective investigation of childhood intelligence and future health. *Public Health, 117*, 187–195.

Hart, C.L., Taylor, M.D., Davey Smith, G., Whalley, L.J., Starr, J.M., Hole, D.J., Wilson, V., & Deary, I.J. (2003). Childhood IQ, social class, deprivation and their relationships with mortality and morbidity risk in later life. *Psychosomatic Medicine, 65*, 877–883.

O'Toole, B.J. (1990). Intelligence and behavior and motor vehicle accident mortality. *Accident Analysis and Prevention, 22*, 211–221.

O'Toole, B.J., & Stankov, L. (1992). Ultimate validity of psychological tests. *Personality and Individual Differences, 13*, 699–716.

Taylor, M.D., Frier, B.M., Gold, A.E., & Deary, I.J. (2003). Psychosocial factors and diabetes-related outcomes following diagnosis of Type 1 diabetes. *Diabetic Medicine, 20*, 135–146.

Taylor, M.D., Hart, C.L., Davey Smith, G., Starr, J.M., Hole, D.J., Whalley, L.J., Wilson, V., & Deary, I.J. (2003). Childhood mental ability and smoking cessation in adulthood. *Journal of Epidemiology and Community Health, 57,* 464–465.

Whalley, L.J., & Deary, I.J. (2001). Longitudinal cohort study of childhood IQ and survival up to age 76. *British Medical Journal, 322,* 1–5.

Williams, M.V., Baker, D.W., Parker, R.M., & Nurss, J.R. (1998). Relationship of functional health literacy to patients' knowledge of their chronic disease. *Archives of Internal Medicine, 158,* 166–172.

Williams, M.V., Parker, R.M., Baker, D.W., Pirikh, N.S., Pitkin, K., Coates, W.C., & Nurss, J.R. (1995). Inadequate functional health literacy among patients at two public hospitals. *Journal of the American Medical Association, 274,* 1677–1682.

Critical Thinking Questions

1. When IQ and SES are studied together, what do the findings suggest about each of their effects on longevity?

2. What is the link between smoking history, intelligence scores and health outcomes?

3. List four reasons that may explain the link between intelligence scores and health.

This article has been reprinted as it originally appeared in *Current Directions in Psychological Science*. Citation information for this article as originally published appears above.

Resilience and Vulnerability to Daily Stressors Assessed via Diary Methods

David M. Almeida[1]
The Pennsylvania State University

Abstract

Stressors encountered in daily life, such as family arguments or work deadlines, may play an important role in individual health and well-being. This article presents a framework for understanding how characteristics of individuals and their environments limit or increase exposure and reactivity to daily stressors. Research on daily stressors has benefited from diary methods that obtain repeated measurements from individuals during their daily lives. These methods improve ecological validity, reduce memory distortions, and permit the assessment of within-person processes. Findings from the National Study of Daily Experiences, which used a telephone-diary design, highlight how people's age, gender, and education and the presence or absence of chronic stressors in their lives predict their exposure and reactivity to daily stressors. Finally, future directions for research designs that combine laboratory-based assessment of stress physiology with daily-diary methods are discussed.

Keywords

daily hassles; diary designs; well-being

> Any idiot can handle a crisis—it's this day-to-day living that wears you out.
>
> —Anton Chekhov

Anyone who has recently experienced a crisis such as job loss, marital disruption, or the death of a loved one would certainly disagree with Chekhov's contention. Indeed, these major life stressors require significant adjustment on the part of the individual and adversely affect psychological and physical health (Brown & Harris, 1989). Major life events, however, are relatively rare, and thus their cumulative effect on health and well-being may not be as great as that of minor yet frequent stressors, such as work deadlines and family arguments (Lazarus, 1999; Zautra, 2003). Daily stressors are defined as routine challenges of day-to-day living, such as the everyday concerns of work, caring for other people, and commuting between work and home. They may also refer to more unexpected small occurrences—such as arguments with children, unexpected work deadlines, and malfunctioning computers—that disrupt daily life.

Tangible, albeit minor, interruptions like these may have a more immediate effect on well-being than major life events. Major life events may be associated with prolonged physiological arousal, whereas daily hassles may be associated with spikes in arousal or psychological distress confined to a single day. Yet minor daily stressors affect well-being not only by having separate, immediate, and direct effects on emotional and physical functioning, but also by piling up over a series of days to create persistent irritations, frustrations, and overloads that may result in more serious stress reactions such as anxiety and depression (Lazarus, 1999; Zautra, 2003).

VULNERABILITY AND RESILIENCE TO DAILY STRESSORS

Some stressors are unhealthier than other stressors, and some individuals are more prone to the effects of stressors than other individuals. Recent improvements in the measurement of daily stressors and in study design have allowed researchers to address (a) how different types of stressors and personal meanings attached to these stressors affect well-being and (b) how sociodemographic factors and personal characteristics account for group and individual differences in daily-stress processes. Figure 1 provides a model for these two areas of inquiry.

The right side of the figure represents daily-stress processes that occur within the individual. To understand these processes, one must consider both the objective characteristics of daily stressors and individuals' subjective appraisal of stressors. Objective characteristics of daily stressors include their frequency, type (e.g., interpersonal tension, being overloaded or overwhelmed at work), focus of involvement (e.g., whether the stressor involves other persons, such as a sick family member), and objective severity (e.g., degree of unpleasantness and disruption for an average person). Individuals appraise stressors in terms of their perceived severity and in terms of how much they are perceived as

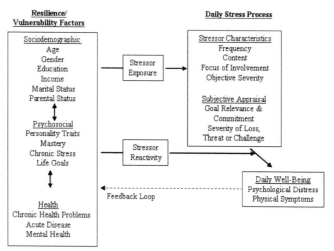

Fig. 1. Model showing how individual resilience or vulnerability factors affect daily-stress processes and well-being. Such factors include socioeconomic, psychosocial, and health characteristics; these influence the likelihood of being exposed to different kinds of stressors and the way individuals appraise stressors. Objective stressor characteristics and stressors' subjective appraisal by individuals in turn influences individuals' psychological and physical well-being. In addition to influencing stressor exposure, resilience or vulnerability factors influence individuals' reactivity to stressors—that is, their likelihood of reacting emotionally or physically. The feedback loop indicates that aspects of stressors and well-being will have subsequent effects on the vulnerability and resilience factors.

disrupting daily goals and commitments. Both objective and subjective components of daily stressors affect daily well-being (Cohen, Kessler, & Gordon, 1997). The objective characteristics of a stressor may play an important role in how that stressor is appraised, which in turn may influence how much distress it causes. Integrating the objective characteristics of stressors with their subjective appraisal allows researchers to investigate whether different kinds of daily stressors elicit different appraisal processes and affect well-being differently.

The left side of Figure 1 represents sociodemographic, psychosocial, and health factors that contribute to individuals' resilience or vulnerability to stress. Resilience and vulnerability factors affect individuals' *exposure* and *reactivity* to daily stressors and, thereby, their daily well-being. Exposure is the likelihood that an individual will experience a daily stressor, given his or her resilience or vulnerability factors. Although daily stressors may be unpredictable, more often they arise out of the routine circumstances of everyday life. The stressor-exposure path illustrates that an individual's sociodemographic, psychosocial, and health characteristics are likely to play a role in determining what kinds of stressors that individual experiences and how he or she appraises them (right side of Fig. 1). Reactivity is the likelihood that an individual will react emotionally or physically to daily stressors and depends on the individual's resilience or vulnerability (Bolger & Zuckerman, 1995). The stressor-reactivity path illustrates that sociodemographic, psychosocial, and health factors modify how daily stressors affect daily well-being. Individuals' personal resources (e.g., their education, income, feelings of mastery and control over their environment, and physical health) and environmental resources (e.g., social support) affect how they can cope with daily experiences (Lazarus, 1999). Finally, the feedback-loop path (dotted arrow from the right to the left of the figure) shows how aspects of stressors and well-being will have subsequent effects on the resilience and vulnerability factors.

DAILY-DIARY METHODOLOGY

The understanding of daily stressors has benefited from the development of diary methods that obtain repeated measurements from individuals during their daily lives. In this method, individuals report the stressors they experienced over the course of several days, as well as their behaviors, physical symptoms, and emotional states on these days. The use of paper-and-pencil diaries has been criticized because some participants may not complete their entries at scheduled times (Stone, Shiffman, Schwartz, Broderick, & Hufford, 2002). However, recent diary methods in which participants respond over the telephone, with personal digital assistants, and on Internet Web pages provide more control over compliance and make it possible to obtain more in-depth information by allowing subjects to skip irrelevant questions and go into greater detail on those that are more relevant to them, for instance by describing experiences in their own words. Diary methods have a number of virtues (Bolger, Davis, & Rafaeli, 2003). By obtaining information about individuals' actual daily stressors over short-term intervals, daily diaries circumvent concerns about ecological validity (applicability to real life) that constrain findings from laboratory research. Further, diary methods alleviate memory distortions that can occur in more traditional questionnaire and interview methods that require respondents to recall experiences over longer time frames.

Perhaps the most valuable feature of diary methods is that they allow assessment of within-person processes. This feature entails a shift from assessing mean levels of stressors and well-being in a group of individuals to charting the day-to-day fluctuations in stress and well-being within an individual, as well as to identifying predictors, correlates, and consequences of these fluctuations (Reis & Gamble, 2000).

Stress is a process that occurs within the individual, and research designs need to reflect this fact. For example, instead of asking whether individuals who encounter many stressors at work experience more distress than individuals with less stressful jobs, a researcher can ask whether a worker experiences more distress on days when he or she has too many deadlines (or is reprimanded) than on days when work has been stress free. This within-person approach allows the researcher to rule out personality and environmental variables that are stable over time as explanations for the relationship between stressors and well-being. In addition, the intensive longitudinal aspect of this design permits researchers to examine how stressors are associated with changes in a person's well-being from one day to the next. By establishing within-person, through-time associations between daily stressors and well-being, researchers can more precisely establish the short-term effects of concrete daily experiences (Bolger et al., 2003; Larson & Almeida, 1999).

EMPIRICAL FINDINGS FROM THE NATIONAL STUDY OF DAILY EXPERIENCES

A recent project called the National Study of Daily Experiences (NSDE) is aimed to investigate the sources of vulnerability and resilience to daily stressors. The NSDE is a telephone-diary study of a U.S. national sample of 1,483 adults ranging in age from 25 to 74 years. Interviews occurred over eight consecutive nights, resulting in 11,578 days of information. Although past research advanced the understanding of daily-stress processes, there are important limitations in these studies that are overcome in the NSDE. First, previous diary studies of daily stressors relied on small and often unrepresentative samples that limited the generalizability of findings. In contrast, the NSDE data come from a representative subsample of adults surveyed in a nationwide study on Midlife in the United States (MIDUS). Second, previous studies of individual differences in vulnerability to stress have typically examined only one source of variability, such as neuroticism (i.e., whether a person is dispositionally anxious). The NSDE, in contrast, uses data on a wide array of personality variables and sociodemographic characteristics collected in the MIDUS survey. Third, previous studies typically have relied on self-administered checklists of daily stressors that only indicate whether or not a given stressor has occurred. The NSDE uses a semistructured telephone interview to measure several aspects of daily stressors, including their objective characteristics as rated by expert coders (e.g., content, severity) and their subjective appraisals by study participants.

Prevalence of Daily Stressors

Respondents reported experiencing on average at least one stressor on 40% of the study days and multiple stressors on 10% of the study days (Almeida, Wethington, & Kessler, 2002). Table 1 provides a breakdown by various stressor categories. The most common stressors for both men and women were interpersonal arguments and tensions, which accounted for half of all the stressors. Gender differences were also evident. Women were more likely than men to report network stressors—stressors involving their network of relatives or close friends—whereas men were more likely than women to report stressors at work or at school. On average, the respondents subjectively rated stressors as having medium severity, whereas objective coders rated the stressors as having low severity. It is interesting that objective and subjective severity were only moderately correlated ($r = .36$). As appraised by respondents, daily stressors more commonly posed a threat to respondents' daily routines than to other domains of their lives (e.g., their finances, health, and safety). The threat dimensions refer to

Table 1. *Results from the national study of daily experiences: measures of stressors*

	Total	Men	Women
	(N = 1,031)	(n = 469)	(n = 562)
Stressor content (% of events)[a]			
Interpersonal tensions	50.0%	49.1%	50.3%
Work or school	13.2	15.7	11.2*
Home	8.2	8.0	8.3
Health care	2.2	1.6	2.7
Network[b]	15.4	12.5	17.8*
Miscellaneous	3.5	4.4	2.7
Type of threat posed by stressor (% of events)			
Loss	29.7	29.9	29.5
Danger	36.2	35.7	36.6
Disappointment	4.2	4.0	4.4
Frustration	27.4	28.3	26.6
Stressor severity (mean)[c]			
Objective assessment	1.8	1.7	1.9
Subjective assessment	2.7	2.5	2.9*
Domain of life potentially disrupted (mean)[d]			
Daily routine	2.3	2.3	2.3
Financial situation	1.3	1.4	1.2*
Way feel about self	1.5	1.4	1.5
Way others feel about you	1.4	1.3	1.4*
Physical health or safety	1.3	1.3	1.3
Health/well-being of someone you care about	1.5	1.5	1.5
Plans for the future	1.4	1.4	1.3

[a]Seven percent of events could not be placed into these content classifications.
[b]Events that happen to other people.
[c]Range: 1–4 (not at all stressful to very stressful).
[d]Range: 1–4 (no risk to a lot of risk).
*Asterisks indicate a significant gender difference, $p < .01$.

stressful implications for the respondent. Approximately 30% of the reported stressors involved some sort of loss (e.g., of money), nearly 37% posed danger (e.g., potential for future loss), and 27% were frustrations or events over which the respondent felt he or she had no control.

Daily stressors also had implications for well-being. Respondents were more likely to report psychological distress and physical symptoms on days when they experienced stressors than on stress-free days. Certain types of daily stressors, such as interpersonal tensions and network stressors, were more predictive of psychological distress and physical symptoms than other types of stressors. Furthermore, severe stressors that disrupted daily routines or posed a risk to physical health and self-concept were particularly distressing.

Group and Individual Differences in Daily Stressors

As previously mentioned, demographic and psychological characteristics affect how resilient or vulnerable individuals are to daily stressors (see Fig. 1). Horn and I initially investigated this issue by assessing age differences in exposure and reactivity to daily stressors (Almeida & Horn, 2004). Young (25–39 years) and middle-aged (40–59 years) individuals reported a greater daily frequency of stressors than did older individuals (60–74 years). Compared with older adults, younger and midlife adults also perceived their stressors as more severe and as more likely to affect how other people felt about them. Overloads (i.e., having too little time or other resources) and demands (i.e., having too much to do) were a greater source of daily stressors for younger and midlife adults than for older adults, although the focus of the demands tended to differ by gender. Younger men's daily stressors were more likely than those of older men to revolve around demands and overloads as well as interactions with coworkers. Women in midlife reported the same percentage of overloads as younger women but had a greater proportion of network stressors. Although overloads were not a common type of stressor for older adults, these respondents had the greatest proportion of network stressors (stressors that happen to other people) and spouse-related stressors.

Socioeconomic factors may also help or hinder individuals in facing daily stressors. Consistent with research on socioeconomic inequalities in health, our analyses indicated that, on any given day, better-educated adults reported fewer physical symptoms and less psychological distress than less-educated adults (Grzywacz, Almeida, Neupert, & Ettner, 2004). In contrast to studies of life-event stressors, this study found that college-educated individuals reported more daily stressors than those with no more than high-school education. However, college-educated respondents were less reactive to stressors, which indicates that socioeconomic differentials in daily health could be attributed to differential reactivity to stressors rather than to differential exposure to stressors.

Finally, it is important to acknowledge that ongoing difficulties in a person's life (e.g., caring for a sick spouse, poor working conditions) not only may expose him or her to stressors, but also may increase his or her reactivity to daily stressors by depleting resources. Participants who experienced chronic stressors were more likely than those who did not to report psychological distress on days when they experienced daily stressors (Serido, Almeida, & Wethington, 2004). For women, the interaction of home hassles and chronic stressors was significant; for men, it was the interaction of work hassles and chronic stressors that was significant.

FUTURE DIRECTIONS: PHYSIOLOGICAL INDICATORS OF WELL-BEING

Most research on resilience and vulnerability to daily stressors has relied on self-reported well-being. Results have had to be qualified by discussions of possible biases in study participants' responses and questions concerning the validity of self-reported well-being measures. Thus, questions regarding the direct relation between daily stressors and physiological functioning remain. One promising avenue for future research concerns *allostatic load,* the biological cost of adapting to stresssors. Allostatic load is commonly measured by indicators of the body's response to physiological dysregulation—responses such as high cholesterol levels or lowered blood-clotting ability—and has been found to be predictive of decline in physical health (McEwen, 1998). Ironically, researchers have conceptualized allostatic load as physical vulnerability caused by the body having to adjust repeatedly to stressors, yet few studies have examined allostatic load in conjunction with individuals' daily accounts of stressors. The combination of daily-stressor data from diaries and data from laboratory tests of physiological reactivity would provide an opportunity to examine how daily stressors map onto physiological indicators of allostatic load.

In conclusion, the study of daily stress provides a unique window into the ebb and flow of day-to-day frustrations and irritations that are often missed by research on major life events. The focus on naturally occurring minor stressors assessed on a daily basis offers an exciting opportunity to understand how people adapt to the challenges of life. Adaptation occurs within an individual, so understanding adaptation requires consideration both of stressors themselves and of the persons they affect. Because daily stressors are real-life issues that require immediate attention, daily-diary study of stressors can provide the micro-level data needed to understand the immediate relationships between stressors and how individuals respond to and interpret them. It is true that day-to-day living can wear you out; however certain days are better than others, and certain people are better equipped to handle stressors than other people are.

Recommended Reading

Affleck, G., Zautra, A., Tennen, H., & Armeli, S. (1999). Multilevel daily process designs for consulting and clinical psychology: A preface for the perplexed. *Journal of Consulting and Clinical Psychology, 67,* 746–754.
Almeida, D.M., Wethington, E., & Kessler, R.C. (2002). (See References)
Bolger, N., Davis, A., & Rafaeli, E. (2003). (See References)
Lazarus, R.S. (1999). (See References)
Zautra, A.J. (2003). (See References)

Acknowledgments—The research reported in this article was supported by the MacArthur Foundation Research Network on Successful Midlife Development and by National Institute on Aging Grants AG19239 and AG0210166.

Note

1. David M. Almeida, Department of Human Development and Family Studies, The Pennsylvania State University, 105 White Building, University Park, PA 16802; e-mail: dalmeida@psu.edu.

References

Almeida, D.M., & Horn, M.C. (2004). Is daily life more stressful during middle adulthood? In O.G. Brim, C.D. Ryff, & R.C. Kessler (Eds.), *How healthy are we? A national study of well-being at midlife* (pp. 425–451). Chicago: University of Chicago Press.

Almeida, D.M., Wethington, E., & Kessler, R.C. (2002). The Daily Inventory of Stressful Experiences (DISE): An interview-based approach for measuring daily stressors. *Assessment, 9,* 41–55.

Bolger, N., Davis, A., & Rafaeli, E. (2003). Diary methods: Capturing life as it is lived. *Annual Review of Psychology, 54,* 579–616.

Bolger, N., & Zuckerman, A. (1995). A framework for studying personality in the stress process. *Journal of Personality and Social Psychology, 69,* 890–902.

Brown, G.W., & Harris, T.O. (1989). *Life events and illness*. New York: Guilford.

Cohen, S., Kessler, R.C., & Gordon, L. (1997). Strategies for measuring stress in studies of psychiatric and physical disorders. In S. Cohen, R.C. Kessler, & L. Gordon (Eds.), *Measuring stress: A guide for health and social scientists* (pp. 3–26). New York: Oxford University Press.

Grzywacz, J.G., Almeida, D.M., Neupert, S.D., & Ettner, S.L. (2004). Stress and socioeconomic differentials in physical and mental health: A daily diary approach. *Journal of Health and Social Behavior, 45,* 1–16.

Larson, R., & Almeida, D.M. (1999). Emotional transmission in the daily lives of families: A new paradigm for studying family processes. *Journal of Marriage and the Family, 61,* 5–20.

Lazarus, R.S. (1999). *Stress and emotion: A new synthesis*. New York: Springer.

McEwen, B.S. (1998). Protective and damaging effects of stress mediators. *New England Journal of Medicine, 338,* 171–179.

Reis, H.T., & Gable, S.L. (2000). Event-sampling and other methods for studying everyday experience. In H.T. Reis & C.M. Judd (Eds.), *Handbook of research methods in social and personality psychology* (pp. 190–222). New York: Cambridge University Press.

Serido, J., Almeida, D.M., & Wethington, E. (2004). Conceptual and empirical distinctions between chronic stressors and daily hassles. *Journal of Health and Social Behavior, 45,* 17–33.

Stone, A.A., Shiffman, S., Schwartz, J.E., Broderick, J.E., & Hufford, M.R. (2002). Patient noncompliance with paper diaries. *British Medical Journal, 324,* 1193–1194.

Zautra, A.J. (2003). *Emotions, stress, and health*. New York: Oxford University Press.

Critical Thinking Questions

1. What are some advantages of daily-diary methods over traditional one-time assessments?

2. Define exposure and reactivity and describe how they may explain both between-subject and within-subject differences when studying how stress influences well-being.

3. Describe how age is related to exposure and reactivity to stressors.

This article has been reprinted as it originally appeared in *Current Directions in Psychological Science*. Citation information for this article as originally published appears above.

Is Caregiving a Risk Factor for Illness?

Peter P. Vitaliano[1]

Department of Psychiatry and Behavioral Sciences, University of Washington

Heather M. Young

School of Nursing, Oregon Health and Science University School of Nursing

Jianping Zhang

Department of Psychology, Indiana University–Purdue University

Abstract

This article focuses on the physical health of persons who provide care to family members and friends with dementia. Such caregivers are under extended chronic stress because of the particular demands that this illness places on them. Caregiver research has made important contributions in two areas of health psychology. First, this research has increased understanding of the impact of chronic illness in families. Second, it has explored the complex relationships between stress and human responses (psychological and physiological) in the context of aging, using caregiving as a prototypic chronic stressor. This article discusses the relationship between distress, health habits, physiological changes, and, ultimately, health risks. There is evidence for greater health risks in caregivers than in non-caregivers. In addition, vulnerabilities and resources influence the relationship between caregiver stressors and health. One of the greatest methodological challenges of research on caregiver health is that the studies occur under natural conditions, so that it is not possible to randomly assign people to be caregivers and then observe changes in their health. Careful designs are required to infer the reasons for health risks.

Keywords

caregiving; dementia; physical health; stress; risk

In this article, we discuss current research on caregiving as a risk factor for physical health problems, theoretical and methodological issues in making inferences from such research, and recommendations for future research. We focus on informal (unpaid) caregivers of persons with dementia. Such caregivers provide the majority of long-term care in the United States, and the market value of this care was estimated to be approximately $196 billion in 1997, dwarfing concurrent national spending on formal home health care ($32 billion) and nursing home care ($83 billion). In the next 20 years, caregivers will be more critical than ever because the prevalence of Alzheimer's disease will increase, as will the prevalence of other chronic diseases. For these reasons, promoting health for caregivers is of potential benefit not only to these individuals, but to society as well.

WHAT DOES CAREGIVING FOR A PERSON WITH DEMENTIA ENTAIL?

Caring for a person with dementia poses specific challenges, including unrelenting psychosocial, physical, and financial demands over an extended period of time (3–15 years), lack of control over the disease, and resulting social isolation. With the progressive intellectual, social, and physical declines associated with dementia, caregivers experience an extended grieving period as they slowly lose a loved one to this illness. Moreover, caregiving can be a full-time job, and many caregivers are themselves older adults with their own chronic health problems or adult children who are balancing competing demands of work and child rearing. Hence, caregiving is conducive to distress, and trying to meet the care recipient's needs can result in perceptions of burden, depressed mood, and the absence of positive experiences.

HOW HAS CAREGIVING BEEN STUDIED?

Caregiving was first recognized as a chronic stressor more than 30 years ago. Early reports were anecdotal, describing the effects of caregiving demands on family members. Research then progressed to examine the psychosocial aspects of caregiving in more detail, and within a few years, investigators were beginning to look at possible effects on self-reported health. An important advance occurred when study designs began to include noncaregiving control groups, so that by comparing groups, researchers could attempt to isolate the effects of caregiving from those of general stressors experienced in the course of daily life. As the research became more sophisticated, investigators began to include more objective measures of health, to augment caregivers' reports of their own health. Finally, prospective designs enabled researchers to examine new health problems that arose during the course of caregiving. Caregiver research has made important contributions in two areas of health psychology. First, this research has increased understanding of the impact of chronic illness in families. Second, it has explored the complex relationships between stress and human responses (psychological and physiological) in the context of aging, using caregiving as a prototypic chronic stressor.

THE CONNECTION BETWEEN DISTRESS AND HEALTH

The unchallenged and implicit assumption of this research has been that the demands of caregiving influence caregivers' distress and health problems. Indeed, much research has shown that in general populations, chronic stress is associated with distress (e.g., depression), sleep problems, risky health habits (e.g., poor diet, sedentary behaviors), and illness progression in persons with existing health problems (Taylor, 1995).

In this regard, there is growing evidence of mind-body connections and the relationship between mental stress and physical responses. Distress and poor health habits elevate levels of stress hormones, thereby stimulating further physiological activity that can lead to negative health outcomes such as hyperglycemia (elevated levels of blood sugar), hyperinsulinemia (elevated levels of blood insulin), higher blood pressure (BP), and poorer immune functioning. If prolonged, these conditions can compromise health (Lovallo, 1997). In particular, physiological indicators of coronary risk and diabetes risk include heightened levels of resting BP, BP reactivity in response to stressors, low levels of high-density (good) cholesterol, high levels of blood fats and sugar, and obesity. Markers thought to reflect poor immune functioning include reduced ability to fight tumor cells, poor antibody production in response to viruses, and slow wound-healing responses.

RESEARCH ON CAREGIVER HEALTH

Schulz, Visintainer, and Williamson (1990) provided one of the first reviews of caregivers' physical and mental health. Most of the 34 studies in their review examined mental health (only 11 examined physical health) and assessed self-reported health rather than using objective measures. Some studies observed that the health of caregivers was similar to that of age- and sex-matched noncaregivers, whereas others found that caregivers rated their health as "poorer" than matched control participants did. Later, Schulz, O'Brien, Bookwala, and Fleissner (1995) reviewed 40 additional studies comparing caregivers with noncaregivers and observed conflicting results regarding self-reported chronic illnesses and medication use.

Given the inconsistent results and the absence of reviews that quantified the degree of added illness risks in caregivers relative to noncaregivers, we (Vitaliano, Zhang, & Scanlan, 2003) performed a meta-analysis of 23 studies, over a 38-year period, that compared 1,594 caregivers of persons with dementia to 1,478 noncaregivers who were similar in their distributions of age and sex. The meta-analytic approach enabled us to combine the results from these studies to estimate quantitative relationships between caregiving and illness risks. Eleven health categories were examined: five categories of self-reported health (global self-reported health, health care use, and reports of symptoms, major and minor illnesses, and medications) and six physiological categories of health. The physiological categories included antibody responses to vaccination and viruses, enumerative cellular immunity (counts of immune-cell markers), functional cellular immunity (ability to fight tumors and viruses), cardiovascular measures (e.g., BP), metabolic measures (e.g., glucose levels, weight), and levels of stress hormones.

The aggregate analysis showed that caregivers reported poorer global health and took more medications for physical problems than noncaregivers did. Furthermore, they had 23% higher levels of stress hormones, and a 15% lower level of antibody responses. These findings are important because prolonged physiological reactions to elevated stress hormones can increase one's risk for hypertension and diabetes. Caregivers may also have reduced resistance to viruses because of poorer antibody production. This may be especially critical to older caregivers, who are already at added risk for influenza because of their age.

PROBLEMS WITH THE RESEARCH ON CAREGIVER HEALTH

Theoretical Models

Research on caregiver health has not made full use of stress models that focus on differences between people. For example, differences in vulnerabilities and resources can modify (i.e., moderate) or increase or decrease (i.e., mediate) the effects of stress. Models that incorporate differences between people should improve researchers' ability to explain health problems that may result from caregiving, make it possible to identify high-risk caregivers, and allow for a better understanding of factors that mediate or moderate the relationship of caregiving with health problems.

We have proposed a model of caregiver health in which stressors and individual differences interact to influence the caregiver's level of distress (e.g., perceived hassles, depression, burden, few positive experiences) and health habits (e.g., amount of exercise, diet, substance abuse), which in turn mediate health outcomes (Vitaliano et al., 2002). Vulnerabilities, which include being a man, having a hostile disposition, and having coexisting medical conditions (e.g., hypertension, heart disease), are typically hard-wired or relatively static characteristics that exist prior to caregiving. Resources, such as coping skills, social supports, and income, are more mutable, and availability of resources is generally predictive of better health. The model predicts that caregivers who are high in vulnerabilities and low in resources will have greater distress and poorer health habits than caregivers with fewer vulnerabilities and more resources (Vitaliano, Russo, Young, Teri, & Maiuro, 1991).

Individual Differences in Research on Caregiver Health

In our meta-analysis, the relationships between caregiving and self-reported health were greater for older than for younger participants. Perhaps this was true because greater age is accompanied by increases in physical illnesses and disabilities, and these may be exacerbated by distress. This analysis also showed that for women, caregiving was related much more strongly to self-reported global health than to a physiological measure combining cardiovascular, metabolic, and stress hormone data; the relationship between caregiving and the physiological measure was minute. In contrast, for men, caregiving was related to both the combined physiological measure and self-reported health. These results are especially meaningful to clinicians, researchers, and policymakers because the analysis was strictly limited to studies that simultaneously compared male caregivers with male noncaregivers and female caregivers with female noncaregivers. Such comparisons are important because they provide some control for basic biological differences and differences in self-report tendencies between men and women. Also, if the difference between caregivers and noncaregivers is greater for men than women, but the caregiver-noncaregiver comparisons for men and women come from different studies (i.e., involving different procedures, labs, and samples), it is difficult to evaluate whether the difference is moderated by sex or by study differences.

The relationships between caregiver status and physiological risk may be particularly strong for persons with coexisting health conditions (Vitaliano et al., 2003). For example, caregivers with cancer histories have lower natural killer activity, a defense against tumors, than do noncaregivers with cancer histories, but natural killer activity does not differ for caregivers and noncaregivers who have not had cancer. Also, hypertensive caregivers have greater BP reactivity (while experiencing a potential stressor, such as discussing their relationship with their spouse) than do hypertensive noncaregivers, but caregiver status is not related to BP reactivity in persons with normal blood pressure. Finally, caregivers with coronary disease have higher values on an estimate of the metabolic syndrome than do noncaregivers with heart disease; however, no difference occurs for caregivers and noncaregivers free of heart disease. The metabolic syndrome is important to health because it involves five physical signs that are predictive of both heart disease and the exacerbation of this disease after it occurs. These signs include obesity, elevated BP, high cholesterol, high levels of glucose, and high levels of insulin.

Given the interactions that occur between caregiving and coexisting health conditions, it is unfortunate that most researchers have either excluded persons with coexisting conditions in their designs or have not analyzed the presence/absence of such conditions as moderators of relationships of caregiver/noncaregiver status with health. These practices may limit studies to those caregivers who are least likely to show health or physiological problems, and prevent researchers from discovering relationships between caregiving and disease progression.

Additional Design Issues

Most studies have compared caregivers with noncaregivers after they have already developed health problems. Such studies do not allow one to determine whether illnesses reported preceded caregiving or vice versa. However, some prospective studies have been done. These studies examined only caregivers and noncaregivers who were initially free of health problems and followed them to assess whether caregivers were more likely than noncaregivers to become ill. Shaw et al. (1997) found that over 1 to 6 years, caregivers who provided the most assistance were more likely to develop at least one new health problem than were either caregivers who provided less assistance or noncaregivers. Schulz and Beach (1999) observed that over an average of 4 years, strained caregivers had a 63% higher death rate than noncaregivers. Finally, we (Vitaliano et al., 2002) observed that over 27 to 30 months, male caregivers had a higher rate of new cases of heart disease (8 out of 19 participants) than male noncaregivers (3 out of 20 participants). Distress was related to caregiver status and the care recipients' cognitive and functional deficits, and was further related to poor health habits; in turn, poor health habits predicted greater physiological risk, via the metabolic syndrome, 15 to 18 months later.

Although these prospective studies allow one to conclude that caregiving preceded the outcomes assessed, they were prospective for illness and mortality only, and not for caregiving. That is, the participants were already caregivers and noncaregivers at the start of these studies, so only retrospective data were potentially available for analyzing the precaregiving lifestyle of the caregivers and the lifestyle of the noncaregivers during a similar earlier period of time. Because caregiver research is based primarily on real-world observations and not experiments, characteristics (poor diet and insufficient exercise) that increase health risks may be present in caregivers prior to caregiving and not be the result of caregiving. Indeed, because these characteristics vary across couples and families, it may be these characteristics, and not caregiving per se, that are responsible for greater health problems in caregivers than in noncaregivers.

In an attempt to control for effects of unknown confounders, researchers typically match age and gender in the caregiver and noncaregiver groups they study. However, biases can occur if other important variables are ignored. Income is one such variable because it is negatively related to health, and persons who become caregivers (especially men) may have lower incomes than persons who are eligible to be caregivers but opt out of caregiving and pay for it instead because they have the income to do so (Vitaliano et al., 2003). Bias can also occur because of assortative mating (the tendency to marry someone like oneself) and mutual influences of spouses on each other. For example, spouses tend to have similar health habits (Davis, Murphy, Neuhaus, Gee, & Quiroga, 2000), and poor health habits and distress may increase one's risk for dementia (Leonard, 2001; Skoog, 1998). Thus, prior to caregiving, caregivers may have greater distress and poorer health habits than noncaregivers. In addition, the same experiences that influence the development of dementia in care recipients may influence the development of other illnesses in caregivers, with genetic predispositions affecting how these shared risk factors are manifested.

Only studies that are doubly prospective, that examine a cohort both before caregiving and before a target illness develops, allow one to examine how changes in caregiver status and illness relate to psychosocial, behavioral, and physiological changes. A doubly prospective study could begin with persons who are not caregivers and not ill and then follow them to determine what happens after some become caregivers and others remain noncaregivers. The first question of interest would be whether those who become caregivers develop health problems at a higher rate than those who remain noncaregivers. In addition, researchers could determine whether such higher incidences in caregivers can be explained by variables such as greater demands, greater distress, and poorer health habits in caregivers than in noncaregivers. Combining caregiver research with ongoing population studies should make doubly prospective studies possible. However, illnesses take time to be detected, and extensive follow-up may be necessary.

MEASUREMENT ISSUES

Research on caregiver health began with an emphasis on self-report measures. However, more recent work has also included direct physiological assessments. Although these studies have been conducted primarily in laboratories, ecological validity can be improved by examining measures taken in natural settings, such as the home, over longer time periods. For example, BPs that are taken in the home while caregivers engage in their usual activities may be greater than BPs taken in clinic or work settings, especially when taken in the presence of the persons being cared for (King, Oka, & Young, 1994).

Another benefit may come from medical records. It may be difficult for caregivers to recall and distinguish their use of health care versus that of the persons for whom they are caring. Therefore, collecting such information from alternate sources might be useful. Medical records may not only provide information on doctors' visits, but may also be repositories of other valuable data, such as lab results, dates and nature of diagnoses, information on treatments and medications, and prognoses. Caregivers may not know such information or may not report it accurately. In using medical records, researchers can develop quality-control checklists to document participants' treatments, symptoms, and diagnoses and to assess the reliability of their records and the quality of their data. We also recommend physical exams, because they can uncover problems undetected in medical records. Some reported health measures may be used more productively than in the past. Instead of simply counting illnesses, for example, researchers should assess which illnesses are most related to caregiving. Medication data could be more useful to researchers if they considered frequencies, dosages, and the health implications of such medications.

IMPORTANT NEXT STEPS

Although the observational nature of caregiver research precludes the definitive inference that caregiving is a risk factor for illness, doubly prospective studies and studies that examine disease progression in caregivers and noncaregivers with and without coexisting conditions should be useful for clarifying potential causes of the added risk caregivers appear to experience. Using theoretical models in research will promote identification of factors amenable to change and development of targeted interventions that might promote overall health for caregivers by improving their health-related behaviors and stress management.

Although the research reviewed here focused on caregivers of persons with dementia, caregivers of persons with cancer, coronary disease, injuries, and mental illnesses are also under stress. The model we have presented could be extended to them, and differences among types of caregiving situations could be explored. By helping caregivers to maintain their health, such studies and interventions should also help care recipients and society. The added health risks for caregivers are provocative because there are more than 5 million caregivers of persons with dementia in the United States and another 4 million care recipients that will be affected if their caregivers become ill. Finally, caregiver's own illnesses are a major reason why caregivers institutionalize their care recipients (Deimling & Poulshock, 1985), and improved caregiver health may delay or avoid many institutionalizations.

Recommended Reading

American Association of Retired Persons. (1988). *National survey of caregivers: Summary of findings*. Washington, DC: Author.
Kasl, S.V. (1983). Pursuing the link between stressful life experiences and disease: A time for reappraisal. In C.L. Cooper (Ed.), *Stress research: Issues for the eighties* (pp. 79–102). New York: John Wiley & Sons.
Mechanic, D. (1967). Invited commentary on self, social environment and stress. In M.H. Appley & R. Trumbull (Eds.), *Psychological stress* (pp. 123–150). New York: Appleton-Century-Crofts.
Rowe, J.W., & Kahn, R.L. (1998). *Successful aging*. New York: Pantheon Books.
Vogel, F., & Motulsky, A.G. (1986). *Human genetics*. New York: Springer-Verlag.

Acknowledgments—This research was supported by the National Institute of Mental Health, Grant RO1 MH57663.

Note

1. Address correspondence to Peter P. Vitaliano, Department of Psychiatry and Behavioral Sciences, Box 356560, University of Washington, Seattle, WA 98195-6560.

References

Davis, M.A., Murphy, S.P., Neuhaus, J.M., Gee, L., & Quiroga, S. (2000). Living arrangements affect dietary quality for U.S. adults aged 50 years and older: NHANES III 1988–1994. *Journal of Nutrition, 130*, 2256–2263.

Deimling, G.T., & Poulshock, S.W. (1985). The transition from family in-home care to institutional care. *Research on Aging, 7*, 563–576.

King, A.C., Oka, R.K., & Young, D.R. (1994). Ambulatory blood pressure and heart rate responses to the stress of work and caregiving in older women. *Journal of Gerontology, 49*, 239–245.

Leonard, B.E. (2001). Changes in the immune system in depression and dementia: Causal or co-incidental effects? *International Journal of Developmental Neuroscience, 19*, 305–312.

Lovallo, W.R. (1997). *Stress & health*. Thousand Oaks, CA: Sage.

Schulz, R., & Beach, S.R. (1999). Caregiving as a risk factor for mortality: The Caregiver Health Effects Study. *Journal of the American Medical Association, 282*, 2215–2260.

Schulz, R., O'Brien, A.T., Bookwala, J., & Fleissner, K. (1995). Psychiatric and physical morbidity effects of dementia caregiving: Prevalence, correlates, and causes. *The Gerontologist, 35*, 771–791.

Schulz, R., Visintainer, P., & Williamson, G.M. (1990). Psychiatric and physical morbidity effects of caregiving. *Journal of Gerontology: Psychological Sciences, 45*, 181–191.

Shaw, W.S., Patterson, T.L., Semple, S.J., Ho, S., Irwin, M.R., Hauger, R.L., & Grant, I. (1997). Longitudinal analysis of multiple indicators of health decline among spousal caregivers. *Annals of Behavioral Medicine, 19* (1), 101–109.

Skoog, I. (1998). Status of risk factors for vascular dementia. *Neuroepidemiology, 17*, 2–9.

Taylor, S.E. (1995). Health psychology (3rd ed.). New York: McGraw Hill.

Vitaliano, P.P., Russo, J., Young, H.M., Teri, L., & Maiuro, R.D. (1991). Predictors of burden in spouse caregivers of individuals with Alzheimer's disease. *Psychology and Aging, 6*, 392–401.

Vitaliano, P.P., Scanlan, J.M., Zhang, J., Savage, M.V., Hirsch, I., & Siegler, I.C. (2002). A path model of chronic stress, the metabolic syndrome, and coronary heart disease. *Psychosomatic Medicine, 64*, 418–435.

Vitaliano, P.P., Zhang, J., & Scanlan, J.M. (2003). Is caregiving hazardous to one's physical health? A meta-analysis. *Psychological Bulletin, 129*, 946–972.

Critical Thinking Questions

1. Describe several differences in the physical health of caregivers versus their noncaregiver counterparts.

2. What are some gender differences in caregiving outcomes that have been reported in the literature?

3. What are some reasons for the worse physical health among caregivers versus same-age noncaregiving adults.

This article has been reprinted as it originally appeared in *Current Directions in Psychological Science*. Citation information for this article as originally published appears above.